When States Take Rights Back

When States Take Rights Back draws on contributions by international experts in history, law, political science, and sociology, offering a rare interdisciplinary and comparative examination of citizenship revocation in five countries, revealing hidden government rationales and unintended consequences.

Once considered outdated, citizenship revocation – also called deprivation or denationalization – has come back to the political centre in many Western liberal states. Contributors scrutinise the positions of stakeholders (e.g. civil servants, representatives of civil society, judges, supranational institutions) and their diverse rationales for citizenship revocation (e.g. allegations of terrorism, treason, espionage, criminal behaviour, and fraud in the naturalisation process). The volume also uncovers the variety of tools that national governments have at their disposition to change existing citizenship revocation laws and policies, and the constraints that they are faced with to actually implement citizenship revocation in daily operations. Finally, contributors underscore the extraordinary severity of sanctions implied by citizenship revocation and offer a nuanced picture of the material and symbolic forms of exclusion not only for those whose citizenship is withdrawn but also for minority groups (wrongly) associated with the aforementioned allegations. Indeed, revocation policies target not merely individuals but specific collective categories, which tend to be ethno-racially constructed and attributed specific locations within the international status hierarchy of nation-states.

International and interdisciplinary in scope, *When States Take Rights Back* will be of great interest to scholars of politics, international law, sociology and political and legal history, and human rights. The chapters were originally published in *Citizenship Studies*.

Émilien Fargues is a Max Weber Fellow at the European University Institute and a research associate in the Global Citizenship Governance project at the Robert Schuman Centre for Advanced Studies. He holds a PhD in political science from Sciences Po Paris.

Elke Winter is the William Lyon Mackenzie King Professor of Sociology at Harvard University, Professor of Sociology at the University of Ottawa, and Research Director at the Centre for Interdisciplinary Research on Citizenship and Minorities (CIRCEM). Her research is concerned with questions of migration, ethnic diversity, multiculturalism, and citizenship.

Matthew J. Gibney is Professor of Politics and Forced Migration at the University of Oxford, Official Fellow of Linacre College, Oxford, and Director of the Refugee Studies Centre. He specialises in the political and ethical issues raised by refugees, citizenship, and migration control.

When States Take Rights Back

Citizenship Revocation and Its Discontents

Edited by
Émilien Fargues, Elke Winter and Matthew J. Gibney

Routledge
Taylor & Francis Group
LONDON AND NEW YORK

First published 2020
by Routledge
2 Park Square, Milton Park, Abingdon, Oxon, OX14 4RN

and by Routledge
52 Vanderbilt Avenue, New York, NY 10017

Routledge is an imprint of the Taylor & Francis Group, an informa business

British Library Cataloguing in Publication Data
A catalogue record for this book is available from the British Library

ISBN13: 978-0-367-89645-4

Typeset in Minion Pro
by Newgen Publishing UK

Publisher's Note
The publisher accepts responsibility for any inconsistencies that may have arisen during the conversion of this book from journal articles to book chapters, namely the inclusion of journal terminology.

Disclaimer
Every effort has been made to contact copyright holders for their permission to reprint material in this book. The publishers would be grateful to hear from any copyright holder who is not here acknowledged and will undertake to rectify any errors or omissions in future editions of this book.

Contents

Citation Information

The following chapters were originally published in *Citizenship Studies*. Chapters 2–4 and 6–7 were originally published in *Citizenship Studies*, volume 23, issue 4 (2019). Chapter 5 was originally published in *Citizenship Studies*, volume 20, issue 6–7 (2016). When citing this material, please use the original page numbering for each article, as follows:

Chapter 2

Governing imperial citizenship: a historical account of citizenship revocation
Deirdre Troy
Citizenship Studies, volume 23, issue 4 (2019), pp. 304–319

Chapter 3

Discussing the human rights limits on loss of citizenship: a normative-legal perspective on egalitarian arguments regarding Dutch Nationality laws targeting Dutch-Moroccans
Tom L. Boekestein and Gerard-René de Groot
Citizenship Studies, volume 23, issue 4 (2019), pp. 320–337

Chapter 4

The politics of un-belonging: lessons from Canada's experiment with citizenship revocation
Elke Winter and Ivana Previsic
Citizenship Studies, volume 23, issue 4 (2019), pp. 338–355

Chapter 5

Denaturalisation and conceptions of citizenship in the 'war on terror"
Patrick Sykes
Citizenship Studies, volume 20, issue 6–7 (2016), pp. 749–763

Chapter 6

Simply a matter of compliance with the rules? The moralising and responsibilising function of fraud-based citizenship deprivation in France and the UK
Émilien Fargues
Citizenship Studies, volume 23, issue 4 (2019), pp. 356–371

Chapter 7

The concept of allegiance in citizenship law and revocation: an Australian study
Helen Irving
Citizenship Studies, volume 23, issue 4 (2019), pp. 372–387

For any permission-related enquiries please visit:
www.tandfonline.com/page/help/permissions

Notes on Contributors

Tom L. Boekestein, LLM (cantab), is a PhD candidate at the University of Cambridge. His research focusses on the impact of human rights guarantees on EU Citizenship, particularly in the context of Member State withdrawal. He has been writing contributions on Dutch nationality law for the GLOBALCIT project since 2016.

Gerard-René de Groot is Professor Emeritus of Comparative Law and Private International Law at Maastricht University and Professor of Private Law at the University of Aruba (West Indies). His main research focus is on nationality law. He has published more than 400 books, articles, and case notes in that field.

Émilien Fargues is a Max Weber Fellow at the European University Institute and a research associate in the Global Citizenship Governance project at the Robert Schuman Centre for Advanced Studies. He holds a PhD in Political Science from Sciences Po Paris.

Helen Irving is Professor of Law at the University of Sydney Law School. She writes and researches on constitutional law and history, gender and constitutional design, and constitutional citizenship. Her most recent publications include *Citizenship, Alienage and the Modern Constitutional State: A Gendered History* (2016); as editor, *Constitutions and Gender* (2017); and, as co-editor with Ruth Rubio-Marin, *Women as Constitution-Makers: Case Studies from the New Democratic Era* (2019).

Janie Pélabay is FNSP tenured Research Fellow at Sciences Po, Centre for Political Research (CEVIPOF), CNRS. In the field of political philosophy, she investigates the theoretical and practical challenges posed by pluralism to liberal democracy, and the contemporary debates on state neutrality, multiculturalism and patriotism. Her current research focuses on the political uses of "shared values" in public discourses and policies related to civic education, immigration, European integration.

Ivana Previsic received a PhD in sociology from the University of Ottawa in 2018. Her SSHRC funded doctoral thesis explored the post-9/11 experiences of Bosnian and Albanian muslim immigrants in Canada.

Réjane Sénac is a CNRS permanent senior Research Fellow at Sciences Po, Centre for Political Research (CEVIPOF). Her researches bring political theory and a cognitive approach to public policy together to examine the tensions between republican and liberal notions of equality and liberty as well as their intertwining with identity issues. They focus on public justifications for equality policies (parity, diversity, same-sex marriage, etc.) and the principles of justice at stake in the latter.

Patrick Sykes is a senior energy market reporter (LNG, Gas, Power) at Independent Commodity Intelligence Services (ICIS). He received a first-class degree in English Literature from the University of Cambridge, and an MA in political science and international relations from Boğaziçi University, Turkey.

Deirdre Troy is a PhD candidate in the School of Politics and International Relations, Queen Mary University of London. Her research explores histories of citizenship and subjecthood, particularly in the context of the British Nationality Acts.

Elke Winter is Professor of Sociology at the University of Ottawa, research director at the Centre for Interdisciplinary Research on Citizenship and Minorities (CIRCEM) and, in 2019–20, the William Lyon Mackenzie King Chair for Canadian Studies at the Weatherhead Center for International Affairs, Harvard University. Professor Winter's research is concerned with questions of migration, ethnic diversity, integration and citizenship.

Conditional membership: what revocation does to citizenship

Émilien Fargues and Elke Winter

Abstract

The variety of contexts in which citizenship revocation is being discussed and applied confronts us with a complex map. Drawing on contributions at the crossroads between history, law, political science and sociology, this volume offers an interdisciplinary and comparative examination of this political instrument, revealing hidden rationales and consequences at the material and symbolic levels. In this introduction, we argue that the contributions to the volume expand the scope of the existing literature in terms of the social actors that are investigated, as well as the rationales for citizenship revocation that are investigated. We also introduce three levels of analysis according to which authors have explored revocation: conditionality, consequentiality and bordering processes. We then outline the contributions of the articles reassembled here at these three levels.

Citizenship revocation has been brought back onto the political agenda of many countries across the globe. Public debate on the need to revoke the citizenship of alleged terrorists took place not only in Europe (France in 2015, Turkey in 2016, the Netherlands in 2017, to name a few) and North America (Canada in 2014), but also in the Middle East (Israel in 2008 and, more recently, Bahrain and Oman in 2014) and the Southern Hemisphere (Australia in 2015). Debate on citizenship revocation is not confined to terror-related issues. After a number of failed attempts to legalise citizenship revocation in the United States (Sykes *this volume*), the Trump administration recently announced the creation of a 'denaturalization task force' to struggle against alleged fraudulent acquisitions of citizenship (Wessler 2018).

The variety of the contexts in which citizenship revocation is being actively put in practice and discussed as a potential solution to real or assumed societal ills presents us with a complex map. At a time when native populations often endorse citizenship revocation as a seemingly simple, effective and just means to get rid of those who are no longer wanted,[1] it seems all the more necessary to clarify the many issues that this policy instrument raises: how far can governments go in extending their leeway to revoke citizenship? What strategies do they follow? Do these strategies vary from one state to another? Are there limits to citizenship revocation that states have to obey? These are just some of the questions that this volume addresses.

In recent scholarship, the controversial character of citizenship revocation has mostly been discussed from legal and normative viewpoints. Legal scholars have examined whether citizenship revocation conflicts with specific rules that states ought to respect, such as non-discrimination. Macklin, for instance, has made the case that citizenship revocation discriminates between single and dual nationals (Macklin 2014). Indeed, statelessness as a result of citizenship revocation has been prohibited by the United Nations' Convention Against Statelessness since 1961. This privileges those who – as single nationals – are in a 'monogamous relationship' (Rubinstein and Lenagh-Maguire 2014) with the state that they were born in. Only they possess a secure national membership that cannot be withdrawn. While this legal argument may be true for a large number of countries, the divisions that citizenship revocation draws between individuals may not be the same depending on the contexts in which it is implemented. Most importantly, the British case has shown that statelessness may not always be regarded as an insuperable obstacle to citizenship revocation. In 2014, an amendment was made to the British Nationality Act allowing the Home Secretary to strip citizenship from individuals who allegedly pose a threat to the 'public good' even though this results in statelessness. However, only naturalised citizens now face the consequence of statelessness, not British-born citizens (Mills 2016). Therefore, single nationals (depending on how they became citizens) are not necessarily protected from statelessness. In short, legal analysis is important, but a purely legal approach to citizenship revocation risks leaving aside sociological divisions (based on class, gender, or race) that often become entangled with the distinctions that law creates between citizens, but that sometimes only partly overlap with them.

Normative debates have focused on the circumstances under which citizenship revocation could be considered a legitimate form of punishment (Gibney 2013; Joppke 2016; Lavi 2011; Macklin and Bauböck 2015). Drawing on different conceptions of citizenship (citizenship as a contract, citizenship as an unconditional right), scholars have reached contradictory conclusions. Joppke (2016), most prominently, holds that there are circumstances where individuals repudiate their allegiance to the political community they belong to (which arguably is the case in 'Islamist terror'). He argues that the reciprocal relationship between the state and these individuals is broken up in these circumstances, and hence it becomes legitimate to revoke citizenship.[2] In stark contrast, emphasising the responsibility that states have towards their citizens (including their 'bad guys') and doubting the effectiveness of the measure to counterterrorism, Bauböck (2015) maintains that the revival of citizenship revocation in the context of terrorism cannot be regarded as a legitimate form of punishment.

These are important questions, and this volume is indeed interested in understanding with which legal rules and normative values citizenship revocation is likely to conflict. It also aims to uncover which conceptions of citizenship drive policy changes in this domain (see Pélabay and Sénac, *this volume*). However, our goal here is neither to determine whether revocation is legal under certain national and international standards nor to debate whether it represents a just punishment. Rather, the contributions assembled here use the legal and normative controversies that citizenship revocation raises as a springboard to develop a discussion on the different dimensions of citizenship as a concept.

Drawing on Joppke (2007) and Carens (2000), we distinguish between three main dimensions of citizenship. The first dimension refers to the *legal bond* that ties an individual to a given state (citizenship in the legal sense of 'nationality'). Other states recognise this legal bond, which confers rights and duties upon all the individuals who possess the same status. Second, citizenship can be also characterised as *practices of participation* in a political community. As Winter and Previsic remind us in this volume, some of these practices are identified as 'good' forms of behaviour in the community, while others are held as unacceptable and are therefore likely to give rise to sanctions (including citizenship revocation). Citizenship's third dimension refers to *identity* or *belonging*. This dimension operates at the symbolic level. It links citizenship to the idea of the nation as an 'imagined community' (Anderson 2006). The chapters in this volume speak to all three levels of citizenship as they pertain to citizenship revocation. In the afterword, Pélabay and Sénac further explain that these three dimensions of citizenship can be, respectively, linked to different political theories (liberalism, republicanism and communitarianism) and used as analytical tools to investigate the 'thinner' or 'thicker' character that citizenship revocation gives to national membership.

In the remainder of this introduction, we first circumscribe the theoretical approach to citizenship that guides the contributions of this volume. We then distinguish between three levels of analysis in the ways in which citizenship revocation affects the three dimensions that are inherent to the concept of citizenship.

We approach citizenship as a mechanism of 'social closure' (Brubaker 1992) that not only differentiates between 'citizens' and 'aliens' but that also draws a line between 'desirable' and 'undesirable' citizens (Byrne 2014). The laws and practices defining citizenship produce such categories that often intertwine with divisions based on race, gender or class (Anderson 2013; Isin 2002). While citizenship rules and procedures are not necessarily path dependent in a deterministic sense, uncovering their historical emergence helps us to better understand how the boundary between 'desirable' vs. 'undesirable' citizens is conceived in a given national context today (Bertossi and Duyvendak 2012). Citizenship rules and procedures have both a material and a symbolic significance. They do not only have very concrete effects on people's lives, but they also feed into societal norms and representations of otherness. Based on a principle of 'exclusive inclusion' that includes some individuals and rejects others (Turner 2014), citizenship can thus serve as a technique for managing the 'undesirable' subjects (see Troy, *this volume*).

The chapters in this volume investigate how the 'exclusionary function' of citizenship (Nyers 2009) plays out in revocation policies; they also locate this function within larger governing strategies. Identifying which governing strategies are at stake in revocation policies allows analysis of how they affect the three aforementioned dimensions of citizenship at the empirical and at the theoretical level. For example, the liberalisation of citizenship, which is seen as the main driver of policy changes over the second half of the twentieth century (Hansen and Weil 2001), is said to have transformed national identities into 'thin and procedural forms' (Joppke 2010, 12) and reduced the gap between citizens' and foreign residents' rights (especially with respect to social rights). At the same time – and in contradiction – a 'renationalisation' of citizenship (Joppke 2010; Mouritsen 2012) is said to have taken place where integration' is seen as a condition of citizenship (and not as its consequence), and where 'good citizenship' is increasingly linked to the adherence to specific moral or cultural values (Pélabay 2017). As a result, we now have (more) reason to believe that citizenship matters not only in terms of rights and duties but also in terms of a common conduct or culture (see Sykes *this volume*) that newcomers are required to adopt in order to be considered eligible for citizenship. This points to the 'promotion of a thick conception of membership, whether republican or communitarian', that challenges the liberal branding of both contemporary citizenship policies and the states that implement them (see Pélabay and Sénac, *this volume*, 114). The chapters in this volume clarify which governing strategies apply to revocation policies. They show what consequences these strategies have not only for the people being targeted, but also for society at large. They also locate revocation policies within the rules, discourses and practices that govern migration and citizenship policies more broadly and are therefore able to identify logics of convergence and divergence.

Drawing on contributions at the crossroads between history, law, political science and sociology, this volume offers an interdisciplinary and comparative examination of citizenship revocation, which reveals hidden rationales and consequences at the material and symbolic levels. More specifically, the contributions presented here significantly expand the scope of the existing literature on citizenship revocation, in at least in three respects. First, they focus on a wide range of social actors, not only on national governments. They question the roles of parliamentarians and civil society in the reconfiguration of revocation policies (Winter and Previsic, as well as Sykes), the discretion that bureaucrats enjoy in their implementation (Fargues), and the protections that supranational institutions provide to individuals (Boekestein and de Groot). Second, rather than concentrating purely on citizenship revocation related to terrorism, the authors included in this volume also investigate other grounds of citizenship revocation (Fargues, Troy). Third, they put recent legislative changes and revocation practices into historical perspective (Irving, Troy) in order to identify continuities and/or ruptures with the past and to situate citizenship revocation within broader changes in citizenship policies.

Furthermore, the chapters presented here showcase a number of different methodological perspectives. Citizenship revocation is investigated on the basis of three levels of analysis: (1) conditionality, (2) consequentiality and (3) bordering processes.

1. Conditionality raises two main questions: what amount of discretion do governments have in their hands in revocation processes? Has the executive's latitude been extended or limited in recent years and what have been the arguments brought forward to expand or constrain it?
2. Consequentiality has to do with the consequences that revocation has for people's lives. It also relates to the different (material and symbolic) objectives that states pursue through revocation policies.
3. Bordering processes refer to the boundaries that revocation draws between individuals and/or groups and the categories it creates or perpetuates. We can investigate whether these categories are conceived politically, morally and/or culturally.

The chapters assembled here offer contributions at all three levels. First, as far as conditionality is concerned, the contributions demonstrate the high variability of the legal constraints that bind national governments either in the changes that they wish to bring to citizenship revocation or in the way that they implement this instrument. The limits that domestic and international law set forth in citizenship revocation (especially with respect to the prevention of statelessness) vary greatly depending on the specificities of national contexts and procedures. As has already been mentioned above with respect to citizenship revocation in the United Kingdom (UK), the prevention of statelessness is not necessarily considered as an insuperable obstacle to citizenship revocation.[3] Moreover, as Fargues (*this volume*) reveals, the prohibition of statelessness does not apply solely to citizenship revocation based on national security concerns but also to citizenship revocation on grounds of fraud. Although statelessness as a consequence of fraud-based citizenship revocation is allowed by international law, states will sometimes organise the revocation procedure in such a way that the citizens targeted will not normally become stateless. In

France, for example (contrary to the UK), the judges from the Council of State exercise direct control over fraud-based revocation orders, which allows them to prevent those that would result in statelessness. This also shows that we have to go beyond the legal analysis of international agreements. Rather, to understand more accurately what constrains the exercise of discretionary power scholars need to examine how citizenship revocation is bureaucratically organised. The difficulties faced by those who wish to resist increasing revocation powers are also underlined in other chapters in this volume. Boekestein and de Groot show that while international observers have brought strong indications of discrimination affecting Dutch-Moroccans in the Netherlands, the legislation remains unchanged, and is thereby in contradiction with the European Convention of Human Rights. These authors make a valuable contribution to the scholarship examining the effectiveness of international law in protecting individuals against revocation orders (Mantu 2018). As Pélabay and Sénac (*this volume*, 115) argue in the afterword, the weakening of legal protections that comes with the revival of citizenship-stripping is part of a larger 'return of patriotism' that holds 'the rule of human rights and humanitarian law' as an obstacle to 'national security'. Interestingly, in many countries, public opinion tends to support legislative changes expanding citizenship revocation. Furthermore, governments often keep their practices secret, thereby preventing a broad and informed public debate on the topic.[4] However, there are also cases where public opposition and political campaigns against citizenship revocation have resulted in the blockage or withdrawal of legislations that were seen as one-sided and discriminatory. This was the case in the United States in 2014 (see Sykes *this volume*) and Canada in 2016 (see Winter and Previsic, *this volume*).

With respect to consequentiality, the chapters in this volume highlight the material significance of the sanctions implied by citizenship revocation. Revocation has important consequences for people's lives; however, these consequences differ depending on the national context and the procedures at stake. The comparison between revocation policies based on national security concerns and those based on grounds of fraud reveals important differences in this respect. States may pursue removal strategies in the first type of revocation (see Boekestein and de Groot, *this volume*), but not in the latter (see Fargues, *this volume*). Differences between cases also emerge with regard to statelessness, as has already been mentioned above. These material effects of citizenship revocation are not disconnected from its more symbolic consequences. A common feature in the cases presented here lies in the symbolic use that governments make of citizenship-stripping as a 'technology of reassurance' (Fortier 2008), which aims at calming down the native population and at threatening those who are deemed to not behave as they should. In this regard, revocation policies illustrate the 'exclusionary potential of affective citizenship' (Di Gregorio and Merolli 2016). They exemplify the ways in which governments exploit unease and anxieties to pit those whom they claim to protect against those who should fear the threat of retaliation. Revocation policies thereby feed into existing 'us' vs. 'them' narratives. Winter and Previsic (*this volume*, 56) define citizenship revocation as 'an act of un-belonging, which removes the convicted individual not only from society (as imprisonment would do), but also from the national community (withdrawal of legal status) and its collective imaginary (denial of belonging)'. Similarly, Irving (*this volume*) reflects on the symbolic dimension of citizenship-stripping. More specifically, she observes that governments tend to justify citizenship revocation by means of a rhetoric based on 'allegiance', 'loyalty' and 'national values'. Irving invites us to ponder whether and to what extent these discourses revive a conduct-based conception of citizenship.

The insights offered by this volume into the material and symbolic forms of exclusion caused by citizenship revocation open up a broader discussion of the underlying bordering processes. Sykes (*this volume*) situates the debates about citizenship revocation within the broader policy convergence in public discourses and policy making away from multiculturalism and towards assimilation or 'civic integration'. Within this convergence (Mouritsen, Kriegbaum and Larin 2019), citizenship revocation appears thus as the ultimate exclusion of those who do not or cannot assimilate. Indeed, a finding common to all chapters is that revocation policies implicitly or explicitly target not merely individuals but specific collective categories. These categories are often racially constructed, and history is the key to understand how they emerge and operate. In the case of the UK, Troy (*this volume*) argues that the 'undesirable' subjects that citizenship revocation constructs (together with other citizenship policies, such as naturalisation policies) can be traced back to the colonial conferences that led to the introduction of revocation powers in 1914. In many of the forthcoming chapters, Muslims surface as the most obvious target of the legislative changes invoking terror-related concerns as reasons for denationalisation. With respect to the Netherlands, Boekestein and de Groot (*this volume*) explain that revocation can only be used against individuals who have allegedly joined one of the three organisations identified as 'Islamist'. Being suspected of having joined other 'terrorist' organisations – such as the Partiya Karkerên Kurdistanê (PKK), which is considered as 'terrorist' by the European Union – cannot result in the loss of one's citizenship. Focusing on the public discourses on citizenship revocation in Canada, Winter and Previsic (*this volume*, 55) further show that Muslims have been targeted 'not as individual criminals, but as a group'. This echoes concerns raised by other scholars (Choudhury 2017; Mazouz 2016) who claim that the revival of citizenship revocation in the context of the 'war against terror' legitimises forms of exclusion specifically directed against Muslims. In fuelling suspicions about Muslims being 'terrorists' who should be banned from the 'national community', revocation policies portray them as a threatening homogeneous group and encourage Islamophobia (Hajjat and Mohammed 2013). Pélabay and Sénac (*this volume*, 121) further explain that the emphasis on allegiance to so-called 'national values' in contemporary citizenship policies presents Muslims as 'ethical dissidents' and points to a process of 'ethicisation-cum-ethnicisation of citizenship'. With this notion, Pélabay and Sénac shed light on how the reference to a common culture that would allegedly bind the citizens of a given state together justifies the exclusion from citizenship of specific categories of migrants who are being assigned to a different cultural sub-group than the majority. Authors contributing to this volume argue that the targeting of certain groups and the propagation of racial stereotypes is not specific to terror-related types of revocation. Similar processes can be seen in revocation policies on the grounds of fraud (Fargues, *this volume*) and when crimes are cited to justify citizenship-stripping (Troy, *this volume*).

To conclude, there is a commonality to the multiplicity of contexts and cases of citizenship revocation rules, discourses and practices examined here. The 'unmaking' of citizenship through revocation constructs two classes of citizens: it creates a category of 'accidental' citizens – that is, citizens whose participation and belonging into the political community remain debatable – and opposes them to 'essential' citizens, whose membership is never called into question (Nyers 2006). The chapters assembled in this volume invite us to further explore the extent to which such categories overlap with other categories based on class, gender or race.

Notes

1. The expansion of citizenship revocation to all dual nationals was largely supported in France in 2015 (more than 80% of people were in favour of the expansion).
2. However legitimate, Joppke nevertheless argues that citizenship revocation involves too many practical issues and should not be implemented.
3. Even though – to date – no case of citizenship revocation based on 'public good' grounds leading to statelessness has ever been reported in the UK.
4. The investigations of journalists from *The Bureau of Investigative Journalism* (URL: www.thebureauinvestigates.com) have been crucial in publicising the extent of the revocation policy in the UK, which would have otherwise remained hidden.

Acknowledgements

The preparation of this volume and the introduction benefited from various sources of support from (in alphabetical order) the Alexander von Humboldt Foundation, the Canada Program, Weatherhead Center for International Affairs at Harvard University, the Centre of Excellence 'Cultural Foundations of Integration' at the University of Konstanz, the Fonds France Canada pour la Recherche, and a Mitacs Globalink Research Scholarship. The guest editors would like to thank Dr. Réjane Sénac and Dr. Janie Pélabay for their respective roles as chair and discussant of the 2018 IPSA panel 'When States Take Rights Back: Questioning the Public Justifications of Citizenship Revocation' (RC14.34), which served as a springboard to this publication project. The guest editors are grateful for the critiques received from numerous anonymous reviewers and from the *Citizenship Studies* editors: your investment made this endeavour better! The remaining errors and omissions are solely ours.

Disclosure statement

No potential conflict of interest was reported by the authors.

References

Anderson, B. 2006. *Imagined Communities: Reflections on the Origin and Spread of Nationalism*. London: Verso.

Anderson, B. 2013. *Us and Them? The Dangerous Politics of Immigration Control*. Oxford: Oxford University Press.

Bauböck, R. 2015. "Whose Bad Guys Are Terrorists?" In *The Return of Banishment: Do the New Citizenship Revocation Policies Weaken Citizenship?*, edited by A. Macklin and R. Bauböck, 27–30. Florence: European University Institute.

Bertossi, C., and J. W. Duyvendak. 2012. "National Models of Immigrant Integration: The Cost for Comparative Research." *Comparative European Politics* 10 (3): 237–247. doi:10.1057/ cep.2012.10

Boekestein, T., and G.-R de Groot. 2020. "Discussing the Human Rights Limits on Loss of Citizenship: A Normative-Legal Perspective on Egalitarian Arguments Regarding Dutch Nationality Laws Targeting Dutch-Moroccans." *When States Take Rights Back: Citizenship Revocation and Its Discontents*, edited by É. Fargues, E. Winter and M. J. Gibney, 26–43. Abingdon: Routledge.

Brubaker, R. 1992. *Citizenship and Nationhood in France and Germany*. Cambridge: Harvard University Press.

Byrne, B. 2014. *Making Citizens: Public Rituals and Personal Journeys to Citizenship*. Basingstoke: Palgrave Macmillan.

Carens, J. 2000. *Culture, Citizenship, and Community: A Contextual Exploration of Justice as Evenhandedness*. Oxford: Oxford University Press.

Choudhury, T. 2017. "The Radicalisation of Citizenship Deprivation." *Critical Social Policy* 37 (2): 225–244. doi:10.1177/0261018316684507

Di Gregorio, M., and J. Merolli. 2016. "Introduction: Affective Citizenship and the Politics of Identity, Control, Resistance." *Citizenship Studies* 20 (8): 933–942. doi:10.1080/13621025.2016.1229193

Fargues, E. 2020. "Simply a Matter of Compliance with the Rules? The Moralising and Responsibilising Function of Fraud-Based Citizenship Deprivation in France and the UK." *When States Take Rights Back: Citizenship Revocation and Its Discontents*, edited by É. Fargues, E. Winter and M. J. Gibney, 77–92. Abingdon: Routledge.

Fortier, A.-M. 2008. *Multicultural Horizons: Diversity and the Limits of the Civil Nation*. London: Routledge.

Gibney, M. 2013. "Should Citizenship Be Conditional? The Ethics of Denationalization." *The Journal of Politics* 75 (3): 646–658. doi:10.1017/S0022381613000352

Hajjat, A., and M. Mohammed. 2013. *Islamophobie. Comment Les Élites Françaises Fabriquent Le "Problème Musulman"*. Paris: La Découverte.

Hansen, R., and P. Weil. 2001. *Towards a European Nationality. Citizenship, Immigration and Nationality Law in the EU*. Basingstoke: Palgrave Macmillan.

Irving, H. 2020. "The Concept of Allegiance in Citizenship Law and Revocation: An Australian Study." *When States Take Rights Back: Citizenship Revocation and Its Discontents*, edited by É. Fargues, E. Winter and M. J. Gibney, 93–108. Abingdon: Routledge.

Isin, E. 2002. *Being Political: Genealogies of Citizenship*. Minneapolis: University of Minnesota Press.

Joppke, C. 2007. "Transformation of Citizenship: Status, Rights, Identity." *Citizenship Studies* 11 (1): 37–48. doi:10.1080/13621020601099831

Joppke, C. 2010. "The Inevitable Lightening of Citizenship." *European Journal of Sociology* 51 (1): 9–32. doi:10.1017/S0003975610000019

Joppke, C. 2016. "Terror and the Loss of Citizenship." *Citizenship Studies* 20 (6–7): 728–748. doi:10.1080/13621025.2016.1191435

Lavi, S. 2011. "Punishment and the Revocation of Citizenship in the United Kingdom, United States, and Israel." *New Criminal Law Review: An International and Interdisciplinary Journal* 13 (2): 404–426.

Macklin, A. 2014. "Citizenship Revocation, the Privilege to Have Rights and the Production of the Alien." *Queen's Law Journal* 40 (1): 1–54.

Macklin, A., and R. Bauböck, Eds. 2015. *The Return of Banishment: Do the New Denationalisation Policies Weaken Citizenship?*. Florence: European University Institute.

Mantu, S. 2018. "'Terrorist' Citizens and the Human Right to Nationality." *Journal of Contemporary European Studies* 26 (1): 28–41. doi:10.1080/14782804.2017.1397503

Mazouz, S. 2016. "Politiques de la Délégitimation: De la Remise en Cause de la Double Nationalité au Projet d'Extension de la Déchéance de Nationalité." *Mouvements*. 88: 159–167. doi:10.3917/mouv.088.0159.http://mouvements.info/politiques-de-la-delegitimation-de-la-remise-en- cause-de-la-double-nationalite-au-projetdextension-de-la-decheance-de-nationalite/

Mills, B. 2016. *'A Privilege, Not a Right': Contemporary Debates on Citizenship Deprivation in Britain and France*. Oxford: COMPAS Working Paper.

Mouritsen, P. 2012. "Beyond Postnational Citizenship: Access, Consequence, Conditionality." In *European Multiculturalisms: Cultural, Religious and Ethnic Challenges*, edited by A. Triandafyllidou, T. Modood, and N. Meer, 88–115. Edinburgh: Edinburgh University Press.

Mouritsen, P., Kriegbaum J. K., and Larin, S. J. (2019). "Introduction: Theorizing the Civic Turn in European Integration Policies." *Ethnicities*, 19(4): 595–613. doi:10.1177/1468796819843532

Nyers, P. 2006. "The Accidental Citizen: Acts of Sovereignty and (Un)Making Citizenship." *Economy and Society* 35 (1): 22–41. doi:10.1080/03085140500465824

Nyers, P., ed. 2009. *Securitizations of Citizenship*. London: Routledge.

Pélabay, J. 2017. "La République Des «Valeurs»: Entre Public Et Privé, Quel Lien Citoyen?" In *La Démocratie De L'entre-Soi*, edited by P. Perrineau, 119–132. Paris: Presses de Sciences Po.

Pélabay, J., and Sénac, R. 2020 "Citizenship Revocation: A Stress Test for Liberal Democracy." *When States Take Rights Back: Citizenship Revocation and Its Discontents*, edited by É. Fargues, E. Winter and M. J. Gibney, 109–125. Abingdon: Routledge.

Rubinstein, K., and Lenagh-Maguire, N. 2014. "More or Less Secure? Nationality Questions, Deportation and Dual Nationality." In *Nationality and Statelessness under International Law*, edited by A. Edwards and L. Van Waas, 264–291. Cambridge: Cambridge University Press.

Sykes, P. 2020. "Denaturalisation and Conceptions of Citizenship in the 'War on Terror'". *When States Take Rights Back: Citizenship Revocation and Its Discontents*, edited by É. Fargues, E. Winter and M. J. Gibney, 62–76. Abingdon: Routledge.

Troy, D. 2020 "Governing Imperial Citizenship: A Historical Account of Citizenship Revocation." *When States Take Rights Back: Citizenship Revocation and Its Discontents*, edited by É. Fargues, E. Winter and M. J. Gibney, 10–25. Abingdon: Routledge.

Turner, B. 2014. "Testing the Liberal Subject: (In)Security, Responsibility and 'Self-Improvement' in the UK Citizenship Test." *Citizenship Studies* 18 (3–4): 332–348.

Wessler, S. F. 2018. "Is Denaturalization the Next Front in the Trump Administration's War on Immigration?" *New York Times*. www.nytimes.com/2018/12/19/magazine/naturalized-citizenship-immigration-trump.html

Winter, E., and I. Previsic. 2020. "The Politics of Un-Belonging: Lessons from Canada's Experiment with Citizenship Revocation." *When States Take Rights Back: Citizenship Revocation and Its Discontents*, edited by É. Fargues, E. Winter and M. J. Gibney, 44–61. Abingdon: Routledge.

Governing imperial citizenship: a historical account of citizenship revocation

Deirdre Troy

ABSTRACT

In recent years, citizenship revocation has become synonymous with terrorism, regarded as a practice reserved for the most dangerous of citizens. Yet in the UK revocation has a much longer history, spanning over 100 years, with a narrative that extends beyond the nation-state and into Empire. This paper asks what may be learned from a historical account of citizenship revocation? Exploring its emergence as part of the British Nationality and Status of Aliens Act 1914, this account suggests that revocation should not be analyzed in isolation but as a practice embedded in polices of immigration, naturalization, and emigration. This paper illustrates the ways in which these policies code subjects based on race, class and gender in order to govern their mobility. From this study, it argues that citizenship revocation cannot be explained solely through security claims and suggests that the 2018 cases should be considered in the context of revocation's history.

Introduction

In an interview with the Associated Press following his capture in February 2018, one of 'ISIS' infamous British fighters'[1], Alexanda Amon Kotey, expressed surprise at the ability of the UK government to revoke his citizenship, saying, '"I was born in the UK… My mother was born in the UK. I have a daughter there in the UK… I probably never left the UK more than 3 months" before coming to Syria' (Associated Press, 30 March 2018). But for those who have studied the evolution of citizenship revocation as a technology of government from 2002, Kotey's case is one that fits comfortably within current security discourse. Since amendments were made to the British Nationality Act in 2002, parliamentary debates, press conferences and media coverage have all contributed to the meaning applied to revocation – that it is primarily a technology of national security, one to be used against terrorists. This, in turn, positions the analysis of revocation within a framework of exception, suggesting a practice reserved for the most dangerous and undesirable of citizens.

In accepting this framework of exception, some scholars critique the practice as one that potentially weakens citizenship, arguing that citizenship becomes less secure if retaining the status is contingent on performance (Macklin 2018). Others, building on the dangerous citizen rhetoric, debate how violent or threatening a citizen must be before they should lose their status (Barry and Ferracioli 2016; Joppke 2016). In effect, each of these arguments locates revocation outside of, or separate to, citizenship, as something that is done to the institution rather than a practice that is a part of it.

A study of the history of citizenship revocation in the UK calls for pause on this framing. Tracing a narrative that extends beyond the nation-state and into Empire, this study positions revocation not as an exception to citizenship, but as a practice that represents the logic of citizenship – a logic that divides and codes subjects, categorizing them as desirable or undesirable. In what follows, I ask what may be learned from a historical account of citizenship revocation? Exploring the conditions of its emergence as part of the British Nationality and Status of Aliens Act (BNSAA) 1914, this account illustrates that citizenship revocation was a practice that belonged not to national security but to citizenship, and this study draws us away from the exception and into an imperial strategy of governing subject mobility. The following analysis demonstrates three points: it removes the BNSAA and the introduction of revocation from a state-centric focus and positions it firmly within an imperial framework. Secondly, it places citizenship revocation within a series of practices that developed through the governing of British Empire and argues that it should not be analyzed in isolation, but as a technology embedded in imperial polices of immigration, naturalization, and emigration, policies which governed the mobility of subjects. Thirdly, calling the framework of exception into question, this analysis points to changes in 2018 in how citizenship revocation is used and suggests that these changes be explored in the context of revocation's history.

The paper begins by looking at citizenship revocation in the UK from 2002 and identifies how revocation became synonymous with terrorism in public discourse. It then introduces theoretical and methodological frameworks through which revocation will be analyzed. Following this, the paper turns to a historicization of this practice. Beginning with a background to the colonial negotiations and the ways in which mobility was governed before the BNSAA, it then contextualises the Act with a critical study of the colonial conferences (a series of meetings that British imperial authorities initiated with a view to reaching agreement with the self-governing colonies on the governing of Empire) that preceded the passing of this legislation. The negotiations surrounding immigration, naturalization, and emigration are examined before the conditions of revocation are explored. Focusing on the codification of subjects, this paper highlights the racial, class and gendered thinking behind the BNSAA and argues that revocation must be critiqued not in exceptionalist terms, but as another component of the laws and practices that produce the citizen.

Citizenship and security

In 2003, Home Secretary David Blunkett announced on BBC 4's flagship news and current affairs show, 'Today', that Muslim cleric Abu Hamza was to lose his British status[2] (*BBC News*, 5 April 2003). The announcement followed months of debates in parliament over the perceived threat of international terrorism where Abu Hamza and others were singled out as using their 'position at the mosque to promote a message of violent and radical extremism' (HC Deb 16 October 2001 vol 372 cc1087). Calls were made for the Home Secretary's revocation powers to be extended (HC Deb

16 October 2001 vol 372 cc1088). Once amendments were drafted, the Nationality, Immigration and Asylum Bill 2002 was passed and inserted into the British Nationality Act 1981 to toughen conditions of naturalization and broaden the scope for the revocation of status. Unique to the 2002 amendments was the inclusion of a provision that allowed for the revocation of status of natural-born citizens holding dual-nationality. Until this point, the law was only applicable to naturalized and registered citizens.

Since the Abu Hamza case, MPs have turned to revocation at moments of heightened national security, positioning the revocation of citizenship within a counter-terrorism narrative. At a press conference held in 2005, after the bombings of 7/7, then Prime Minister Tony Blair announced that 'the rules of the game are changing' and revealed new security measures drafted by the government. Blair pointed to existing powers to strip citizenship and stated '[w]e will now consult on extending these powers, applying them to naturalized citizens engaged in extremism, and making the procedures simpler and more effective' (*The Guardian*, 5 August 2005).

In 2014, as part of the government's 'Hostile Environment' strategy, further amendments under a new Immigration Act strengthened the hand of government. In introducing the Bill, then Prime Minister David Cameron declared that what was needed was 'targeted, discretionary power to allow us to exclude British nationals from the UK' (HC Deb 1 September 2014 vol 585 cc26). In his address, the Prime Minister was careful to mention that the new revocation powers outlined in the Bill would not apply to 'those who are solely British nationals, who could be rendered stateless if deprived of citizenship' (ibid.). This aligned the new Immigration Act with international standards laid down by the European Convention of Human Rights and the European Convention on Nationality, restricting states from rendering citizens stateless[3]. In effect this new power targeted naturalized citizens disproportionately, establishing the legal right to remove the status of a naturalized citizen if the Secretary of State believed citizenship could be attained elsewhere (GOV.UK 2014, 66).

In 2018 the rules seemed to change once again. Though the cases of citizenship revocation from 2002 were framed as terror-related, 2018 saw the removal of status of three citizens involved in the Rochdale child exploitation scandal (*The Guardian*, 8 August 2018). At the Conservative Party conference, Home Secretary Sajid Javid hinted at stricter immigration and citizenship laws and stated that he would now use revocation powers to strip the status of 'some of those who are convicted of the most grave criminal offences'. '[O]ur message to the very worst criminals is clear', he continued, 'if you grossly abuse the laws of this country, you will no longer be welcome in our home' (CCHQ Press, 2 October 2018). With the government's line shifting, the scope for the removal of citizenship broadened to incorporate those involved in criminal activity more generally.

In the following sections, I explore citizenship revocation's history before returning to the 2018 cases and Javid's comments in the discussion below. The argument of this paper is not that the security logic has no place in an analysis of revocation. Instead, it suggests that when it becomes the dominant narrative, security obscures revocation's longer history, presenting the practice as something new and exceptional, overshadowing its position alongside other laws and practices that represent the logic of citizenship. The following historical account situates the Nationality Act and the rules governing subject mobility within a wider imperial context. Drawing on the work of Engin Isin and Bridget Anderson, the paper explores the production of the undesirable subject through their codification based on race, class and gender.

Disrupting categories of subjects

In arguing for citizenship revocation to be reconceptualized, this paper draws on the work of Isin (2002) and Anderson (2013). Both scholars interrogate the categories of citizen and non-citizen and challenge the seemingly binary relation between, for example, citizen and alien or citizen and migrant. Rather than viewed as distinct, these categories should be considered together. Isin explores the thesis of citizenship as alterity which accounts for the multiple relational positions of non-citizens to citizens within a political space. Questioning the reproduction of powerful imagery and narratives associated with the citizen, Isin examines the other categories produced each time citizenship is constituted and draws on the struggles and conflicts surrounding citizenship (Isin 2002). Anderson seeks to disrupt categories produced by what she terms the 'community of value' – a concept indicating how modern states portray themselves. The volatility and instability of categories are exposed as Anderson compares the Good Citizen with the Failed Citizen (the Criminal or Benefit Scrounger) or the Tolerated member (hard-working Migrant). Such categories are continuously in tension as subjects attempt to break out of or differentiate themselves from these prescribed categories (Anderson 2013).

For these scholars, behind the creation of these categories are struggles over power. Technologies and strategies of citizenship are shown to engage in the creation of difference (Isin 2002) with the laws and practices revealed as producing rather than reflecting a particular status (Anderson 2013). As a result, we cannot understand the citizen without looking at the categories that are simultaneously produced alongside the citizen. By linking the relation of 'privilege, power, and poverty to questions of mobility and state development' (p. 179), the work of these scholars encourages us to continually question the meaning behind the production of categories and ask how such categories are embedded in power relations.

This paper refers to this process by which laws and practices produce different categories as the logic of citizenship. This logic is a rule that underpins citizenship, that simultaneously produces multiple categories alongside the citizen through practices such as immigration, revocation, naturalization. The types of categories outlined by Isin correspond to those found in this history, and in the study below take the form of 'indigenous', 'poor', 'immigrant', 'alien'. As these subjects are rejected by governing powers, these codes eventually translate to 'undesirable' while subjects in the desirable category are often coded as 'white', 'educated' or 'wealthy' etc. These desirable and undesirable categories define one another. At the same time, they are fluid, accommodating race, class, gender, immigrants, aliens, and subjects. Coding subjects in this way facilitated the governing of subject mobility and indicated whether a subject would have their ability to migrate blocked through immigration law, or whether they could be granted a naturalization certificate. It indicated what rights and privileges a subject could expect. Following this theoretical perspective, it is argued that the practice of revoking status belongs to the logic of citizenship that divides and codes subjects.

Rather than framing it as an exception, revocation should be analyzed alongside practices such as immigration, naturalization and emigration.

To argue this thesis, this paper draws on a close reading of the colonial and imperial conference minutes of 1897, 1902, 1907 and 1911. These contain the negotiations that preceded the passing of the BNSAA. Exploring the imperial narrative serves two purposes: while the 1914 Act is often read as a national Act, it was an Act of Empire and was designed to govern the mobility of multiple populations within imperial territories. Positioning the BNSAA in an imperial framework offers a clearer insight into the class and racial coding hidden within the Act. The second benefit of exploring this imperial framework is that it illustrates how these practices were used together to govern subject mobility. While immigration, naturalization, emigration and revocation may sometimes be analyzed as disparate practices, the conference minutes show how these were designed to overlap and work together, creating desirable and undesirable categories.

Imperial codification of subjects

The strategy of governing mobility through the division and codification of subjects was one familiar to the imperial government. From the seventeenth to the early twentieth century, the British governed mobility utilizing cruder technologies such as convict transportation, the slave trade, and indentured labor. Evident in all three, and particularly true of convict transportation, was the codification of subjects which facilitated the movement of convicts around imperial territories. In Ireland and England, subjects classed as rebels, vagrants and petty thieves were among those who could expect to be transported. Talk of dangerous, immoral, incorrigible, lazy, diseased subjects necessitated their removal from society and helped to sustain a need for transportation (Gwynn 1932; Beattie 1974; Maxwell-Stewart 2010). This banishing practice saw 380,000 subjects forcibly moved around British territories[4]. From the 1780s, with the establishment of penal colonies in Australia and South and Southeast Asia, a further gradation entered this imperial code and at every opportunity authorities worked to divide convicts based on ethnic origin. Transported indigenous subjects of India and Australia were consistently positioned at the bottom of the order of transported subjects, resulting in worse treatment when compared with their European counterparts[5].

Yet the Empire was transforming, challenging the power Britain once had. From the mid-19th century, the white settler colonies began to seek more control over their own borders. Careful not to repeat mistakes made in the 1770s with the American colonies, and conscious of global political and economic developments that could threaten the Empire, the British government allowed the colonies of Canada, Australia, New Zealand, and South Africa to move towards self-governing status (Burbank and Cooper 2010, 300; Kendle 1967). These self-governing colonies, eventually termed 'Dominions' in 1907 to signal a shift to a commonwealth logic, were given some control over domestic affairs, while an additional layer of rule at imperial level remained (Burbank and Cooper 2010, 300).

Not long after a new administration was established in Australia in the 1850s, the Australian penal colonies of New South Wales, Van Diemen's Land and Western

Australia closed, ending transportation of European subjects on a large scale. In India, where transportation continued, a century-long resistance to British rule culminated in the first major challenge in 1857. Though the rebellion was defeated, independence movements and uprisings continued, threatening imperial control (Chandra et al. 2016). In light of these events, new efforts were made to consolidate the Empire. During the 1870s and 1880s, a system was devised which could regulate relations between Britain and the Dominions, resulting in the establishment of colonial conferences (Kendle 1967). Over the course of these conferences, Britain sought agreement on the mobility of subjects, and these lengthy negotiations led to the BNSAA and the introduction of citizenship revocation in the UK.

Exploring the logic of imperial citizenship

As this paper turns to the conference minutes, it details the arrangements made under each of the practices of citizenship. In particular, the analysis of these minutes provides two insights: no longer separate to citizenship, it repositions revocation within a series of practices, highlighting how immigration, naturalization, emigration and revocation were designed to work together to divide and code subjects. Secondly, in demonstrating how the category of undesirable subject is created through these laws, it calls to question the narrative that describes the subject suitable for revocation as exceptionally dangerous or undesirable.

Before the Act of 1914 was passed, a series of colonial, later named imperial, conferences were held in London[6]. Attended by representatives of Britain and the Dominions, these meetings were used to discuss matters relating to Empire and appeared increasingly constitutional in nature, covering everything from defence, trade, communications, taxation, and the mobility of subjects. The negotiations that precipitated the passing of the BNSAA focused on the possible codification of subjects based on race, class and gender. In many cases, the unofficial reason behind the rejection of subjects was racial though racial reasons were concealed and often reframed as an issue of class, renamed as one of character.

Immigration

Over the course of the negotiations, it was evident that Britain sought closer unity with the increasingly powerful Dominions. In 1902, Joseph Chamberlain called on their support in the administration of Empire, which they were told, 'is yours as well as ours' (CC 1902, 4). This invitation to share in the governing of Empire was also an attempt to regularise the mobility of subjects within the British territories. But Britain's proposed rules were frequently challenged as each Dominion arrived at the conference with their own border demands. Undoubtedly the greatest challenge facing agreement on imperial mobility, repeated at every conference, was the 'colour question' – Dominions' ability to discriminate against race. Following the Indian rebellion, the British government was reluctant to insert any official mention of race into imperial legislation (CC 1897, 14), and sought a new solution for the desires expressed by conference participants. The solution came in two parts: the first saw the agreement that immigration law could undermine naturalization legislation, while the second was a recoding of race as class, which appeared in legislation under character. Referencing character was a way of rejecting specific subjects without having to explicitly name them in law.

In controlling the mobility of imperial subjects, immigration law worked in tandem with naturalization legislation and was encouraged by the British authorities to be used in such a way (IC 1907, 538; IC 1911, 268). It was agreed during the conference of 1911 that immigration restrictions would undermine whatever inclusivity may have been constituted through the overarching naturalization legislation, with the resolution reading: '[n]othing now proposed would affect the validity and effectiveness of local laws regulating immigration and the like or differentiating between classes of British subjects' (IC 1911, 16).

Though it was agreed that immigration and naturalization legislation would operate in this way, the Dominions were told that their immigration laws, which explicitly named subjects of color, were not acceptable to the imperial government (CC 1897, 13). Mindful of the threats to British control in India, Chamberlain told the conference participants that the inclusion of race would offend Indian subjects, particularly those who had 'saved Empire by their loyalty' during the Indian rebellion. In place of the racialized language, Chamberlain proposed a new way of describing those the Dominions wished to exclude (CC 1897, 14). Instead of legislating for colour, as it was so crudely put, Chamberlain encouraged the self-governing colonies to target the character of the immigrant, suggesting that,

> It is not because a man is of a different colour from ourselves that he is necessarily an undesirable immigrant, but it is because he is dirty, or he is immoral, or he is a pauper, or he has some other objection which can be defined in an Act of Parliament, and in which the exclusion can be managed with regard to all those whom you really desire to exclude (CC 1897, 14).

The description not only bore similarities to the characterization of the banished convict decades previous, it also resembled words commonly used to describe the 'native' regardless of where they were from (Mangan 2012).

This covert codification of race through carefully worded legislation was an imperial strategy used under South African immigration law – known as the Natal Formula – of which Chamberlain was a keen proponent. This policy, requiring new immigrants to have £25 and a knowledge of a European language, avoided the insertion of race into law (Daniels 1995, 40). The laws framed under this policy could be non-discriminatory in their body 'because the real teeth would be secreted in the regulations governing their administration, well hidden from public view' (Huttenback 1973a, 112). In his discussion of immigration legislation, Chamberlain commended the colony of Natal on coming up with a solution that gave them 'all that they want' as far as restrictions were concerned, and encouraged the other participants to 'arrange a form of words which will avoid hurting the feelings of any of Her Majesty's subjects', while at the same time 'amply protect the Australian Colonies against any invasion of the class to which they would justly object' (CC 1897, 14). Thereby, Chamberlain introduced to the conference the possibility of coding for class and character to account for race, and thus sanctioned the exclusion of millions of subjects from the self-governing colonies.

Naturalisation

Naturalization is often positioned as the opposite of revocation – simply put, the granting of citizenship is explained as rights-giving and revocation as the removal of these rights. But when the negotiations leading to the Nationality Act in 1914 are examined, the logic underpinning these ostensibly opposing policies remained the same. Though naturalization law sought to determine the conditions under which someone could be granted status, the discussion throughout the conferences, for the most part, focused on who could be refused imperial subjecthood. While the British government pushed for unity, though not inclusivity, the protestations raised by the Dominions resembled those that arose under immigration, emigration and revocation and once again, using a different form of legislation, the conference participants discussed who could be kept out if an imperial Bill was passed.

The objections to the Bill as proposed to the conference centered on the potential naturalization of undesirable aliens in one part of the Empire, and the expected validation of that certificate in another[7]. The arguments made were heavily racialized, and just as it emerged under the discussion of emigration, outlined below, the Dominions wished to only admit subjects of European descent. Speaking for Australia, Alfred Deakin plainly stated that the only difficulty the naturalization question raised in his State was 'the admission of coloured races, and particularly coloured aliens' (CC 1907, 535). General Botha of Transvaal requested that the Bill should contain a clause that the certificate would 'have effect beyond the borders of such Colony only when granted to a person of European birth or descent' (CC 1907, 536). Botha also suggested that anyone whose father was an indentured servant of non-European descent should be excluded from the naturalization process – a direct attempt to target Indian subjects residing in South Africa. Joseph Ward of New Zealand raised objections broadly along similar lines to others and sought assurance that New Zealand would 'avoid the mixing up and the contamination of the races... by preserving it for white men' (CC 1907, 539).

Answering the Dominion concerns, the British government assured participants that British principles were as robust as any other. On the point of non-Europeans, Herbert Gladstone stated that the UK had admitted very few of non-European decent, and reminded the Dominions that Natal, which already had a policy of blocking non-Europeans from naturalization, accepted the UK's naturalization certificates as valid, thereby suggesting that there was no cause for concern over who the British chose to naturalize (CC 1907, 181). Further clarifying the difference between classes of subjects, Winston Churchill spoke of the discretionary nature of rights under naturalization. He stressed that a certificate of status did not guarantee equal treatment in the UK or in any Dominion within the British Empire and referred to the 'distinctions in this country between different classes of white British subjects' (IC 1911, 257). Responding to Wilfrid Laurier's suggestion that the issue of race was not really an issue for the UK as it did not face the same 'rush of immigration' the Dominions were experiencing (a point that proved poignant when an increase in migration into the UK resulted in a series of immigration Acts in the 1960s), Churchill attempted to reassure him that there was a strong feeling in the UK that aliens should not be able to obtain naturalization easily (IC 1911, 263). Adding to this, Solicitor General John Smith suggested that in the case of a natural-born British subject who was also a person of colour, the proposed laws did 'not in the least affect the legislative power of each and every Dominion either to exclude him or, if he comes inside the area of a Dominion, to deny him privileges which white people or persons speaking a European language enjoy' (IC 1911, 268).

Emigration

The rejection of specific subjects evident under immigration and naturalization was juxtaposed with the desire to attract others, and as with revocation, together these policies produced categories of desirable and undesirable subjects. Though the Dominions refused to accept immigrants from certain parts of the Empire, they were eager to attract other subjects, specifically white British subjects, in order to populate the self-governing colonies. Movement of subjects within the Empire continued on a large scale, with estimates of over 1.6 million leaving the UK in the 1880s, increasing as the years progressed (Constantine 2003, 19).

During the conferences, the Dominions, keen to grow their relatively small populations, appealed to Britain to keep the flow of migration coming from the UK exclusively within the boundaries of Empire, not wishing to draw their supply of immigrants from 'foreign sources' (IC 1911, 42). In response to the individual statements provided by the Dominion's representatives on emigration, the British government presented a long list of numbers, accounting for subjects who had emigrated from their shores. The discussion that accompanied these numbers reveals the implicit part played by the British government in maintaining and supporting the predominantly white appearance of the desirable imperial subject. The figures presented to the conference also emphasized the fact that mobility was open to those of the accepted race.

The president of the Local Government Board, John Burns, pointed to the increase in movement of subjects and announced that over four years Britain experienced a rise in emigration from 191,671 leaving in 1906 to 233,911 leaving in 1910. Burns projected total numbers in 1911 to reach 300,000 with an estimated 230,000 to stay within the Empire (IC 1911, 200). The Dominions were then warned not to expect more: 'with a diminishing birth rate and with an increasing emigration of fertile people, the Mother Country cannot safely go beyond 300,000 a year' (IC 1911, 200). Dominions were entitled to the surplus, they were told, but 'must not diminish the seed plot' of the Mother Country (ibid.).

Adding to the numbers of British subjects relocated to other parts of Empire were thousands of children sent through the boards of guardians and agencies such as Dr. Barnardo's (IC 1907, 172). Praising the British system of sending children to the self-governing colonies, Burns shared with the conference, 'in my judgment, [children] are perhaps the best form of emigrants and settlers looking ahead, that the Colonies could possibly have' (ibid.). Dominions were told that there were 650 boards of guardians working with the department of Local Government, sending to the self-governing colonies 'absolutely all the children they emigrate' (IC 1911, 201). Over 21 years, 9,300 poor law children had been relocated. Many of the children went to Canada, with Dr. Barnardo's sending close to 18,000 (CC 1907, 172).

As these three policies show, immigration, naturalization and emigration all responded to the same logic. Efforts were made by each of the imperial parties to reject subjects using the available governing practices, and this rejection was premised on the way in which subjects were coded. In Chamberlain's words, this took the form of dirty, immoral or poor, or as the Dominions suggested, simply non-European. Depending on how subjects were coded, they would either have their mobility restricted or facilitated by the British and Dominion governments. The final practice examined is revocation, officially introduced into the UK in 1914. When positioned alongside the practices analyzed above, it is clear that revocation carries with it the language and logic of the discussions on imperial citizenship.

Revocation

As with naturalization, revocation was positioned under Part II of the BNSAA – the section applicable to the Dominions should they chose to adopt it. While loss of subject status could occur under the Naturalisation Act of 1870 through either renunciation or automatic loss (if naturalized in another country), it was under the 1914 Act that revocation was first officially introduced into Britain (Fransman 2011, 5.7.1). It was, however, a policy already in practice in some of the Dominions. For example, Australia's Commonwealth Act II of 1903 blocked subjects from Asia, Africa or the Pacific Islands from naturalization, and empowered the governor general to revoke naturalization certificates already issued, without having to show cause for the removal of status (Huttenback 1973b).

Revocation orders under Section 7 of the BNSAA allowed the Secretary of State to strip status off naturalized subjects where a certificate was 'obtained by false representations or by fraud'. In 1918, powers were extended, and new provisions were added to allow for the revocation of status if the naturalized subject acted or spoke in a disloyal manner or communicated with or assisted the enemy during wartime. Those who were imprisoned, fined or served a term of penal servitude within 5 years of receiving a certificate would also lose their status (GOV.UK 1914, 7.2). Included was a provision that allowed for revocation if it was thought that the individual was not of good character at the time of naturalization (despite good character being a prerequisite for naturalization). And Section 7A stripped subjecthood off married women if their spouse was revoked of theirs. In any of the above, the status would be removed when the continuance of the certificate was 'not conducive to the public good' (GOV.UK 1914, 7).

One function of revocation after legislation was amended in 1918 was to target naturalized Germans following WWI (Gibney 2013). In parliamentary debates over the extension of powers, German naturalization was presented as a major concern, as one MP stated, 'I think the naturalised British subject of German birth is in many cases more dangerous than the alien enemy' (HL Deb 25 November 1914 vol 18 cc133). Yet, despite the voiced anxieties in parliament and the new amendments ushered in, the extension of powers in 1918 did not lead to a large number of revocation cases (Gibney 2013, 644).

While this was to be one function of revocation once introduced into the national setting, the legislation also bore marks of the imperial discussions of 1897–1911, and many of the points raised by conference participants under discussions of the three practices detailed above reappeared under citizenship revocation. One example was in the debate over the potential naturalization of criminals. The Dominions were apprehensive about the naturalization of a subject in one part of the Empire and the supposed recognition of that certificate in all parts of the Empire. In the anxieties expressed over the executive power granted to the Secretary of State, it was suggested to the British government that, 'there was nothing in the law to prevent in the Mother Country a certificate of naturalization being given to undesirables who might even be criminals, and in the second place to persons of non-European descent' (CC 1907, 180). After assuring that the Dominions' needs would be met, Gladstone suggested that it would be quite possible to consider whether certain 'classes of criminal undesirables' would be named in the Bill as being disqualified for naturalization, so as to 'express in law what, in fact, has been our practice in its administration in this country' (CC 1907, 180–181). Official mention of criminals was not inserted under naturalization but appeared under revocation. It was unofficially captured by the power to remove any certificate on the basis of false representation or fraud at the time of naturalization, while a clause covering convictions was added in 1918.

The inclusion of a character clause under both naturalization and later revocation continued the imperial logic behind its initial use and as mentioned above, character became code for all those imperial powers wished to exclude. The substitution of class for race expressed as a character was captured by Major Newman in his parliamentary address in 1918. Addressing the House of Commons, speaker Newman stated that he did not agree that the revocation clause was directed against naturalized German subjects (HC Deb 17 July 1918 vol 108 cc1140). He believed that Section 7 was the beginning of a series of measures that would 'make British citizenship something worth having'. To acquire it, 'one must have shown himself worthy of it' and once the subject was naturalised, they must show themselves 'worthy of keeping it' (ibid.), pointing to the permanently precarious position of naturalized subject under revocation laws.

He claimed that the introduction of this power would provide the government with an 'opportunity' to deal with undesirables, and he hoped that this Act would be the 'first of a series of Acts' under which the British government would not, as before, 'allow any man or woman to come to this country on the very flimsiest excuse without examination of their character, antecedents, and mode of living' (HC Deb 17 July 1918 vol 108 cc1141). He warned that Britain was 'largely now reaping where we sowed' on account of granting asylum to those who 'lowered the mode of living of great masses of our own citizens by their mode of living and their character' (ibid.) and suggested that the question should be put as to whether the naturalized man would make a good citizen (HC Deb 17 July 1918 vol 108 cc1142).

Elsewhere in the Act, a provision for the revocation of women's status was included. Though the removal of women's subjecthood was not included under section 7 until 1918, it existed in a different part of the Act in 1914. Under section 10, which legally counted as an automatic loss (Fransman 2011, 5.7.2) though could be argued as revocation[8], women would have their British citizenship removed if they married an alien, a re-enactment of a law passed under the Naturalisation Act of 1870. In 1918, these powers were brought under Section 7A and extended, granting the Secretary of

State the power to strip the status of wife and minor children if the spouse or father had their status revoked.

The desire to regulate marriage of British subjects was discussed towards the close of the 1911 conference, when the issue of Indian immigration was raised. What ended up a discussion on the preservation of the white race and the desire to keep 'every coloured race in its own zone' (IC 1911, 401) began with objections to interracial, named as 'alien', marriage. Speaking on behalf of the British government, the Earle of Crewe acknowledged the objections 'which are felt by many to a close intercourse between the white and the coloured races'. Crewe claimed that the 'disapproval of marriage of a white man with a native woman, and still more the marriage between a white woman and a man of a native race, affects superior people to the greatest extent' (IC 1911, 396). Objections to this marriage became stronger, Crewe continued, among the 'more educated and more generally superior'.

Despite the objections towards marriage of a 'white man with a native woman', only women were subjected to revocation following interracial marriage. Fears and prejudices around race and Empire created a rhetoric that 'identified women with the role of preserving, perpetuating, and enhancing the physical quality, and the numbers, of the race in their role as mothers' (Thane 1998, 31). Revoking the status of women was a way of discouraging interracial marriage, playing to the suggestion that the white race should be preserved and that governments should keep 'every coloured race in its own zone'. Though men were allowed more freedom to choose who they married, women were penalized heavily if they married an undesirable subject, thus rendering themselves undesirable.

As these examples demonstrate, the logic and language of the imperial negotiations are visible throughout legislation covering revocation. From penalizing the criminal class; removing the status of undeserving citizens of undesirable character; restricting interracial marriage of a white women to a 'native' man, it is evident that revocation relied upon the same coding through which mobility was restricted or facilitated as described in the other practices above.

Discussion

Following from the analysis above, this section asks how a historical account of revocation can inform our understanding of the practice today? The paper began by identifying the meaning often applied to revocation – that it is a technology of national security, one to be used against terrorists. It pointed to questions raised by scholars regarding the weakening of the institution of citizenship and to queries of how threatening a citizen must be before they lose their status. This framing accepts the narrative of an exceptional practice for exceptional cases. Yet its history raises questions for how we approach the study of revocation. Firstly, the archival research demonstrates that rather than a practice that existed separate to citizenship, the logic underpinning immigration, naturalization, emigration and revocation remained the same. The desire of governing authorities to divide and code subjects, determining their mobility, continued throughout this series of practices. As a result, this calls on us not simply to question revocation, but to question citizenship and the laws and practices associated with it. But what of the argument of the exceptional cases?

This paper draws on the studies of Isin and Anderson to provide analytical tools through which to read this history. Each scholar argues that categories appearing alongside the citizen should not be analyzed in discrete or binary ways, but should be considered together, as new categories appear each time citizenship is constituted. In exposing the power struggles behind the positioning of the dominant class, they challenge given narratives behind categories such as 'immigrant' or Failed Citizen. How can their research speak to the study of revocation? Their theories encourage the dismantling of accepted narratives behind the dangerous and undesirable citizen and support a critical evaluation of how laws and practices are involved in the creation of difference.

The archival research illustrates how this creation of difference manifested. In particular, it reveals the administrative practices hidden behind legislation. The underlying intention was to restrict mobility based on how subjects were coded and this was clear from Chamberlain's encouragement of the use of class and character to code for race, Churchill's assurances that even within naturalization, a difference in treatment existed between classes of white British subjects, and Gladstone's suggestion that the discrimination against criminal classes existed in practice in government administration if not in legislation. This research calls on us to recognize the layers of class, gendered and racial thinking that established the undesirable category.

While it may be shown that once powers were expanded in 1918, they were used to target the 'enemy German', and from 2002 they were used in the context of terror, the argument of this paper is that the logic underpinning revocation transcends particular security contexts. How then are we to understand the cases of Alexanda Amon Kotey and the Rochdale citizens? Though it may be argued that Kotey's revocation is a response to threats to national security, the analysis provided in this paper pushes us to ask whether terror alone explains his revocation.

The Rochdale case presents something else. While the argument of national security and the framework of exception dominates current literature and public discourse on revocation (Barry and Ferracioli 2016; Joppke 2016; Rainer 2018), in 2018 we witnessed a shift in the use of this practice. In his speech, the Home Secretary stated that citizenship revocation was a power for 'extreme and exceptional cases' (CCHQ Press, 2 October 2018). However, in revoking the status of citizens involved in the Rochdale case, we witness a broadening of the application of revocation from terrorism to criminality. Previous efforts of scholars to explain the conditions of revocation by way of terror, where it is understood that 'terror is not like ordinary crime, to be sanctioned under ordinary penal law' (Joppke 2016, 731) now require additional reasons as to why these citizens had their status revoked.

Revocation's history in the UK and British Empire has shown it to be another practice of citizenship that divides and codes subjects according to race, class and gender. It therefore suggests that in seeking answers as to why some subjects have their status revoked, we should look beyond arguments of the 'very worst criminals' who are convicted of the 'most grave criminal offences' and look for other explanations for the revocation of citizens' status.

Conclusion

This paper has shown that the colonial conference minutes offer a rare glimpse into the governing of Empire, and the negotiations expose the logic that underpinned decisions that were taken and laws that were passed. These minutes serve as a reminder that the BNSAA sought to legislate for multiple populations within the Empire. This legislation did not only affect the Dominions directly involved in the negotiations of the Act, but also all other subjects who would simultaneously be coded as undesirable. The codification of subjects was a continuation of a logic that developed through the slave trade, convict transportation and indentured servitude and persisted during the negotiations surrounding the laws and practices governing citizenship. The studies of Isin and Anderson encourage us to challenge given narratives behind established categories and to interrogate how such laws and practices are used. In asking what may be learned from a historicization of revocation, this archival research suggests that analysis of revocation should move beyond the framework of national security to both challenge given narratives about exceptionally bad citizens and examine other motivations behind revocation's use.

Notes

1. As named in *The New York Times* (*The New York Times*, 8 February 2018).
2. Despite attempts to remove his citizenship, the UK government was ultimately unsuccessful as the Egyptian government had already revoked his Egyptian citizenship (*The Guardian*, 5 November 2010).
3. For further reading see Mantu (2018).
4. This figure is an estimate of those banished over the course of 330 years, from 1615 to 1939 (for table, see Anderson 2016). Many cases were not recorded (Maxwell-Stewart 2010).
5. As Anderson et al. note, an explicit ban was put in place to prohibit the transfer of Indian subjects to Australian colonies and any mixing of European convicts with those from Asia and Southeast Asia. Other examples of treatment can be found in (Anderson et al. 2015; Yang 2003; Finnane and John 2001) who describe how transportation continued in South and Southeast Asia long after it ended for European subjects. Other forms of punishment such as public hanging also continued for indigenous Australians after it was abolished for Europeans.
6. From 1911 the conferences were published as imperial conferences.
7. Many of the objections can be found here: (CC 1907, 178 – 182).
8. This is if one takes today's legal definition of revocation as that which 'occurs where the secretary of state removes a person's British citizenship irrespective of that person's wishes in the matter' (Fransman 2011, 19.5).

Acknowledgments

I would like to thank the editors of this Special Issue for their constructive feedback, two anonymous reviewers for their revisions, and Kimberly Hutchings and Engin Isin for their insightful and encouraging comments on an earlier version of this paper.

Disclosure statement

No potential conflict of interest was reported by the author.

References

Primary Sources

Colonial Conference. 1902. "(CC 1902)." Papers Relating to a Conference between the Secretary of State for the Colonies and the Prime Ministers of Self-Governing Colonies. Cmd 1299.

Colonial Conference. 1907. "(CC 1907)." *Minutes of Proceedings.* Cmd 1299.

Conference between the Colonial Secretary and Premiers of Self-Governing Colonies. 1897. "(CC 1897)." *Proceedings.* C 8596.

GOV.UK. 1914. "British Nationality and Status of Aliens Act 1914." C 17. 4 & 5 Geo.

GOV.UK. 2014. "Immigration Act 2014." C 22.

Imperial Conference. 1911. "(IC 1911)." Precis of the Proceedings. Cmd 5741.

Reference

Anderson, B. 2013. *Us and Them?: The Dangerous Politics of Immigration Control.* Oxford: Oxford University Press.

Anderson, C., C. M. Crockett, G. Christian, D. Vito, T. Miyamoto, K. Moss, K. Roscoe, and M. Sakata. 2015. "Locating Penal Transportation: Punishment, Space and Place C. 1750–1900." In *Historical Geographies of Prisons: Unlocking the Usable Carceral Past*, edited by K. Morin and D. Moran, 147–167. Abingdon: Routledge.

Anderson, C. 2016. "Transnational Histories of Penal Transportation: Punishment, Labour and Governance in the British Imperial World, 1788–1939." *Australian Historical Studies* 47 (3): 381–397. doi:10.1080/1031461X.2016.1203962.

Barry, C., and L. Ferracioli. 2016. "Can Withdrawing Citizenship Be Justified?" *Political Studies* 64 (4): 1055–1070. doi:10.1177/0032321715606569.

Beattie, J. M. 1974. "The Pattern of Crime in England 1660–1800." *Past & Present* 62: 47–95. doi:10.1093/past/62.1.47.

Burbank, J., and F. Cooper. 2010. *Empires in World History: Power and the Politics of Difference.* Princeton: Princeton University Press.

Chandra, B., M. Mukherjee, A. Mukherjee, K. N. Panikkar, and S. Mahajan. 2016. *India's Struggle for Independence.* New Delhi: Penguin.

Constantine, S. 2003. "British Emigration to the Empire-Commonwealth since 1880: From Overseas Settlement to Diaspora?" *The Journal of Imperial and Commonwealth History* 31 (2): 16–35. doi:10.1080/03086530310001705586.

Daniels, R. 1995. "The Growth of Restrictive Immigration Policies in the Colonies of Settlement." In *The Cambridge Survey of World Migration*, edited by R. Cohen, 39–44. Cambridge: Cambridge University Press.

Finnane, M., and M. John. 2001. "The Uses of Punishment and Exile: Aborigines in Colonial Australia." *Punishment & Society* 3 (2): 279–298. doi:10.1177/14624740122228339.

Fransman, L. 2011. *Fransman's British Nationality Law. Third Edition.* Haywards Heath: Bloomsbury Professional.

Gibney, M. J. 2013. "A Very Transcendental Power": Denaturalisation and the Liberalisation of Citizenship in the United Kingdom." *Political Studies* 61: 637–655. doi:10.1111/j.1467-9248.2012.00980.x.

Gwynn, A. 1932. "Documents Relating to the Irish in the West Indies." *Analecta Hibernica* 4: 139–286. www.jstor.org/stable/25510930

Huttenback, R. A. 1973a. "The British Empire as a 'White Man's Country'—Racial Attitudes and Immigration Legislation in the Colonies of White Settlement." *Journal of British Studies* 13 (1): 108–137. doi:10.1086/385652.

Huttenback, R. A. 1973b. "No Strangers within the Gates: Attitudes and Policies Towards the On-White Residents of the British Empire of Settlement." *The Journal of Imperial and Commonwealth History* 1 (3): 271–302. doi:10.1080/03086537308582379.

Isin, E. 2002. *Being Political: Genealogies of Citizenship*. Minneapolis: University of Minnesota Press.

Joppke, C. 2016. "Terror and the Loss of Citizenship." *Citizenship Studies* 20 (6–7): 728–748. doi:10.1080/13621025.2016.1191435.

Kendle, J. E. 1967. *The Colonial and Imperial Conferences, 1887–1911: A Study in Imperial Organization*. London: Published for the Royal Commonwealth Society by Longmans.

Macklin, A. 2018. "The Return of Banishment: Do the New Denationalisation Policies Weaken Citizenship?" In *Debating Transformations of National Citizenship*, edited by R. Baubock, IMISCOE Research Series, 163–172. Cham: Springer.

Mangan, J. A. 2012. "Images for Confident Control: Stereotypes in Imperial Discourse." In *The Imperial Curriculum: Racial Images and Education in the British Colonial Experience*, edited by J. A. Mangan, 6–22. London: Routledge.

Mantu, S. 2018. "Terrorist' Citizens and the Human Right to Nationality." *Journal of Contemporary European Studies* 26 (1): 28–41. doi:10.1080/14782804.2017.1397503.

Maxwell-Stewart, H. 2010. "Convict Transportation from Britain and Ireland 1615–1870." *History Compass* 8 (11): 1221–1242. doi:10.1111/j.1478-0542.2010.00722.x.

Rainer, B., ed. 2018. *Debating Transformations of National Citizenship*. IMISCOE Research Series. Cham: Springer.

Secondary Sources

Thane, P. 1998. "The British Imperial State and the Construction of National Identities." In *Borderlines: Genders and Identities in War and Peace 1870–1930*, edited by B. Melman, 29–45. New York: Routledge.

Yang, A. A. 2003. "Indian Convict Workers in Southeast Asia in the Late Eighteenth and Early Nineteenth Centuries." *Journal of World History* 14 (2): 179–208. doi:10.1353/jwh.2003.0029.

Discussing the human rights limits on loss of citizenship: a normative-legal perspective on egalitarian arguments regarding Dutch Nationality laws targeting Dutch-Moroccans

Tom L. Boekestein and Gerard-René de Groot

ABSTRACT

In its efforts to counteract terrorist threats and contain the risks posed by returning foreign fighters, the Netherlands, like several other European states, has enacted legislation introducing denationalisation as a counter-terrorism measure. The Dutch measures target convicted terrorists and foreign fighters alike, the latter without the prior involvement of the judiciary. This practice not only challenges traditional conceptions of citizenship, but also raises several human rights concerns, of which discrimination is the most pressing. This Article therefore examines the measures taken by the Netherlands and analyses their compatibility with Articles 14 and P12-1 of the European Convention on Human Rights, to assess the measures' disproportionate focus on Dutch-Moroccans from a legal perspective. Based on this conclusion of inequality, the Article then ventures beyond purely legal analysis to discuss the Dutch legislation more broadly, before linking the legal argument with normative critiques on the denationalisation of terrorists, and foreign fighters in particular. Taken together, the legal and normative findings establish that denationalisation as a counter-terrorism measure in the Netherlands cannot be reconciled with the legal or normative dimension of the equality principle.

Introduction

The wave of terrorist attacks that has hit Europe in recent years has led to the adoption and expansion of denationalisation laws targeting terrorists in several European states, including France, the Netherlands and the United Kingdom. In essence, these countries now deprive individuals of their nationality if they are convicted of a terrorist offence or more generally facilitate terrorism. While these measures have met strong criticism in academic literature (Macklin 2014; Gibney 2013; Bauböck and Paskelev 2015), some scholars have sought to justify them by reference to new conceptions of citizenship (Lavi 2011; Joppke 2016). The conceptual divide underlying the discourse can be illustrated well through the International Court of Justice's characterisation of citizenship in *Nottebohm* (1955, 23) as 'a legal bond having as its basis a social fact of attachment, a genuine connection of existence, interests and sentiments, together with the existence of reciprocal rights and duties'. Opponents of denationalisation generally argue for citizenship as an unconditional right or status (Macklin 2014), whereas proponents tend to stress reciprocity of duties and conditionality instead (Joppke 2016).

Regardless of the position on denationalisation one adopts, it is important to acknowledge the limitations to such an approach in practice. Critics have long questioned its effectiveness (Bauböck 2014) or challenged its legality (Jessurun d'Oliveira2017). Pursuing the latter angle, this Article evaluates Dutch denationalisation laws against the prohibition of discrimination under the European Convention of Human Rights (ECHR) to discuss the implications of the 'social divisiveness of citizenship stripping', as developed by Joppke in his defence of denationalisation (2016, 745). Although Joppke recognises that by targeting dual-nationals with an immigration background, denationalisation creates two classes of citizens,[1] he finds this to be a necessary consequence of international law (Idem., 744–745). While he qualifies his defence by recognising that this social divisiveness would interfere with equality as a fundamental principle of citizenship (Idem.), from a legal perspective, Joppke's analysis understates the importance of the equality principle. After all, it not only constitutes a fundamental principle of citizenship, but a binding *human right* guaranteed through the prohibition of discrimination. Thus, if Dutch denationalisation laws were indeed in violation of that right, this would endow challenges based on the equality principle (Carey 2018) with legal force by challenging the perception that the distinction between certain groups of citizens is merely an 'unavoidable consequence of abiding by international law' (Joppke 2016, 745). The well-accepted prohibition of statelessness could then no longer be invoked as an excuse for the distinction,[2] and justifications of denationalisation of terrorists would have to take account of broader legal requirements.[3]

This Article will address the issue of discrimination in the context of Dutch denationalisation laws from a legal and normative perspective. Its legal analysis will be centred around an assessment of discrimination as defined in European Convention on Human Rights (ECHR), taking into account empirical studies on the background of Dutch foreign fighters in establishing discrimination and normative proposals when assessing proportionality. Based on the outcome, the strengths and limits of the human rights law will be discussed. This Article then approaches the matter from a normative perspective, which supports and enriches the legal analysis, but also highlight non-legal considerations that ought to inform the decision to introduce denationalisation as a counter-terrorism measure.

The focus will be on the Netherlands for several reasons: Firstly, the Country has ratified a wide range of supranational human rights instruments, including the ECHR and the European Convention on Nationality (ECN). Secondly, the Dutch Nationality Act (DNA) includes both proactive and reactive forms of denationalisation, so that a wide range of conclusion can be drawn from a discussion thereof, that can then be applied to other Council of Europe (CoE) jurisdictions. Thirdly, the Dutch legal system is monist, meaning that domestic legislation can be juxtaposed against the aforementioned international instruments directly (Dutch Constitution, Articles 93–94) without being influenced by domestic implementing legislation. Fourthly, there is no constitutional review in the Netherlands, which minimises the risk of domestic review interfering with the application of the international law prohibition of discrimination (Dutch Constitution, Article 120). Fifthly, the CoE and academia have raised similar concerns regarding discrimination (CoE Commissioner for Human Rights 2016; De Groot and Vonk 2015a; Groen 2016). Jesserun d'Oliveira (2016) has touched upon several of the issues to be discussed more extensively below and de Leeuw (2016) has conducted a legal examination of the Dutch approach, supporting several of the initial concerns. These concerns are further substantiated by the fact that the four denationalisations in which the second nationality of the individual was made public all concerned Dutch-Moroccans. Finally, litigation against similar measures under French law is currently pending before the ECtHR (Ghoumid et al. v France 2016). While it is true that domestic litigation against denationalisation in the Netherlands has recently been dismissed, it should be noted that the Court did so because it deemed the automatic review mechanism under Article 22a(3) DNA underlying the case as incompatible with EU law (SGR 17/6834 and 17/15049 2018).

Legal analysis

Legislative context: revocation of Nationality under Dutch law

The legal analysis of Dutch nationality law below will be based on a distinction between proactive and reactive denationalisation (Boekestein 2019). While both types of denationalisation can have pre-emptive effects and could be triggered by the same type of conduct, they differ with regard to the degree of judicial involvement. The defining element is whether a criminal conviction is a prerequisite for denationalisation or not, i.e. whether it takes effect autonomously or whether indirect judicial authorisation is required.

Under Dutch law, reactive denationalisation seeks to prevent the use of citizenship to facilitate terrorism and to punish those who have done so (Bill 31813 (R1873), nr. 6 nota naar aanleiding van het verslag 2008), whereas proactive denationalisation specifically targets foreign fighters abroad by revoking their right to return (Bill 34356 (R2064), nr. 3 Memorie van Toelichting 2015). Denationalisation decisions are adopted at the discretion of the Minister of Security and Justice (hereinafter 'the Minister'), not *ex lege*. The personal scope of application is limited to dual-nationals, as Article 14(8) DNA prescribes the avoidance of statelessness.[4]

The reactive arm: article 14(2) DNA

Article 14(2) specifies a final conviction for one of the offences subsequently referred to as a prerequisite for denationalisation. Subsection (a) refers to the crimes listed in Article 92 – 130b Dutch Criminal Code (hereinafter DCC): Crimes against national security, against the dignity of the King, against the heads and representatives of foreign states, and against the exercise of the powers of the state, provided they are sanctioned with a term of at least eight years of imprisonment. Subsection (b) refers to Articles 83, 134 and 205 DCC, of which the former two are of particular importance.[5] Article 83 defines a wide range of offences, such as murder or kidnapping, as terrorist offences if committed pursuant to a terrorist objective as defined in Article 83a DCC. Article 134 sanctions certain preparatory conduct, such as the (attempted) acquisition of information, means, or skills for the purpose of committing a terrorist offence. An individual whose conviction is upheld at final instance under either of these provisions may subsequently be denationalised. Notably, the denationalisation takes effect by administrative decision and is separate from the underlying criminal conviction. Although not explicitly specified in the DNA, the denationalisation will usually be accompanied by declaring those concerned *personae non grata*, thereby criminalising their presence in the Netherlands.

The emphasis of the reactive dimension of the Dutch approach lies primarily on prevention of actual harm, given that it can be triggered by a range of preparatory offences. Carrying out an actual terrorist attack is not necessary. The underlying rationale is simple: Once removed from the country, an individual will encounter additional difficulties in supporting or carrying out a terrorist attack in the Netherlands. Although the conduct triggering the reactive deprivation of nationality under Article 14(2) may be very remote from actual harm, it still involves prior examination and adjudication by a criminal court and must at least qualify as a preparatory offence. This link no longer exists under proactive denationalisation, discussed next, where loss of citizenship can be triggered by conduct that is not criminalised.

The proactive arm: article 14(4) DNA

The prerequisites for proactive deprivation of nationality are more elusive. Article 14(4) DNA allows for the denationalisation of individuals above the age of 16 whose conduct indicates that they have joined a terrorist organisation whilst residing outside the Netherlands. The list of organisations to which this provision applies is created by the Minister. It currently contains three organisations, all of which are Islamist: Al-Qaeda and associated organisations, ISIS and associated organisations, and Hay'at Tahrir al-Sham (2017).[6] The Minister will revoke someone's citizenship based on information provided by various security and intelligence agencies, the accessibility of which is likely limited (Bill 34356 (R2064), nr. 3 Memorie van Toelichting 2015, 6). Since persons whose nationality is revoked are *ipso facto* not residing in the Netherlands, they are not served with the decision, which is instead published in the official government gazette.

Despite similar effects, there are apparent differences between proactive and reactive denationalisation. Article 14(4) greatly exceeds the scope of Article 14(2). Whereas the latter responds to a terrorist threat that has materialised itself to a degree that warrants criminal law sanction imposed by the judiciary, Article 14(4) can be triggered by the Minister once the individual's conduct indicates that a terrorist organisation has been joined. This ambiguous prerequisite arguably does not require the actual preparation or facilitation of terrorist efforts in the Netherlands, nor is the revocation itself subject to (indirect) prior judicial authorisation. The purpose of this extension is to address the threat posed by returning foreign fighters (Bill 34356 (R2064), nr. 3 Memorie van Toelichting 2015). Denationalising these individuals upon their affiliation with a terrorist organisation abroad deprives them of their right to return. Herein lies the rationale of the measure: If foreign fighters cannot return to the Netherlands, they will not be able to carry out attacks there either.

However, such reasoning may be overly simplistic and create a false sense of security. As will be discussed more extensively below, proactive denationalisation can only prevent legal, but not factual return. The low threshold of application also raises issues: As a final criminal conviction is not required, it does not have to be established in accordance with the criminal law standard of proof whether the individual concerned has joined a terrorist organisation. While it is true that a decision to revoke nationality may be subject to administrative appeal, the standard of review in such a procedure is not equivalent to that of a criminal trial, despite the seriousness of the sanction at stake. Review is also hindered by the individual's absence from the Netherlands, which will further impede the ability to challenge such a decision, especially since the automatic appeal mechanism has been found incompatible with EU law by a Dutch court (SGR 17/6834 and 17/15049 2018). The procedure under Article 22a DNA, whereby the Minister requests the review of his own denationalisation decision under Article 14(4) DNA within four weeks if the addressee had not challenged it, no longer applies.

Legal analysis: discrimination under articles 14 taken together with 8 ECHR

Interference with the prohibition of discrimination

In assessing whether the Dutch measures are compatible with the ECHR, the focus will be on the material dimension of discrimination. The requirements for the applicability of both anti-discrimination provisions of the Convention, Article 14 and Protocol 12, are met. Revocation of nationality under the DNA clearly falls within the scope of Article P12-1's independent protection against discrimination (Council of Europe 2000, §22; Council of Europe Treaty Office 2017). While the applicability of Article 14 is dependent on that of another Convention right (Biao v Denmark 2016, §88), there can be little doubt that denationalisation falls within the ambit of Article 8 ECHR, given that the ECtHR held in *Ramadan v Malta* (2016, §85) that 'loss of a citizenship [...] can have the same (and possibly a bigger) impact [as denial of acquisition] on a person's private and family life'. Since Articles 14 ECHR and P12-1 are intended to be complimentary and interpreted harmoniously, they will be analysed together. This is essential given that the limited ECtHR jurisprudence on Protocol 12 must be supplemented by case law on Article 14.[7] Furthermore, applying the two provisions together ensures that the findings made here are relevant to the 27 CoE States that have not ratified Protocol 12 as well.

The ECtHR distinguishes between two types of discrimination: Differences in treatment and general policies or measures having disproportionately prejudicial effects on a particular group, even if they are not aimed at that group in particular (Biao v Denmark 2016, §§90–1). Either will violate the ECHR unless objectively and reasonably justified (Idem., §§89–90). This duality resembles that between direct and indirect discrimination commonly used in EU law.[8]

Both Articles 14(2) and 14(4) are directly discriminatory, because under Article 14(8) the application of both provisions is subject to the objective distinction of having a second nationality. This has been confirmed to fall within the ambit of Article 14 taken together with Article 8 ECHR (Gaygusuz v Austria 1996, §§42–50). This conclusion finds support in the UK House of Lords' *Belmarsh* case (2004, §68), where the expulsion of only non-British terrorism offenders was found to be discriminatory and incompatible with Article 14 ECHR due to a distinction based on nationality.

In addition, Article 14(4) also raises concerns of indirect discrimination against certain dual-nationals, which are shared by the UN Special Rapporteur on Racism (2018). *Prima facie*, any dual-national can be denationalised, irrespective of their background or how they obtained Dutch Citizenship. As the Dutch Government states: '[R]ace or religion play no role in the statutory criteria for application' (Dutch Ministers of the Interior and Kingdom Relations and Security and Justice 2016, 9). However, the absence of an express distinction does not preclude a *de facto* adverse effect on a narrower sub-group of dual-nationals (De Groot and Vonk 2015b, 44–5). The legal analysis establishing indirect discrimination must thus consider the factual impact of the measure under review. To this end, the use of statistical evidence, especially official statistics, has been accepted by the ECtHR (D.H. and Others v The Czech Republic 2007, §§180, 188), provided that it 'appear[s] on critical examination to be reliable and significant'.[9]

Dutch–Moroccans may indeed be more likely to be denationalised under Article 14(4) than other Dutch nationals (De Groot and Vonk 2015b). This concern is based on three factors. Firstly, as discussed, Article 14(4) DNA only applies to individuals joining one of the three Islamist terrorist organisations (Minister of Security and Justice 2017; De Groot and Vonk 2015a). In practice, this limits the scope to foreign fighters who have left for Syria, as these groups draw the majority of their foreign fighters to this area. Secondly, due to the limitation imposed by Article 14(8) DNA, the measure can only be applied to dual-nationals, thus shielding Dutch mono-nationals from denationalisation. Consequently, the measure can only be applied to Dutch dual-nationals who become foreign fighters for one of the three previously listed organisations, primarily in Syria. Whether these individuals could renounce their second nationality to avoid losing their Dutch one is irrelevant; the ECtHR held in Andrejeva v Latvia (2009) that such hypotheticals will not impact a finding of discrimination. This is where the third factor becomes relevant. Assuming that the share of Dutch foreign fighters in Syria who have a Dutch ethnic background *and* a second nationality is insignificant,[10] Dutch nationals with a Moroccan ethnic background make up the majority of Dutch foreign fighters in Syria (55%). The second largest group, individuals with a Turkish background, makes up only 14% of Dutch foreign fighters. The remaining 31% consist of several smaller groups, none of which exceeds 8% (Groen 2017). These figures are drawn from The Hague Centre for Strategic Studies and largely coincide with the findings of Bakker and de Bont (2016). They are striking, as Dutch-Moroccans only make up 2.2% of the Dutch population (CBS 2015, 2016). Yet, they are likely the primary target of proactive denationalisation. This finding must be distinguished from de Leeuw's (2016, 40), who concluded that there was no risk of indirect discrimination against Dutch-Moroccans. However, his findings were based on a broader examination of the percentage of Dutch dual-nationals who have a non-western or Arabic background. De Leeuw did not consider the high percentage of Dutch-Moroccan foreign fighters or the narrowly construed scope of application of Article 14(4).

Recent reports suggest that 15 people have lost their Dutch citizenship because of terrorism-related activities, 10 of which under Article 14(4) DNA (Kouwenhoven 2019; Immigratie- en Naturalisatiedienst 2018, 52). Of the four whose second nationality is known, all were Dutch-Moroccans (Immigratie- en Naturalisatiedienst 2017). This provides initial support for the concerns raised, though it would have to be substantiated through information on the other six individuals. Although it is acknowledged that the data underlying the above findings are limited, it must be stressed that the law has only been enacted very recently and is subject to ministerial discretion. Particularly in light of the five-year sunset clause, it is impossible to predict the total number of cases in which Article 14(4) will eventually be applied. Further, the ECtHR does not adopt an evidentiary standard of absolute certainty. Rather, the Court has favoured a '*rebuttable presumption*' of indirect discrimination, which is then to be rebutted by the respondent (here the Dutch Government) (D.H. and Others v The Czech Republic, §§186,8–9). The Court supports this shifting of the burden of proof by reference to the 'specificity of the facts and the nature of the allegations made'. Although it is true that both *D.H.* and the case law cited therein concerned racial discrimination against Roma, the seriousness of the measure, narrow target group, and nationality context in the case at hand justify similar considerations, especially since security concerns severely limit access to detailed information. The lack of information is further amplified by the fact that the Netherlands no longer records the second nationality of dual-nationals. While it would ultimately be for the ECtHR to decide on the adequacy of the above analysis, the presumption of indirect discrimination it establishes is strong enough to at least warrant a discussion of possible justifications.

Justifications for the interference

From a legal perspective, even an irrefutable difference in treatment does not lead to a violation of the prohibition of discrimination if there is an objective and reasonable justification for it (D.H. and Others v The Czech Republic 2006, §196; Biao v Denmark 2016, §91). The ECtHR has clarified that justification requires a 'legitimate aim' and a 'reasonable relationship of proportionality' between the measure and the aim (Stec and Others v The United Kingdom 2006, §51; S.A.S. v France 2014, §161). The state enjoys a margin of discretion in determining the justifications for an interference, the width of which depends on the nature of the distinction. The nature of the distinction, or ground of discrimination, under Articles 14(2) and (4) taken together with (8) is debatable. The UN Special Rapporteur has argued for the indirect discrimination to be based on ethnic origin (2018, 16–18), which is equivalent to racial discrimination under the ECHR and only justifiable under the strictest scrutiny (Schabas 2016, 578). This is less clear with regard to direct discrimination, where the distinction could also be based on national origin (Stec and Others v The United Kingdom 2006, §§85–88; Andrejeva v Latvia 2009), i.e. having a second nationality. Although 'very weighty reasons' must be put forward for a distinction based on national origin (Biao v Denmark 2016, §93), this standard is less strict than that applicable in cases of racial discrimination. Since the lack of a justification under the lower standard will also fail the higher standard, the former will be adopted for the purposes of the following analysis. In assessing justifications, direct and indirect discrimination will be addressed together if possible, since they relate to similar measures that pursue similar aims.

Foremost, it must be noted that prevention of statelessness is not a legitimate aim or justification by itself nor is compliance with a rule of international law. If compliance with international law obligations sufficed to justify interferences with human rights, states could simply conclude treaties to undermine the binding force of human rights law (Soering v The United Kingdom 1989). Thus, contrary to what Joppke seems to suggest, the prohibition of statelessness does not justify either form of discrimination; it is simply a legal limitation on the personal scope of denationalisation. Instead, the aim of the measures can be defined as the protection of national security, as articulated in the explanatory memoranda (2008, 2015) and recognised under Article 8(2) ECHR.

Next, it must be examined whether the measure is proportionate to its aim. Under ECHR law, proportionality consists of subsidiarity, suitability and proportionality proper. This requires a normative evaluation of the measure in light of the narrow margin of appreciation, taking into account its factual impact, effectiveness and the availability of appropriate alternatives (Grabenwarter 2014, 354–5).

With regard to subsidiarity, several alternatives to denationalisation have been proposed. Jessurun and Ulrich (2017) have suggested recourse to the Dutch Passport Act, arguing that it would achieve similar results whilst placing a lighter burden on the individuals affected. For example, invalidating the passports of foreign fighters would hinder them in returning to the Netherlands, or even from leaving in the first place. This approach could also be adjusted or reversed more easily (Esbrook 2016, 1319–20). While one may argue that the same discrimination arguments raised above would apply to the invalidation of passports, several considerations mitigate this concern. Firstly, the measure could be applied to both mono- and dual-nationals, removing direct discrimination. Secondly, while it is true that Dutch-Moroccans could still be the primary targets of the measure, the invalidation of passports is currently not restricted by law to certain terrorist organisations. Finally, it must be recalled that the harm caused by the invalidation of passports is significantly less than that caused by denationalisation. Thus, even if discriminatory, the interference is likely justified as a less intrusive alternative. Interestingly, the Passport Act is indeed being used, and the Dutch National Counter-terrorism Coordinator has stated that almost 300 passports had been revoked by early 2017 (NPO Radio 1 2017). This raises conceptual questions outside the legal analysis, which will be returned to in the normative second part of this Article.

Furthermore, the Institute for Strategic Dialogue has recommended that foreign fighters should be allowed to return, as this allows the threat they pose to be addressed directly through criminal sanction and rehabilitation (Briggs and Silverman 2014, 37–8). This would lastingly address the threat, rather than relocating it to another country (Canadian Association of Refugee Lawyers 2014, 9). The Institute suggests that rehabilitation efforts should be combined with measures taken by intelligence services and other authorities immediately upon the return of a foreign fighter. Existing Dutch efforts already offer a basis for such an approach, including both increased surveillance of individuals returning from, e.g. Syria and the incarceration of returnees for a limited period of time (Actieprogramma Integrale Aanpak Jihadisme 2014, 5). Further, the preparation of terrorist acts is already extensively criminalised under the Dutch Criminal Code (Articles 83 and 134a), which by itself will have strong preventive and deterrent effects. If these efforts were complemented by active efforts to have foreign fighters return to the Netherlands to rehabilitate and reintegrate them, this could be a lasting and comprehensive solution to the threat (Tweede Kamer 2016).

With regard to suitability, it must be questioned whether, given the seriousness of the sanction, denationalisation should indeed take effect through *administrative* law. Bauböck and Paskelev (2015, 72–3) argue that it should instead be administered through the criminal law system, as it is better equipped to weigh the burden imposed on the individual against the societal harm to be prevented. This would also imply a higher standard of proof and better juridical review, which would be appropriate given the seriousness of the measure. Relying on criminal law and its appeal system would significantly reduce any fair trial and double jeopardy concerns, and remedy issues related to the high degree of discretion currently enjoyed by the Minister.[11] After all, the lack of involvement of criminal courts raised due process and judicial review concerns during the debate in the Dutch Lower House (Tweede Kamer 2016, esp. positions of D66 and GL).

Another suitability issue is raised by the fact that denationalisation measures may, ironically, interfere with the effectiveness of existing counter-terrorism efforts (Bauböck and Paskelev 2015, 72–3). Where an individual has been convicted of a (preparatory) terrorism offence in the Netherlands, the added value of reactive denationalisation is questionable. Similar considerations apply to proactive denationalisation. Either, deprivation of nationality prevents return, thus rendering existing criminal law and rehabilitation measures obsolete (De Groot 2016, 32). Or, as de Leeuw (2016, 57–8) stresses, foreign fighters return covertly, in which case denationalisation would be ineffective. Indeed, Dutch Intelligence Services confirm that returning foreign fighters usually use counterfeit passports (AIVD 2017b, 3).

Issues also arise regarding proportionality. Although numbers differ slightly, it is estimated that about 300–340 foreign fighters have left the Netherlands, of which 160–185 remain in Syria and Iraq as of March 2018. A total of 60–97 foreign fighters have been killed, 50–57 have returned to the Netherlands (AIVD 2017b, 3, Nationaal Coordinator Terrorismebestrijding en Veiligheid March 2018, 4).[12] According to this information, no new foreign fighters have left the Netherlands since June 2017 and the number of successful recent returns is said to be marginal. It is unclear whether this decrease is due to the new Article 14(4) or recent developments in the war in Syria, so far only 10 foreign fighters have been denationalised (Immigratie- en Naturalisatiedienst 2017). In addition to the limited use of the measure so far, doubts regarding its adequacy are raised by estimations that only one in five hundred returnees actually commit a terrorist offence (Hegghammer and Nesser 2015, 101). While Dutch Intelligence Services have not published data on this, they confirm that only a small group of returnees actually pose a significant threat (AIVD 2017b, 3). Furthermore, the Minister has confirmed that IS does not facilitate the return of foreign fighters (Tweede Kamer 2016, 26). The foregoing reinforces concerns that the Dutch measures are disproportionate to the actual threat posed by returnees.

Proportionality concerns are further amplified by the severity of the effects of denationalisation. Those who have their nationality revoked are likely torn from their social environment and placed within a foreign country they have potentially never lived in. The US Supreme Court has described denationalisation as 'the total destruction of the individual's status in organised society' (Trop v. Dulles 1985). These concerns are even stronger under Article 14(4), where the conduct triggering the revocation at most constitutes an indirect threat to national security. All of the above results in the conclusion that the Dutch denationalisation laws could hardly be justified if distinguishing on the basis of national origin, let alone in case it constitutes racial discrimination as discussed above. Thus, it is evident that the distinction between mono- and dual-nationals under Articles 14(2) and (4) is incompatible with the ECHR, whereas the compatibility of Article 14(4) with the prohibition of indirect discrimination will depend on the finding of a distinction in treatment.

Evaluation and supporting normative and empirical considerations

Strengths and limits of the human rights law analysis

The above analysis has also revealed two limitations that arise in particular regarding the narrower issue of indirect discrimination against Dutch-Moroccans in the case study at hand. Firstly, for the legal assessment to establish indirect discrimination it cannot be self-contained, but must necessarily take external data into account, such as statistics regarding the background of the individuals affected and the impact of the measure on specific groups. This applies equally to both limbs of the legal analysis. However, as has been acknowledged above that issues arise where such data are limited, yet it has also been found that the ECtHR has shown a willingness to alleviate this issue by lowering the evidentiary standard that it applies. Still, at this point, it remains impossible to conclude that there is more than a significant indication for indirect discrimination against Dutch-Moroccans. This leads to the second shortcoming. Given that the legal analysis derives its strength from applying the *lex lata*, it is unable to overcome the aforementioned shortcomings through a proposal on the approach the Court ought to adopt. Instead, it accepts that distinctions in treatment which fall outside the Court's approach, or that are justifiable, cannot be challenged on the ground of discrimination from a legal perspective, regardless of other normative considerations to the contrary. Consequently, the legal analysis cannot provide a definite answer to the policy question of whether states should denationalise (certain) foreign fighters. Instead, it can only establish the human rights limitations to such policies.

Despite these two inherent limitations of the purely legal approach to discrimination, its strength must also be emphasised: The binding force on the Dutch State of the sources on which it is based. The Netherlands would be legally obliged to abandon the use of these measures simply because it has bound itself to respect the principle of non-discrimination. Still, normative and empirical considerations remain relevant to the extent that they can inform the legal assessment. Thus, a wider normative assessment within the parameters set by the ECtHR can further inform both the demonstration of indirect discrimination and assessment of justifications as part of the legal analysis conducted above.

Filling the gaps: normative considerations

In light of the foregoing conclusions, the subsequent sections serve a dual purpose. Firstly, they seek to propose a remedy to the shortcomings of the legal analysis by providing additional evidence and support for establishing indirect discrimination against Dutch-Moroccans. It is argued that the ECtHR would take these sources into account given the stance it has taken in *Georgia v Russia (I)* (2014, §84) when relying on a range of reports and findings of international organisations as evidence.[13] Although that case did not concern the prohibition of discrimination, there is nothing to suggest that different rules apply with regard to the evidence that it considers in the context of Article 5 ECHR and Article 14 ECHR. Instead, the Court's decision to use a combination of official (international) reports and statistical evidence is consistent with its general stance towards such evidence (Schabas 2016, 811–12). Secondly, the normative considerations that will be identified offer a challenge to denationalisation on grounds of effectiveness. They inform the above legal discussion on the justifiability under the second limb of Article 8 ECHR by further substantiating the subsidiarity and suitability considerations with an assessment of the impact of the measure. Importantly, this also constitutes an independent normative policy challenge that applies regardless of whether discrimination can be established.

The public discourse on article 14(4) DNA

The concerns addressed by the legal analysis are widely shared, most notably and recently by the UN Special Rapporteur on Racism (2018), but also the CoE Commissioner for Human Rights (2016), Amnesty International (2017), the Dutch Human Rights Institute (College voor de Rechten van de Mens 2015) and the Dutch Advisory Body for Migration (*Adviescommissie voor Vreemdelingenzakenn* 2015). Amnesty and the Dutch Human Rights Institute further argue that denationalisation fosters the alienation of certain groups, with the former further suggesting that this may in turn fuel radicalisation and terrorist recruitment. In legal scholarship, D'Oliveira (2016, 2017) echoes these concerns. Politically, the high controversiality of the Bill is apparent from the debates in both Houses of Parliament. In the Lower House, the provision likely passed only after the Social Democrats successfully introduced a sunset clause to the Bill. Accordingly, Article 14(4) will be abolished automatically five years after it entered into force, unless Parliament decides to maintain it (Tweede Kamer 2016). During the debate in the Lower House, parties on the left side of the political spectrum in particular raised serious concerns against the proposal, questioning its effectiveness, proportionality, and the availability of judicial review of the Minister's decisions in practice (Tweede Kamer 2016). In the Upper House, similar positions were taken, with even the party of the then incumbent Minister of Security and Justice questioning the measure's effectiveness (Eerste Kamer 2017a). Ultimately, the Upper House adopted the proposal by a margin of one vote (Eerste Kamer 2017b). Finally, recent developments in the Parliamentary Assembly of the Council of Europe (PACE 2019a, 2019b) reaffirm the concerns raised so far. Addressing i.a. the Dutch measures, PACE urges states to refrain from denationalising terrorists and foreign fighters, reiterating concerns regarding discrimination, the lack of involvement of the judiciary, and the largely symbolic, yet practically ineffective nature of these measures (Resolution 2263 2019, mns. 5–8). PACE followed this resolution with a recommendation for a comparative study on denationalisation in counter-terrorism and less intrusive alternative measures (Recommendation 2145 2019). Outside the legal and political community and the aforementioned organisations, no notable reactions to the legislation were identified. The Cooperative of Dutch-Moroccans (Samenwerkingsverband van Marokkaanse Nederlanders), which runs campaigns to prevent the radicalisation of Dutch-Moroccans by terrorist organisations, did not react to the new legislation. However, given that the organisation rarely releases statements addressing specific legislative developments, the absence of an opposing statement should not be interpreted as support for denationalisation. Rather, its de-radicalisation campaigns would suggest *tacit* rejection of the law in light of the discussion on its impact below. Ultimately, the fact that the concerns raised in Section 1.2 above are supported by international human rights observers reinforces the presumption of an indirect discrimination claim, on grounds previously discussed (Georgia v Russia (I) 2014, §84).

The factual impact of denationalisation

As stated, a narrow legal analysis by itself cannot establish discrimination, nor can it address the societal impact of proactive and reactive denationalisation beyond the *lex lata*. While the scope and purpose of this Article preclude an extensive sociological assessment of the measure, the risk of denationalisation fostering 'us-versus-them' narratives must be discussed briefly, to raise important policy considerations and implications for the legal analysis. As Winter's research on Canada has shown, such narratives may arise even from less specific measures targeting dual-nationals in general.[14]

Under Dutch law, Article 14(4)'s focus on Dutch-Moroccans may contribute to generally associating the group with terrorism. Notably, such alienation may well be counterproductive to counter-terrorism efforts (Funk and Said 2004). A first issue is that Article 14(4) represents a collectivist approach to the denationalisation of foreign fighters: Whether individuals can have their citizenship revoked does not depend on an individual assessment of the threat they pose to public security in the Netherlands. Instead, it is the joining of a certain terrorist organisation that renders Article 14(4) applicable. Although one could argue that in light of recent threat assessments (Nationaal Coordinator Terrorismebestrijding en Veiligheid September 2018), this limitation of scope shows that the Netherlands is conscious of the seriousness of denationalisation and determined to apply it only to what it perceives as the greatest threats to national security, the new measure also implies that Islamist foreign terrorist fighters are *per se* the biggest threat to national security and that other foreign fighters are *a contrario* a lesser threat. The personal scopes of application of proactive and reactive denationalisation fuel this perception: Only Islamist foreign fighters are subject to denationalisation at ministerial discretion. Any other foreign fighter or terrorist can only be denationalised *after* a criminal trial.[15] This subjects Islamist foreign fighters to general suspicion, whereas criminal law standards of proof apply to all other foreign fighters.

'Us-versus-them' narratives are further fuelled by the normative conceptions of citizenship underlying denationalisation. As discussed, the Netherlands has adopted Articles 14(2) and (4) despite the possibility of achieving the same security aims through the Passport Act. This suggests that denationalisation in the context of terrorism is not only a security consideration, but also an affirmation of a loyalty-based concepts of citizenship (Sykes 2016, 751–2). Sykes (2016, 759–60) and Gibney (2013, 650–2) have alternatively labelled this as republican conceptions of citizenship. According to these conceptions, citizenship is conditional upon a contractual or reciprocal relationship between state and individual based on the latter's loyalty to the former.[16] Indeed, this cannot be articulated through the Passport Act, as it would only limit the exercise of citizens' rights, but leave the status from which they derive unaffected. Denationalisation, on the other hand, could achieve the security aims whilst also articulating and sanctioning the breach of loyalty. This is consistent with the statements made by the government party (VVD) in the debate in the Lower House, where it argued that citizens who turn against their own country lose their *right* to citizenship (Tweede Kamer 2016, 4). Whilst this would explain the rejection of less intrusive alternatives, such as the Passport Act, it also implies that questions of loyalty only arise against dual-nationals, but not mono-nationals, which in turn fuels discriminatory narratives.

This risk of alienating dual-nationals, especially Dutch-Moroccans, and us-versus-them narratives in turn challenges the effectiveness of Dutch denationalisation measures. Cole (2015) notes that these narratives actually support the efforts of terrorist organisations: '[I]f [terrorist organisations] can get non-Muslim[s] to be beastly to ethnic Muslims on the grounds that they are Muslims, [terrorist organisations] can start creating a common political identity around grievance against discrimination.' This issue is reiterated in by recommendations that counter-terrorism efforts should focus on the disruption of terrorist narratives and propaganda and create counter-narratives portraying the grim realities of conflicts such as Syria (Briggs and Silverman 2014). Especially where denationalisation and terrorist recruitment target the same group, there is a real risk of a feedback loop that continuously fuels radicalisation (McBridge 2011; Malik 2015). Discriminatory laws and measures fuel alienation, which in turn sustain further radicalisation and recruitment, which in turn trigger more intrusive (denationalisation) laws to address the increasing number of foreign fighters, and so forth. In light of these concerns, note should be taken of legislative developments in Canada in mid-2017, where concerns about us-versus-them narratives were a driving factor behind the abolition of reactive deprivation of nationality only applicable to dual-nationals (Canadian Citizenship Act 1985, version prior to amendment by Bill C-6, Section 10(2)(b)).

Conclusion

In the Netherlands, revoking the nationality of citizens who have been convicted of terrorist offences or who have affiliated themselves with a terrorist organisation as foreign fighters, has been viewed as an effective addition to traditional counter-terrorism policy. However, both proactive and reactive denationalisation raise serious human rights concerns, particularly with regard to discrimination. While the legal analysis here has shared these concerns and indicated that both Articles 14(2) and (4) are incompatible with the prohibition of direct discrimination, it has also revealed that the information on the background of Dutch foreign fighters currently available is insufficient to establish indirect discrimination against Dutch-Moroccans specifically with certainty. Nevertheless, empirical data and reports by international observers strongly indicate discrimination against Dutch-Moroccans in particular, which is unlikely to be justifiable under the ECHR. These findings are relevant beyond the Netherlands (De Groot and Vonk 2015b). Firstly, they suggest that similar discrimination issues may arise in other countries where the background of foreign fighters is similar, such as Belgium (Bakker and Roel 2016, 54), and in countries that only revoke citizenship obtained by naturalisation, such as France (French Civil Code, Article 25). Secondly, the proportionality analysis has revealed that it may generally be difficult to justify denationalisation interfering with Article 14 taken together with 8 ECHR. New insights are likely to be gained from the case of *Ghoumid et al. v France* on the reactive denationalisation of naturalised foreign fighters currently pending before the ECtHR.

The evaluation of the legal analysis highlighted both its strengths and weaknesses and reiterated the importance of the use of empirical and normative findings both as part of the legal analysis and in supplementation thereto. The ensuing normative discussion offered further support for the finding of indirect discrimination and revealed that even if compatible with the ECHR, the fact that denationalisation measures primarily target a specific group is likely to limit their effectiveness by being counterproductive. The effectiveness concerns were echoed in the discussion of the parliamentary debate surrounding the enactment of the measures. Ultimately, the Article arrived at the conclusion that denationalisation in its current form is hardly reconcilable with the principle of equality as reflected in the prohibition of discrimination.

Finally, the enactment of proactive and reactive denationalisation in the Netherlands must be viewed in light of broader academic observations regarding the changes in conceptions of citizenship. Returning to the definition given by the ICJ in *Nottebohm*, it has become clear that the Netherlands emphasises the element of 'reciprocal rights and duties' rather than the 'social fact or attachment' or the 'genuine connection of existence', indicating a shift away from the concept of citizenship as an unconditional right.

Notes

1. For the purposes of this Article, dual-nationals will include individuals with more than two nationalities.
2. With the narrow exception regarding 'conduct seriously prejudicial to the vital interests of the state' under Article 8(3) 1961 Convention on the Reduction of Statelessness, which only allows denationalisation in force at the time of ratification, statelessness is only an acceptable consequence where fraudulently acquired nationality is revoked. However, this Article discusses denationalisation on grounds of public security.
3. Other human rights concerns include: double jeopardy and interferences with the rights to private and family life (Article 8 ECHR), to an effective remedy (Article 13 ECHR), or to fair trial (Article 6 ECHR).
4. This exception does not apply where denationalisation responds to fraudulent acquisition or a conviction by the ICC.
5. Article 205 Dutch Criminal Code (*Wetboek van Strafrecht*) criminalises entering into service of foreign armed forces.
6. For a discussion see GR De Groot, *Towards a Toolbox for Nationality Legislation* (Maastricht, Nexus Legal, 2016), 33.
7. The ECtHR has so far rendered five judgements under Article 1 Protocol 12, none of which concerned nationality.
8. This distinction is also maintained in European Union Agency for Fundamental Rights and Council of Europe, 'Handbook on European non-discrimination law' (2018 Edition, Publications Office of the European Union, 2018).
9. Such evidence must then be rebutted by the respondent.
10. The data relied upon does not indicate a significant number of foreign fighters with such a background.
11. A discussion of these concerns would exceed the scope of this article by far, see instead Boekestein 2017.
12. It is unclear whether this number only counts men or also includes women and children.
13. In *Nachova and Others* (2005), the ECtHR held that there are no restrictions to the types of evidence it accepts.

14. Elke Winter and Ivana Previsic, 2019, 'The politics of un-belonging: lessons from Canada's experiment with citizenship revocation'.
15. Since only Article 14(2) DNA is applicable.
16. Helen Irving's, 2019, 'The concept of allegiance in citizenship law and revocation: an Australian study'.

Disclosure statement

No potential conflict of interest was reported by the authors.

References

A and Others v Secretary of State for the Home Department (*Belmarsh case*). 2004. 56 (UKHL).

Adviescommissie voor Vreemdelingenzaken. 2015. *Advies Voorstel Wijziging Rijkswet Op Het Nederlanderschap i.v.m. Intrekken Van Het Nederlanderschap in Het Belang Van De Nationale Veiligheid.* Den Haag: Adviescommissie voor Vreemdelingenzaken.

AIVD. 2017a. *Jaarverslag.* Ministerie van Binnenlandse Zaken en Koninkrijksrelaties.

AIVD. 2017b. *Terugkeerders in Beeld.* Den Haag: AIVD.

Amnesty International. 2017. *Netherlands: Counter-Terrorism Bills Would Violate Human Rights and Undermine Rule of Law.* Amnesty Interntional.

Andrejeva v Latvia. 2009. App no 55707/00 (ECtHR, 18 February).

Bakker, E., and D. B. Roel. 2016. "Belgian and Dutch Jihadist Foreign Fighters (2012–2015): Characteristics, Motivations, and Roles in the War in Syria and Iraq." *Small Wars & Insurgencies* 27(5): 837.

Bauböck, R. 2014. *The Return of Banishment: Whose Bad Guys are Terrorists?* Florence: EU Observatory on Citizenship.

Bauböck, R., and V. Paskelev. 2015. "Cutting Genuine Links: A Normative Analysis of Citizenship Deprivation." *Georgetown* 30: 48.

Biao v Denmark. 2016. App no 38590/10 (ECtHR, 24 May).

Bill 31813 (R1873), nr. 6 nota naar aanleiding van het verslag. 2008. *Wijziging van de Rijkswet op het Nederlanderschap met betrekking tot meervoudige nationaliteit en andere nationaliteitsrechtelijke kwesties.*

Bill 34356 (R2064), nr. 3 Memorie van Toelichting. 2015. *Wijziging van de Rijkswet op het Nederlanderschap in verband met het intrekken van het Nederlanderschap in het belang van de nationale veiligheid.*

Boekestein, T. L. 2019. "Deprivation of Nationality as a Counter-Terrorism Tool: A Comparative Analysis of Canadian and Dutch Legislation." *Transnational Human Rights Review* 5, 23.

Briggs, R., and T. Silverman. 2014. *Western Foreign Fighters: Innovations in Responding to the Threat.* London: Institute for Strategic Dialogue.

Canadian Association of Refugee Lawyers. 2014. *Bill C-24, an Act to Amend the Citizenship Act and to Make Consequential Amendments to Other Acts.* Canadian Association of Refugee Lawyers.

Canadian Citizenship Act. 1985. version prior to amendment by Bill C-6

Carey, B. 2018. "Against the Right to Revoke Citizenship." *Citizenship Studies* 22 (8): 897. doi:10.1080/13621025.2018.1538319.

CBS. 2015. *Aantal Nederlanders Met Dubbele Nationaliteit Gestegen Naar 1,3 Miljoen.* 4 August. Accessed 22 October 2018. https://www.cbs.nl/nl-nl/nieuws/2015/32/aantal-nederlanders-met-dubbele-nationaliteit-gestegen-naar-1-3-miljoen

CBS. 2016. *Bevolking Naar Migratieachtergrond.* 21 November. Accessed 22 October 2018. https://www.cbs.nl/nl-nl/achtergrond/2016/47/bevolking-naar-migratieachtergrond

CoE Commissioner for Human Rights. 2016. *Letter to Dutch Ministers of the Interior and Kingdom Relations and Security and Justice.* Strasbourg: Council of Europe.

Cole, J. 2015. *Sharpening Contradictions: Why al-Qaeda Attacked Satirists in Paris.* 1 July. Accessed 22 October 2018. https://www.juancole.com/2015/01/sharpening-contradictions-satirists.html

College voor de Rechten van de Mens. 2015. *Advies: Conceptwetsvoorstel tot Wijziging van de Rijkswet op het Nederlanderschap in Verband met het Intrekken van het Nederlanderschap in het Belang van de Nationale Veiligheid.* College voor de Rechten van de Mens.

Convention on the Reduction of Statelessness. 1961.

Council of Europe. 2000. "Explanatory Report to thProtocol No. 12 to the Convention for the Protection of Human Rights and Fundamental Freedoms." Explanatory Report.

Council of Europe Treaty Office. 2017. *Chart of Signature and Ratifications of Treaty 177 – Protocol No. 12 to the Convention for the Protection of Human Rights and Fundamental Freedoms.* 3 May. Accessed 23 October 2018. https://www.coe.int/en/web/conventions/full-list/-/conventions/treaty/177/signatures?p_auth=lVSIhhvv

D.H. and Others v The Czech Republic. 2006. App no 57325/00 (ECtHR, 7 February).

D.H. and Others v The Czech Republic. 2007. App no 57325/00 (ECtHR [GC], 13 November). doi:10.1094/PDIS-91-4-0467B.

De Groot, G. R. 2016. *Towards a Toolbox for Nationality Legislation.* Maastricht: Nexus Legal.

De Groot, G. R., and O. Vonk. 2015b. "Jihad En Ontneming Van Nationaliteit – Nederlandse Plannen in Vergelijkend Perspectief." In Pauline Kruiniger (Ed.), *Jihad, Islam en Recht: Jihadisme en reacties vanuit het Nederlandse en Belgische Recht: 35.*Den Haag: Boom juridisch.

De Groot, G.-R., and O. Vonk. 2015a. "De Ontneming Van Het Nederlanderschap Wegens Jihadistische Activiteiten." *Tijschrift Voor Religie, Recht En Beleid.*

de Leeuw, R. 2016. *Intrekken Nederlanderschap Uitgereisde Jihadisten: Toetsing Aan Internationale Mensenrechten: Recht Op Een Nationaliteit, Discriminatieverboden En Rechtsbescherming.* Weert: Celsus.

Dutch Constitution. 1814. *Grondwet.*

Dutch Criminal Code. 1881. *Wetboek Van Strafrecht.*

Dutch Ministers of the Interior and Kingdom Relations and Security and Justice. 2016. "Response to the CoE Commissioner for Human Rights' Letter of 2 November 2016." 25 November.

Dutch Ministry of Security and Justice; National Coordinator Counterterrorism and Security; Minister of Social Affairs and Employment. 2014. "Actieprogramma Integrale Aanpak Jihadisme."

Dutch Nationality Act. 1984. *Rijkswet Op Het Nederlanderschap.*

Eerste Kamer. 2017b. "Verslag Van De Vergadering Van 7 Februari 2017." Parliamentary Report 2016/2017 nr. 17.

Eerste Kamer. 2017a. "Verslag Van De Vergadering Van 31 Januari 2017." Parliamentary Report 2016/2017 nr. 16.

Esbrook, L. 2016. "Citizenship Unmoored: Expatriation as Counter-Terrorism Tool." *Journal of International Law* 37 (3): 1273.

European Convention on Nationality. 1997. "

French Civil Code. 1804. *Code Civil.*

Funk, N. C., and A. A. Said. 2004. "Islam and the West: Narratives of Conflict and Conflict Transformation." *International Journal of Peace Studies* 9: 1.

Gaygusuz v Austria. 1996. App no 17371/90 (ECtHR, 16 September).

Georgia v Russia (I). 2014. App no 13255/07 (ECtHR, 3 July).

Ghoumid et al. v France. 2016. App nos 52273/16, 52285/16, 52290/16, 52294/16, 52302/16 (ECtHR, 2016 September).

Gibney, M. J. 2013. "Should Citiznehsip Be Conditional? the Ethics of Denationalisation." *The Journal of Politics* 75 (3): 646. doi:10.1017/S0022381613000352.

Grabenwarter, C. 2014. *European Convention on Human Rights: Commentary*. Munich: CH Beck.

Groen, J. 2016. "De Wetsvoorstellen Ter Uitvoering Van Het Actieprogramma Integrale Aanpak Jihadisme." *Tijdschrift Voor Constitutioneel Recht.*

Groen, J. 2017. *Jihadgangers Zijn Relatief Vaak Bekeerlingen; 45 Procent Is Van Marokkaanse Komaf.* 5 July. Accessed 22 October 2018. https://www.volkskrant.nl/nieuws-achtergrond/jihadgangers-zijn-relatief-vaak-bekeerlingen-45-procent-is-van-marokkaanse-komaf~bb147bf6/

Hegghammer, T., and P. Nesser. 2015. "Assessing the Islamic State's Commitment to Attacking the West." *Perspectives on Terrorism* 9 (4): 14.

Immigratie- en Naturalisatiedienst. 2017. "Intrekking Nederlanderschap." *Staatscourant nr. 52440.* 10 March.

Immigratie- en Naturalisatiedienst. 2018. *Monitor naturalisatie en optie 2014-2017.* Ministerie van Justitie en Veiligheid.

Jessurun D'Oliveira, Hans Ulrich. 2016. "Nationaliteitsrecht Als Wapen in De Strijd Tegen De Jihad." *NJB 2014/1908.*

Jessurun D'Oliveira. Hans Ulrich. 2017. "Geen Directe Werking Europees Nationaliteitsverdrag? so What?" *NJB 2017/98.*

Joppke, C. 2016. "Terror and the Loss of Citizenship." *Citizenship Studies* 20 (6–7): 728. doi:10.1080/13621025.2016.1191435.

Kouwenhoven, A. 2019. *Minister Neemt Tegen Advies in Jihadisten Nationaliteit Af.* 7 January. Accessed 18 January 2019. https://www.nrc.nl/nieuws/2019/01/07/minister-neemt-tegen-advies-in-jihadisten-nationaliteit-af-a3128215

Lavi, S. 2011. "Citizenship Revocation as Punishment: On the Modern Duties of Citizens and Their Criminal Breach." *University of Toronto – Jean-Philippe Julien* 61 (4): 783. doi:10.3138/utlj.61.4.783.

Liechtenstein v Guatemala (Nottebohm). 1955. ICJ 1 (ICJ).

Macklin, A. 2014. "Citizenship Revocation, the Privilege to Have Rights and the Production of Aliens." *Queen's Law Journal* 40 (1): 1.

Malik, N. 2015. *Charlie Hebdo: The "Them and Us" Narrative Is a Dangerous Downward Spiral.* 8 January. Accessed 22 October 2018. https://www.theguardian.com/commentisfree/2015/jan/08/charlie-hebdo-them-and-us-clash-of-civilisations

McBridge, M. K. 2011. "The Logic of Terrorism: Existential Anxiety, the Search for Meaning, and Terrorist Ideologies." *Terrorism and Political Violence* 23 (4): 560. doi:10.1080/09546553.2011.575486.

Minister of Security and Justice. 2017. "Besluit Van De Minister Van Veiligheid En Justitie Van 2 Maart 2017, Nr. 2050307." *Besluit tot vaststelling van de lijst met organisaties de een bedreiging vormen voor de nationale veiligheid.*

Nachova and Others v Bulgaria. 2005. App nos 43577/98 and 43579/98 (ECtHR, 6 July).

Nationaal Coordinator Terrorismebestrijding en Veiligheid. March 2018a. "Dreigingsbeeld Terrorisme Nederland 47."

Nationaal Coordinator Terrorismebestrijding en Veiligheid. September 2018b. Dreigingsbeeld Terrorisme Nederland 48.

NPO Radio 1. 2017. *Bijna 300 Passportent Ingenomen Van Jihadgangers.* February 1. Accessed 24 October 2018. https://www.nporadio1.nl/achtergrond/2959-bijna-300-paspoorten-ingenomen-van-jihadgangers

Parliamentary Assembly of the Council of Europe. 2019a. "Recommendation 2145." *Withdrawing Nationalit as a Measuree to Combat Terrorism: A Human Rights-Compatible Approach?*

Parliamentary Assembly of the Council of Europe. 2019b. "Resolution 2263." *Withdrawing Nationalit as a Measuree to Combat Terrorism: A Human Rights-Compatible Approach?*

Ramadan v Malta. 2016. App no 76136/12 (ECtHR, 21 June).

S.A.S. v France. 2014. App no 43835/11 (ECtHR, 1 July).

Schabas, W. 2016. *The European Convention on Human Rights: A Commentary.* Oxford: OUP.

SGR 17/6834 and 17/15049. 2018. (Rechtbank den Haag, 26 June).

Soering v The United Kingdom. 1989. App no 14038/88 (ECtHR, 7 July).

Stec and Others v The United Kingdom. 2006. App nos. 65731/01 and 65900/01 (ECtHR, 12 April).

Sykes, P. 2016. "Denaturalisation and Conceptions of Citizenship in the 'War on Terror'." *Citizenship Studies*, 749.

Trop v. Dulles. 1985. 356 US 86, 101 (USSC).

Tweede Kamer. 2016. "Intrekken Nederlanderschap in Beland Nationale Veiligheid." Report of Plenary Discussion 18 May 2016.

UN Special Rapporteur on Contemporary Forms of Racism, Racial Discrimination, Xenophobia and Related Intolerance. 2018. Amicus Brief, United Nationals Human Rights.

The politics of un-belonging: lessons from Canada's experiment with citizenship revocation

Elke Winter and Ivana Previsic

ABSTRACT

Citizenship revocation has returned to the political agenda. In recent years, many Western democracies have either legislated or considered legislating citizenship revocation for terrorism offences. This paper analyses how Canada's short-lived experiment with citizenship revocation was represented in political, media and online discourses. Specifically, it identifies who has been interpreted a presumed candidate(s) of citizenship revocation, and analyses the discursive strategies employed to associate these targets with specific ethnic, national, or religious groups. We find that references to Muslims dominated public discourses on citizenship revocation. The articulation of these references reveals that Muslims were targeted not as individuals but as a category, indirectly branding them as less Canadian, and thereby symbolically un-belonging them from Canadian citizenship.

Citizenship revocation (or denationalisation, here used interchangeably) as a form of punishment for criminal acts (other than for suspected fraud) has recently returned to the political agenda. It is one of the most serious punishments citizens can face, commonly used by ruling classes since antiquity to jettison political dissidents, convicted criminals, or ethnic and religious minorities. Strikingly, most countries that contemplate enforcing citizenship revocation in the twenty-first century are signatories of the United Nations Convention on the Reduction of Statelessness. The measure is thus in most Western states[1] restricted to dual (or multiple) nationals, applied only to those who would not be rendered stateless by losing one citizenship (Gibney 2017, 366). This allows the respective countries to abide by their international obligations.

While the impact of citizenship revocation's revival may thus appear 'modest', it is also widespread among Western democracies: the UK, Canada and Australia legislated the measure in 2006, 2014 and 2015 respectively. Austria, the Netherlands, and France recently contemplated denationalisation for convicted terrorists (CBC 2016; Joppke 2016; Mills 2016). While practised for a number of reasons by these nation-states, the revocation of citizenship is most often legitimised as a means to enhance national security and public safety. Scholars of citizenship are divided over this phenomenon. Some argue that terrorists repudiate their citizenship by waging a war against citizens (Joppke 2016); others feel that citizenship revocation is punitive, anachronistic and unconstitutional (Macklin 2014). It is also viewed as ineffective, unethical, and as shifting a (rich) state's responsibility for its criminals to another (often failed or failing) state (Bauböck 2015).

In the recent scholarship on citizenship revocation, legal and normative arguments abound. In this paper, we will be contributing to the literature by adopting a sociological point of view. From this perspective, citizenship revocation is, above all, an official act of legally *and* symbolically 'un-belonging'. This symbolism is not solely produced by the legal act itself, but also by surrounding public debates in politics, media and society. This paper examines how symbolic un-belonging is discursively produced and disseminated. We ask: What does legalising the revocation of citizenship do – via discourse – to the public representations of those associated with it? We find that, in public discourse, citizenship revocation is not only associated with individuals and groups, but also with the social categories associated with them, such as dual nationals, immigrants and ethnic minorities. Concentrating on a specific case – Canada's 2014–2016 citizenship revocation rules for dual nationals – we examine *who* parliamentarians, mainstream media and the wider public saw as individuals who may have their Canadian citizenship revoked, and how these presumed targets of the new policy were represented.

Citizenship revocation in Canada

In today's virtually unchallenged system of nation-states, states regulate membership via nationality or citizenship policies. Individuals must have or must seek admission in at least one nation-state. The 1954 United Nations Convention on the Reduction of Statelessness was implemented in reaction to a period Gibney (2017) characterises as citizenship revocation's apogee (1920–1945), which saw mass denationalisations by totalitarian states. In its wake, with the increased repudiation of citizenship revocation due to its potential to cause statelessness, Western countries gradually liberalised citizenship policy, easing naturalisation and increasing the toleration of dual citizenship (Bauböck, Perchinig, and Sievers 2009).

Following the terrorist attacks in the United States on 11 September 2001 and subsequent terrorist attacks in Europe, this liberalisation is increasingly questioned. As more immigrants from non-Western countries adopt their host countries' nationality as their second or third citizenship, their loyalty, as well as their capacity and willingness to 'integrate' are doubted. Citizenship revocation has become associated with the fight against various forms of 'Islamist' terrorism, whether 'home grown' (i.e. committed by native-born citizens) or 'imported' (i.e. committed by naturalised citizens).

In 2014, Canada's Conservative government, following the United Kingdom, legislated citizenship revocation as a counter-terrorism strategy. Two years earlier, Conservative Member of Parliament (MP) Devinder Shory introduced Bill C-425, An Act to Amend the Citizenship Act (Honouring the Canadian Armed Forces), proposing that Canadian citizens are 'deemed to have made an application for renunciation of their Canadian citizenship if they engage in an act of war against the Canadian Armed Forces' (Parliament of Canada 2012). The bill gained traction in February 2013 when, after reports that Canadian citizens participated in bomb attacks in Bulgaria and

Algeria, the Minister of Citizenship and Immigration affirmed the government was considering to revoke the Canadian citizenship of dual nationals involved in acts of terrorism (Parliament of Canada 2013a, 2013b, 2013c). Bill C-425 died when Parliament was dissolved in August 2013 in anticipation of an election. Similar provisions were proposed again six months later, with the new Conservative Citizenship and Immigration Minister insisting that 'citizenship is not a right, it is a privilege' (Parliament of Canada 2014a).[2]

Bill C-24, the 'Strengthening Canadian Citizenship Act', was introduced in February 2014, rushed through Parliament, and made law without any amendments on 19 June 2014 (Citizenship and Immigration Canada 2014). The Minister of Citizenship and Immigration received authorities that once belonged to the Governor in Council, notably to revoke citizenship (formerly, mainly for fraud) or to grant it under non-routine circumstances. Most contentiously, it granted the Minister's office power to revoke the citizenship of dual nationals engaged in actions contrary to Canada's national interests, such as high treason, terrorism and espionage. A Federal Court of Canada decision in May 2015 confirmed the constitutionality of citizenship revocation (for something other than fraud) (Federal Court 2015). Zakaria Amara, convicted to life imprisonment as the ringleader of the 'Toronto 18 terrorist group', became the first person to lose Canadian citizenship. In October 2015, however, only four months after the measure became law, the Conservative Party lost federal elections to the Liberal Party, which had campaigned on repealing Bill C-24 (CBC 2015). In February 2016, the new Minister of Immigration, Refugees and Citizenship introduced a bill reversing the citizenship revocation portion of the previous government's citizenship legislation and restored Zakaria Amara's citizenship (Parry 2016). In June 2017, the Trudeau government officially repealed the provision (Canada 2017). Despite the measure's repeal, however, the idea of banishment as a legal and/or 'desirable' recourse against 'terrorists' gained public traction, both in Canada and abroad.

Debating citizenship revocation

This paper differentiates between four broad streams of academic inquiry into citizenship revocation: legal, historical/comparative, normative and consequential.

First, legal scholars debate citizenship revocation's compliance with various aspects of law. Macklin (2015, 6), most prominently, claims that citizenship revocation restricts the basic right of entering, prevents rehabilitation, and is an illegal form of punishment: among other reasons, because it treats 'mono-citizens' and dual or multiple citizens unequally. If citizenship revocation does not apply to 'mono-citizens', then they retain citizenship as their right, while it becomes a privilege for those who would not become stateless if convicted. Macklin's stance is not undisputed. In the Canadian case, a Supreme Court decision confirmed the constitutionality of citizenship revocation (Galati v. Canada [Governor General], 2015). Hailbronner (2015, 22) holds that Macklin's interpretation of citizenship revocation as 'a (prohibited) form of punishment simply ignores [its] legal nature', pointing out that in about half of the 28 EU member states 'seriously prejudicial behaviour is considered as a ground for deprivation of citizenship'.

Second, historical and comparative scholarship on citizenship revocation argues that '(seemingly impartial) denationalisation laws have often served as a cover for racial and ethnic-based discrimination' (Gibney 2017, 376). Indeed, the revival of citizenship revocation challenges the thesis of increasing citizenship liberalisation (Joppke 2010), recently shown by Fargues (2017) in the cases of Britain and France. Fargues' claim that citizenship revocation in both countries exemplifies citizenship renationalisation also contradicts the view that there are inherent safeguards against discrimination in international law (Hailbronner 2015, 23).

Third, much of the recent scholarly debate ponders normative questions. Scholars ask whether citizenship revocation is just and/or legitimate. Joppke (2016) argues that new global terrorism transcends borders, targets ordinary citizens, aspires for war, and is 'committed by people who explicitly posit themselves outside the secular community of the nation-state'. The involuntary loss of citizenship seems thus a legitimate punishment for 'a special sort of "public" crime called terror' (Joppke 2016, 735). By contrast, most commentators see citizenship revocation as unjust and unethical (e.g. Bauböck 2015; Macklin 2014, 2015; Ziegler 2015). Bauböck (2015) cautions against citizenship revocation because it allows states to deny their responsibility towards individuals, as well as 'towards the rest of the world upon whom they inflict the terrorist threat'. States are also responsible for their 'bad guys', whether they are dictators like Hitler (Bauböck 2015, 29) and Pinochet (Ziegler 2015) or jihadists. Indeed, as Joppke (2016) admits, these latter are 'our problem' too, because 'Islamism's resonance in the West cannot be disconnected from a domestic logic of failing immigrant integration'.

Citizenship revocation is also viewed as harming dual citizens who are treated unequally for the same crime. In fact, the Canadian Bar Association (2014) argues that citizenship revocation of dual nationals makes approximately one million Canadians with multiple citizenships into second-class citizens and subjects 'entire ethnic or national communities' to the provision, depending on citizenship laws of their country of ancestry, some of which do not allow citizenship renunciation.[3] Furthermore, as Macklin (2014) argues, today's targets of denationalisation are not merely dual citizens convicted of terrorism charges. Rather, they are 'the suspected terrorist, or the potential terrorist, or maybe the associate of a terrorist. He [i.e. this person] is virtually always Muslim and male'. Our analysis below corroborates Macklin's claim.

The fourth line of inquiry concerns citizenship revocation's consequences, a question that most commentators consider in terms of the measure's effectiveness regarding national security objectives. They agree that, compared with the criminal justice system, citizenship revocation has little instrumental value (Forcese 2014; Lenard 2016; Macklin 2014, 2015; Paskalev 2015; Spiro 2015). 'Banishing' jihadists to countries they want to go to anyway, and where they may either be tortured or freed – but regardless will likely renew efforts to cause harm – is unethical and less effective than incarcerating them in Western democracies (Paskalev 2015). Moreover, citizenship revocation does not work as a deterrent, because its targets are unlikely to care about losing citizenship (Paskalev 2015).

A review of the above four strands in the literature indicates that the revocation of citizenship is likely to be legal/constitutional, but ineffective in preventing terrorism. Most commentators suggest that while the measure falls within the realm of symbolic politics, it also creates hierarchies among citizens (Choudhury 2017) and bears the potential for abuse of power and harm to dual citizens, and even to 'entire ethnic or national communities' (Canadian Bar Association 2014.) This last dimension, however, is underdeveloped in the literature. How does a law affecting so few individuals harm dual citizens and stigmatize members of ethnic communities? Adopting a sociological perspective, this paper investigates citizenship revocation's symbolic implications and inherent ability to un-belong not only those who are convicted, but those whose ethno(religious) groups are associated with the targeted individuals. Specifically, we ask: What effect does inscribing citizenship revocation into law have on how those associated with the policy are represented via public discourse?

Citizenship revocation's symbolic boundaries

In addressing the aforementioned research questions, this paper offers conceptual clarification on three levels – citizenship, citizenship revocation and interpretative policy analysis.

Citizenship is commonly described as a combination of three elements (Carens 2000, 162–75). First, formal citizenship status or legal membership (nationality) links individuals to particular states and preconditions a set of rights and duties. Sociologists differentiate between status and rights, since merely possessing citizenship status does not necessarily mean accessing or enjoying citizenship rights in practice. Second, political membership (citizenship) comprises various forms of participation in a political community. Certain types of activity are viewed as conducive to 'good citizenship' (e.g. the active law-abiding, self-sufficient citizen, [Anderson 2014]); others as controversial or subversive (Isin and Nielsen 2008). They can enact change or precede status (Bloemraad 2015). Arguably, recalling Joppke's (2015) argument above, certain acts may break the (legal) bond of citizenship. Third, identity-related membership (belonging) refers to individuals' identifying as members of the polity and being seen as such by other members. Belonging describes the symbolic boundaries of citizenship, that is, the collective identity shared by most individuals possessing the same status.

As scholarship on boundary-work has abundantly shown, the relationship between status/rights, participation, and belonging is neither automatic nor necessarily overlapping. These dimensions feed into each other (see Lamont and Virág 2002, as well as Bloemraad 2018 for useful discussions of the relevant literature). Hence, while legal status often generates belonging, the latter is undermined when individuals are excluded from the nation's symbolic boundaries or subjectively feel this way. This, in turn, affects participation and the de facto enjoyment of rights even when individuals' formal citizenship status remains intact. Put differently, symbolic boundaries have material effects, especially when widely disseminated and agreed upon; they translate into social boundaries (i.e. identifiable patterns of exclusion or class or segregation).

By withdrawing an individual's citizenship status and rights, a citizenship revocation is an official act of un-belonging an individual which has both legal/material and symbolic consequences. Even if a 'mono-national' cannot be made stateless, the punishment of revoking someone's citizenship for select crimes indicates that the person (and their crimes) belongs elsewhere. While the legal effects only apply to (potentially few) dual nationals, the symbolic boundaries drawn by legislating citizenship revocation extend to broader social categories associated – in political and public discourse – with these individuals, such as dual nationals, immigrants and members of certain ethno-religious minorities. Research shows that crimes attributed to members of the dominant group are interpreted as acts of deviant individuals, while crimes committed by members of minority groups are viewed as driven by their (cultural, religious or racial) 'nature' (e.g. Guillaumin 1972; Phillips 2003). It is thus critical to examine whether and *how* individuals and groups associated with those 'worthy' of citizenship revocation become guilty by association.

This brings us to the question of how a policy or legal provision gains social meaning. Yanow (1996) argues that policies or laws convey meaning not only through explicit content, but also at the interface between the authors' intentions (in the case of citizenship revocation, the intentions of those proposing the bill) and the experiences 'readers' bring with them when they read, interpret and debate the policy. Readers or commentators of policies are diverse individuals: politicians and parliamentarians, academics, lawyers, various experts and stakeholders, journalists and members of society, including those who write letters to the editor and debate policies online. The social and political context in which policies and laws are implemented and interpreted matters (Fairclough 1999). Furthermore, through seemingly banal references to individuals, events, groups and countries, commentators infuse policy with a specific meaning. Congruence between the references creates a 'semantic field' – 'a set of words belonging to the same conceptual area' (Baker and Ellece 2011, 125) – sometimes accompanied by divergent counter-fields. When they occur, commentators' responses to counter-fields can reinforce dominant fields and interpretations or open avenues to new ones. Policies may thus stereotype particular groups even though the latter are not mentioned in the policy/legal text per se. According to Yanow (1996, xi), 'some of the tacitly known, yet nonetheless communicated meanings may concern the status of particular groups of "others" in the population'. This is precisely what this paper examines: How does citizenship revocation policy affect – qua public discourse – the public representation of those seen as its targets?

Methodology

This paper concentrates on three discursive sites in which policies are debated and meanings created: political debates, mainstream media and online commentary.

First, in order to examine how citizenship revocation was discussed in the House of Commons and the Standing Committee on Citizenship and Immigration, we accessed transcripts through the Parliament of Canada website using the keywords 'C-425', 'C-24' and 'revocation', in English and French. The debates covered from 30 May 2012, when Bill C-425 was introduced, to 19 June 2014, when Bill C-24 was adopted. In total, we collected transcripts of 23 debates and 15 Standing Committee Meetings.

Second, we examined how mainstream newspapers interpreted the measure. While the media are capitalist institutions, they are also promoters of civic literacy. Newspapers represent the key discursive sites that influence public debates (Korteweg and Yurdakul 2009, 224), including the dissemination of information about government action and legislation. More broadly, the newspapers shape the way that immigration is conceptualised in relation to the national 'self' (Pottie-Sherman and Wilkes 2014). Importantly, mainstream media are a key source of knowledge about minority groups (Mahtani 2001). The relationship between the Canadian media and minorities has mostly been strained (Fleras and Kunz 2001). The study used the same combinations of keywords as above to identify relevant articles in the databases Canadian Newsstand Major Dailies and Eureka.cc, analysing *The Globe and Mail, The National Post, The Toronto Star, The Ottawa Citizen, The Sun, 24 Hours, La Presse, Le Devoir*, and *Le Journal de Montréal*. In order to examine coverage of the measure in newspapers representing a variety of ideological perspectives, we included broadsheets and tabloids, as well as national and local daily press from 7 February 2013 (when Bill C-425 made its first appearance in the media) until 7 July 2014 (after Bill C-24 became law and media debates had decreased). The analysis comprised a total of 88 articles in English and only eight in French,[4] with collected data including news reports, editorials, columns and letters.

Third, the study examined the comments sections of online news stories. An increasing number of Canadians read the news online (Vivadata 2015), and many newspapers allow readers to post comments. User comments are often perceived as extensions of news stories and, being part of the mainstream media discourse, may be interpreted as a cue to public opinion (Lee and Yang 2010; Santana 2011). These sections of online news stories also provide an outlet for members of dominant group(s) to express views on matters involving minorities. Importantly, to members of minority groups, comments indicate – accurately or not – how mainstream society perceives them. In turn, members of minorities use these online platforms to engage in interactions with other Canadians, whom they may perceive as representing the 'majority' of Canadians. The study used internet searches to match news stories identified through the databases that were also available online. The study included only stories that tackled citizenship revocation and allowed readers to post comments, identifying ten such online news stories: seven from *The National Post*, two from *The Globe and Mail* and one from *The Toronto Star*.[5] We analysed a total of 2,174 comments.

Qualitative and quantitative approaches were combined to answer the research questions. We used the qualitative data analysis software NVivo to conduct the analysis. The initial step of the analysis (Saldaña 2013) consisted of reading the data through, and coding and categorising relevant references to (1) individuals;(2) events; (3) criminal groups; and (4) ethnic, religious, and national groups referred to as candidates for citizenship revocation.

This initial step of coding revealed that references to Muslims outnumbered those to other groups, leading to additional categorisation of the references into Muslim and non-Muslim 'semantic fields'. A Muslim 'semantic field' consisted of references to (1) individuals with Muslim names; (2) Muslim-majority ethnic and national groups;[6] (3) criminal groups associated with Muslims; and (4) other events, practices and customs typically associated with Muslims. A non-Muslim semantic field included mentions of (1) individuals presumed to be non-Muslim, (2) non-Muslim majority ethnic and national groups and (3) criminal groups not associated with Muslims. These categories were then also used to classify references in the parliamentary debates and online comments. Once identified, in the second, focused step of coding (Saldaña 2013), the keywords were searched in all texts to capture, count and compare all instances of relevant references and representations. Additionally, all references were divided into the categories 'specific' and 'hypothetical': the former applying to 'real' individuals and groups with a (presumed) criminal association, the latter to religious, ethnic and religious groups, or individual members of these groups ('regular' people) who do not have a criminal background.

The production of symbolic boundaries in Canada's citizenship revocation debates

Quantitative findings: Muslims as (potential) targets of citizenship revocation

Our first finding is that the measure of citizenship revocation evolved from being directed at those who commit 'acts of war' against Canada to targeting dual citizens involved in 'high treason', 'terrorism' and 'espionage'. As Table 1 shows, in all three texts, citizenship revocation was reported on and debated primarily in the context of terrorism. Overall, this criminal activity accounted for 67% of all references. Given the current preoccupation of most states with security and terrorism, it is no surprise that terrorism dominated the debates.

Second, and following from above, in terms of *whose* (real or potential) terrorism is at stake and, hence, *who* is targeted by the measure of citizenship revocation, the debates in all three texts overwhelmingly revolved around Muslims: specifically, 714 references to Muslims and 176 to non-Muslims. The former thus make up 80% of all representations of potential targets.

Discourse analysis: drawing boundaries around Muslims

In discussions of candidates for citizenship revocation, commentators employed a variety of discursive strategies. These strategies provided a clear understanding of who the bills target and discursively contributed to the process of drawing symbolic boundaries between Canadian Muslims and non-Muslims.

The findings exposed two main discursive strategies to mark Muslims, *as a group* and *in general*, as more likely to be involved in terrorism and consequently to be targeted by the bill: enumeration and exceptionalising. Enumeration is defined by Dubois and Sankoff (2001, 2085) as a 'cumulative discursive procedure made up of *at least two* different components that belong to the same or equivalent morphological and functional categories. This procedure evokes a homogeneous referential ensemble to which the enumerated constituents refer'. In other words, the enumerated references are perceived as sharing something in common (i.e. being Muslim, or non-Muslim). 'Exceptionalising' has been examined in discourse analysis mostly as a strategy of positioning select individuals as different – and better – than the (minority) group they are associated with, which is typically stereotyped as inferior (Briscoe, Arriaza, and Henze 2009). This study, however, revealed the reverse: individuals – typically criminal offenders – were positioned as atypical from – and worse than – their (culturally dominant) group.

Table 1. Number of references by criminal activity.

	Criminal activity			
Text	'Acts of War'	Espionage	Treason	Terrorism
Bills	6	0	12	10
Debates	129	48	238	750
Newspapers	41	32	104	486
Online comments	3	8	251	547
Total	179	88	605	1793

Enumeration

Analysis of the examples of enumeration of Muslim references reveals that Muslim references, both specific and hypothetical, were generally grouped together in discussions of the proposed bills in *all three* texts. For instance, during a meeting of the Standing Committee on Citizenship and Immigration, a lawyer referred to the cases of Bashir Makhtal and Huseyincan Celil (both Canadian citizens) and Saeed Malekpour (a Canadian resident) as potential recipients of the measure (Parliament of Canada 2013b). At the time of writing, these individuals remain imprisoned in Ethiopia, China and Iran, respectively, on charges of terrorism or treason. Similar instances of enumeration of specific Muslim references emerged in newspaper articles. An article in the *The National Post* on 14 February 2014 argued, 'The inaccurate tarring and incarceration of Messrs. Arar, El-Maati, Almalki and Nureddin suggest that wrongful conviction of Canadian "terrorists" is not such a remote possibility'. *The Ottawa Sun* (1 April 2013), reporting on the measure, cited an intelligence expert stating that 'at various times terrorist groups have been identified in Canada with origins in ethnic, regional and nationalist conflicts as far apart as Egypt, Algeria, Sudan, Afghanistan, Lebanon, the Punjab, Sri Lanka, Turkey and the former Yugoslavia'. Except for former Yugoslavia, Punjab and Sri Lanka, the remaining six enumerated countries and regions have Muslim majorities. References to *hypothetical* Muslims were also enumerated: an article in *The National Post* on 11 February 2014, asked: 'What if Egypt passed such a law? Or Pakistan or Saudi Arabia or Lebanon?'

The strategy of enumerating non-Muslim references – specific or hypothetical – was identified only in one online exchange following an article by Andrew Coyne in *The National Post* on 8 February 2013. Arthur Porter, accused of what many argued was the biggest corruption fraud in Canada's history (CBC 2017), and Jeffrey Delisle, a former sub-lieutenant in the Royal Canadian Navy who in 2012 pleaded guilty to spying and selling secrets to Russia (Puddicombe 2016), were mentioned by two commentators as hypothetically fitting the criteria for citizenship revocation. They also argued that loyalty to Canada may not be correlated with the number of citizenships. However, a commentator under the alias of 'EnglishCanadian' responded to both these comments as follows: 'What in hell are you talking about?' and 'What relevance does that have to removing citizenship from TERRORISTS?', thereby dismissing these non-Muslim references.

While the exchange above was the only instance of a grouping of non-Muslim references, a number of examples of both specific and hypothetical non-Muslim references being grouped *with* Muslim references were observed. For instance, criticising the provision, a Liberal MP noted, 'in my lifetime we've gone from Irish terrorists to Tamil terrorists to Muslim terrorists, and a lot of these terrorist ideas have been … in the eye of the beholder' (Parliament of Canada 2013b). Chris Selley, writing for *The National Post* on 11 February 2014, interpreted the measure to be neither about 'Robert Pickton's nor Paul Bernardo's[7] Canadian citizenship … I'm not the first to notice how well those circumstances align with those of Canada's least favourite 27-year-old, Omar Ahmed Khadr, whose father was born in Egypt'. In the online exchanges following the same article, both Muslim and non-Muslim Canadians were marked as potential recipients of the measure:

> 'ChrisInNepean (0) Khadr's father may have been an Egyptian but does Egypt allow dual citizenship with Canada? In the US it seems that special permission has to be obtained to be a dual American-Egyptian citizen.
>
> Sue McPherson to ChrisInNepean (0)
>
> He is known only as Canadian, as far as I recall, just as Mohamed Fahmy (see Jonathan Kay's piece) and Tarek Loubani and John Greyson, all of whom are called Canadian but come from there. Egypt or thereabouts'.

Unlike in the one instance of grouping of specific non-Muslim references, these combinations were unchallenged by other online commentators, presumably because including Muslim to non-Muslim references made the arguments (more) pertinent and meaningful.

Finally, non-Muslim *hypothetical* references were enumerated with Muslim references. For instance, during Parliamentary debates, an MP representing Bloc Québécois provided the example of three non-Muslim references alongside a Muslim reference:

> What do we do with a young person who is born in Quebec – who is not of French-Canadian or English-Canadian heritage but may be of Italian heritage, for example – who decides to get involved with a terrorist group? In comparison, what do we do with another young person who was not born in Canada – who arrived from Morocco, for example – who also has Canadian citizenship and joins a terrorist group? What do we do with them? (Parliament of Canada 2014a)

Here, the MP inferred that those of Italian heritage would receive different treatment than those of Moroccan heritage and that the provision was unlikely to apply to those of French Canadian or English Canadian origins. In other examples of enumeration of hypothetical non-Muslims alongside Muslims, the association was less clear, and, in fact, both 'groups' were presented as random examples. For instance, during a Committee Meeting, a lawyer argued,

> [There] are many countries that if your parent is from that country and you're born to that parent even in Canada and even if your parent's a Canadian citizen, you automatically have citizenship, for example, the Egyptians, Chinese, Italians, etc. (Parliament of Canada 2014b)

Exceptionalising

While the strategy of exceptionalising was observed mostly for non-Muslim references, findings revealed three instances of Muslim references standing alone. Omar Khadr[8] was the only *specific* case of a Canadian Muslim who was unaccompanied by other references. Given the notoriety of this case in Canada, it is not surprising that the commentators in all three texts did not feel the need to group Omar Khadr with other individuals.

Two instances of *hypothetical* Muslim references being mentioned alone were identified in two newspaper articles by Nicholas Keung in the *The Toronto Star* published on 7 February and 3 March 2014. Two permanent residents from Pakistan and Iran – presumably future Canadian citizens – were asked their opinion on the question of citizenship revocation. Journalists use 'experiential interviews' with members of the public when these individuals are presumed to have had 'some relevant personal experience' in relation to the issue reported (Montgomery 2011). In these two articles, the journalists *chose* to interview residents with Pakistani and Iranian citizenships, presumably because it was deemed that because nationals of these countries could be affected by the measure, they should weigh in on it. In the article where the Iranian national was interviewed, two other Iranian citizens, as well as nationals of India, Russia and Pakistan, were quoted on various other-proposed changes in Canada's citizenship legislation. In theory, any of these permanent residents could have been asked their opinion on citizenship revocation for terrorism offences. In reality, however, reporting the opinion of the Russian national, for instance, would have probably been interpreted by readers as irrelevant to the topic.

A number of specific, non-Muslim references standing alone were also identified. For instance, during a meeting of the Standing Committee on Citizenship and Immigration, a law professor wondered why Russell Williams, an England-born Canadian killer and rapist and a former colonel in the Canadian Forces, was 'worthy of punishment, but not stripping of citizenship. Does that mean that the government doesn't value the victims of his crimes the same way that it values the victims of the crimes being legislated about in this bill?' (Parliament of Canada 2013b). Other examples of exceptionalising of specific non-Muslim references were found mainly in the online comments, and these were also interpreted by most commentators as off-topic.

The findings also identified instances of hypothetical non-Muslims being exceptionalised. For instance, an online user commenting on an article written in *The National Post* on 8 February 2013 suggested that all Canadians holding citizenship of countries with ties to terrorism should give up one of their citizenships; commentator 'Kevin_start' responded: 'Given that there are still "terrorist cells" in Ireland and Northern Ireland, would you advocate ending dual citizenship for people originally from Ireland or the U.K.?'. Responding to this comment, 'revelationman' wrote that the measure could apply to these people if they had 'strong Middle Eastern and African ties while still maintaining their citizenship with those countries', presumably implying that these would be Irish or British citizens of Middle-Eastern background. Clarifying their point, 'Kevin_start' responded: 'I am not certain if you did not understand my comment or whether you are being deliberately disingenuous. I was talking about "organisations" like the Real IRA'. 'revelationman' concluded this exchange by writing: 'what are you on about, apples and oranges, are you saying the IRA are responsible for terrorist attacks around the worl [*sic*]'.

Discussion

This paper examines how public discourses interpret and interact with government policies to enable the drawing or solidification of symbolic boundaries. Specifically, it studies the discussion of Canada's legislation of citizenship revocation for reasons of espionage, treason and terrorism (2015–2017) in three discourses: political debates, mainstream media and online commentary. Findings show that the emergence of symbolic boundaries created by the bills and the legislation does not depend on the execution of specific denationalisation cases. In other words, revoking the citizenship of specific individuals is not necessary for symbolic boundaries to emerge. Furthermore, and most importantly, the social categories commonly associated with citizenship revocation for national security reasons need not be written into the legal text. In the Canadian case, no mention of ethnic or religious denominations was made in any edition of the bills or law.

Rather, the legal provisions gained social meaning by being situated – by all those interpreting it – within a specific historical and geopolitical context. In this sense, finding that Muslim references dominate the three analysed types of discourse is not surprising. After all, most acts labelled as 'terrorism' are currently committed by individuals or groups associated with Muslims. However, this study identifies a differential discursive treatment of Canadian Muslims and non-Muslims that goes beyond the mere quantity of reference. The articulations of interpretations of the policy in the three discourses indicate that the policy targeted Muslims not as individual criminals but as a *group*.

First, references to specific Muslim individuals and groups accused or convicted of acts of terrorism were often grouped together, creating a perception of terrorism being a collective problem. By contrast, when part of a chain, non-Muslim references were frequently collocated with references to Muslims – arguably to convey a sense of randomness or to avoid being accused of bias. Stand-alone references to non-Muslim individuals and groups (mostly in online comments) were sporadic, appeared individually, and were thereby represented as exceptions rather than symptomatic of a group problem. Importantly, despite the severity of their crimes – judging by the commentators' reactions to these references – these perpetrators were represented as not deserving of the act of un-belonging from the Canadian national community.

Second, findings show that identifying potential targets of the measure extends beyond specific terrorism cases into providing hypothetical scenarios, which tend to incriminate Muslims. Commentators do this by (1) providing examples of Muslim-majority countries of second citizenship, often grouped with non-Muslim hypothetical references in examples, arguably in order for the representations to appear random, and (2) by asking Canadian residents who hold citizenship of a Muslim-majority country to weigh in on the measure. Mentioning the (other) citizenships of these (hypothetically impacted) individuals creates a cognitive association between the individual and the (other) country of citizenship, and then with other nationals of these countries. Although this cognitive link within one and the same utterance (speech in parliament, newspaper article, online commentary) may appear precarious (i.e. limited to that one hypothetical dual national in question, and not applicable to all members of the ethno religious group), it is reinforced by similar discursive constructions in other pieces of the same text, as well in the other two analysed types of text.

Third, looking at all three types of texts as one discourse, we find that references to specific cases of terrorism – even when the individuals in question are falsely accused or acquitted – are collocated with random and innocuous (hypothetical) examples of ethnic and national groups associated with Islam. This is what discourse analysts refer to as 'discursive prosody' – when neutral references acquire positive or negative connotations from emotionally charged words that they are collocated with (Baker and Ellece 2011). When a *Toronto Star* editorial (7 February 2013) refers to hypothetical 'Lebanese-Canadian, American-Canadian, Italian-Canadian' and asks 'How would we react to Lebanon stripping Lebanese-Canadian terrorists of their Lebanese citizenship and telling us they are now exclusively our worry?', the guilty, the suspected, the innocent, the acquitted, and the hypothetical are united in the reader's mind into the category of 'Muslims'. It then becomes difficult to distinguish 'the good' from 'the bad'. Placing the 'real' next to the 'hypothetical' – and the frequent enumeration of Muslim individuals, groups and events in the context of terrorism – contributes to the popular suspicion that Canadian Muslims are, at the very least, sympathetic to terrorism and incapable of truly belonging in Canada.

Fourth, while terrorism attacks in Canada are rare, Antonius (2013) observes that the international context provides the underpinning, justification and vocabulary for discussing national issues. In the examined discourses – the 'inside' and 'outside', 'here' and 'there' – are merged together in a way that would be unimaginable if criminal offences not (overtly) associated with any particular ethno-religious group were debated.

To conclude, the representations analysed in these three texts are a snapshot of cumulative 'texts' and 'fields'. Just as these texts were congruent with one another in terms of consistent references and employed strategies, they also match other political, media, online and everyday discourses in which citizenship, immigration and terrorism are debated. In fact, complementary and interacting texts constitute intertextuality and interdiscursivity, and are how congruent semantic fields are created (Baker and Ellece 2011, 64, 125). In this way, a segment of the discourse on citizenship revocation referencing Muslims is linked to another segment that mentions Muslims but that may not tackle citizenship revocation but instead terrorism, and that segment to another, etc. Together, they create a congruent semantic field and provide knowledge that is difficult (but not impossible) to counter. This is how bills and legislation pertaining to citizenship revocation contributed to Islamophobia and to the solidification of symbolic boundaries – and this, despite the facts that the legal texts made no mention of any specific group that only one individual (temporarily) lost his Canadian citizenship, and that the law was eventually overturned. Sadly, the existence of Islamophobia in Canada is 'beyond a doubt' (Wilkins-Laflamme 2018, 105). This study has shown how law and its public repercussions fuelled the victimisation of Muslims.

Conclusion

This paper contributes to three areas of scholarship: the impacts of policy qua public discourse, the consequences of citizenship revocation law, and the un-belonging of Muslims in Western countries. Specifically, we have argued that citizenship revocation is an act of un-belonging, which removes the convicted individual not only from society (as imprisonment would do) but also (through the withdrawal of legal status) from the national community, as well as (by the denial of belonging) from its collective imaginary. Furthermore, by examining how Canada's legislation of citizenship revocation is discussed in three discourses, this study has shown that legislation that is widely characterised as 'symbolic politics'. Symbolic politics, in the words of Faist (2016, 38), shift the problem 'from substantive policies to argumentative strategies and symbolic performances', and 'prioritizes political presentation over political solutions via substantive policies'. Despite its symbolic nature, legislation enacted in this manner has far-reaching social consequences. It affects not only the few who are convicted but the many who are publicly identified as belonging to the same ethno-religious category as those associated with (domestic or international) 'terrorism'.

Scholarship has shown that symbolic boundaries may quickly become social boundaries, producing identifiable patterns of segregation and affecting social and political participation, as well as de facto enjoyment of rights even when individuals' formal citizenship status remains intact (Lamont and Virág 2002). In this way, the politics of un-belonging individuals is extended – qua discourse – to collectively target an already-stigmatised group in Canada and in many Western societies (Perigoe and Eid 2014; Razack 2008). This additional stigmatising of Muslims is not only unnecessary – as citizenship revocation legislation is widely seen as having few tangible security effects – it is also counter-productive, potentially producing or reinforcing the formation of reactive ethnic and religious identities (Ajrouch and Kusow 2007; Berns-McGown 1999; Nagra 2017) and even encouraging religious radicalisation (Lindekilde 2014).

Notes

1. The UK is an outlier in this respect. In 2014, the power of the Secretary of State for the Home Department to deprive dual nationals of citizenship when this would be 'conducive to the public good' was extended from dual to mono citizens who acquired UK citizenship via naturalisation and who could thereby be rendered stateless if deprived of UK citizenship (Mantu 2018).
2. Similar rhetoric was used by the UK Prime Minister Theresa May in 2013 when a statement from the Home Office said: 'Citizenship is a privilege, not a right, and the Home Secretary will remove British citizenship from individuals where she feels it is conducive to the public good to do so.' (Shaw 2018).
3. In 2011, only 2.9% of Canadians held multiple citizenships, 79.5% of these were indeed foreign-born, with most frequently reported other countries of citizenship being the United States (20.3%), the United Kingdom (12.9%) and France (9.6%) (Statistics Canada 2011). Among those born in Canada, 0.7 had multiple citizenships, with the United States (20.3%), the United Kingdom (12.9%) and France (9.6%) being the most frequently reported other countries of citizenship (Ibid).
4. The issue of citizenship revocation was not high on the radar of French-language newspapers. We resume that it was overshadowed by the debates about an important provincial bill, the so-called Charter of values, presented by the Parti Québécois during the same time frame.
5. The comments posted in the conservative-leaning newspaper *the National Post* outnumbered those published on the websites of the more liberal-leaning newspapers *The Globe and Mail* and *The Toronto Star*. As noted earlier, however, even though online comments may be perceived as a cue to the public opinion, they are not statistically representative of the political leanings of Canadians. Moreover, and in line with previous research (Lee and Yang 2010), our analysis revealed that the comments often diverged from the political affiliations of the newspaper or the slant of the article.
6. In marking a national group as Muslim-majority or non-Muslim-majority, we used official statistics on the religious composition of the state. For instance, while referring to Lebanese or Egyptian Canadians as 'Muslim', we also acknowledge the multi-ethnic and multi-religious composition of their ancestral homelands. We also acknowledge that national groups marked as 'non-Muslim', e.g. China or the US, are populated by Muslim minorities.
7. Robert Pickton is a Canadian serial killer sentenced in 2007 to life in prison for murdering six women. Paul Bernardo is a Canadian serial killer and serial rapist sentenced to life in prison in 1995.
8. Omar Khadr is a Canadian who was detained at the United States detention centre at Guantanamo Bay in Cuba for ten years, from the age of 16. He pleaded guilty to the murder of an American soldier, but later appealed his conviction claiming he only signed the plea agreement so that he could return to Canada. In 2010, the Supreme Court of Canada found that Khadr's constitutional rights had been violated. He was transferred to Canada in 2012 and released on bail with strict conditions in 2015. In 2013, Khadr sued the Canadian government for infringing his rights. The government settled the lawsuit in 2017 with a $10.5 million payment and an apology.

Acknowledgments

This research would not have been possible without the generous funding of the Kanishka Project, Public Safety, Government of Canada (2013-2016). One of the authors acknowledges support from the Alexander von Humboldt Foundation and the Centre of Excellence "Cultural Foundations of Integration", University of Konstanz, Germany. The helpful comments from the anonymous reviewers made this paper better, and the remaining errors and omissions are solely ours.

Disclosure statement

No potential conflict of interest was reported by the authors.

References

Ajrouch, K., and A. Kusow. 2007. "Racial and Religious Contexts: Situational Identities among Lebanese and Somali Muslim Immigrants." *Ethnic and Racial Studies* 30 (1): 72–94. doi:10.1080/01419870601006553.

Anderson, B. 2014. *Exclusion, Failure, and the Politics of Citizenship*. Toronto: Ryerson Centre for Immigration and Settlement.

Antonius, R. 2013. "A Mediated Relationship: Media Representations of Arabs and Muslims as A Political Process." In *Targeted Transnationals: The State, the Media, and Arab Canadians*, edited by J. Hennebry and B. Momani, 110–128. Vancouver: UBC Press.

Baker, P., and S. Ellece. 2011. *Key Terms in Discourse Analysis*. London: Continuum.

Bauböck, R. 2015. "Whose Bad Guys Are Terrorists?" In *The Return of Banishment: Do the New Citizenship Revocation Policies Weaken Citizenship?* edited by A. Macklin and R. Bauböck, 27–30. Florence: European University Institute.

BauböCk, R., B. Perchinig, and W. Sievers. 2009. *Citizenship Policies in the New Europe*. Amsterdam: University Press.

Berns-McGown, R. 1999. *Muslims in the Diaspora: The Somali Communities of London and Toronto*. Toronto: University of Toronto Press.

Bloemraad, I. 2015. "Theorizing and Analyzing Citizenship in Multicultural Societies." *The Sociological Quarterly* 56 (4): 591–606. doi:10.1111/tsq.12095.

Bloemraad, I. 2018. "Theorising the Power of Citizenship as Claims-Making." *Journal of Ethnic and Migration Studies* 44 (1): 4–26. doi:10.1080/1369183X.2018.1396108.

Briscoe, F., G. Arriaza, and R. Henze. 2009. *The Power of Talk: How Words Change Our Lives*. Thousand Oaks: Corwin.

Canada. 2017. "Bill C-6 Receives Royal Assent." Accessed 25 October 2017. https://www.canada.ca/en/immigration-refugees-citizenship/news/2017/06/bill_c-6_receivesroyalassent0.html

Canadian Bar Association. 2014. "Bill C-24, Strengthening Canadian Citizenship Act: Submission to the Standing Committee on Citizenship and Immigration." Accessed 25 May 2015. http://www.cba.org/cba/submissions/pdf/14-22-eng.pdf

Carens, J. C. 2000. *Culture, Citizenship, and Community: A Contextual Exploration of Justice as Evenhandedness*. Oxford: Oxford University Press.

CBC. 2015. "Revocation of Citizenship: 5 Things to Know." September 29. http://www.cbc.ca/news/politics/citizenship-revoked-revocation-bill-c-24-1.3248920

CBC. 2016. "François Hollande Drops Bill to Revoke French Citizenship of Convicted Terrorists." March 30. http://www.cbc.ca/news/world/france-drops-terrorism-citizenship-bill-1.3511865

CBC. 2017. "Charges Officially Abandoned against Arthur Porter, Two Years after His Death." August 4. http://www.cbc.ca/news/canada/montreal/arthur-porter-officially-dead-1.4235786

Choudhury, T. 2017. "The Radicalisation of Citizenship Deprivation." *Critical Social Policy* 37 (2): 225–244. doi:10.1177/0261018316684507.

Citizenship and Immigration Canada. 2014. "Government Welcomes Royal Assent of Bill C-24." Accessed 20 June 2014. https://www.canada.ca/en/news/archive/2014/06/government-welcomes-royal-assent-bill-c-24.html?=undefined&

Dubois, S., and D. Sankoff. 2001. "The Variationist Approach Towards Discourse Structural Effects and Socio-Interactional Dynamics." In *The Handbook of Discourse Analysis*, edited by H. E. Hamilton, D. Schiffrin, D. Tannen, and H. E. Hamilton, 282–303. Malden, MA: Blackwell Publishers.

Fairclough, N. 1999. "Linguistic and Intertextual Analysis within Discourse Analysis." In *The Discourse Reader*, edited by A. Jaworski and N. Coupland, 183–212. London: Routledge.

Faist, T. 2016. *Dual Citizenship in Europe: From Nationhood to Societal Integration*. London: Routledge.

Fargues, É. 2017. "The Revival of Citizenship Deprivation in France and the UK as an Instance of Citizenship Renationalisation." *Citizenship Studies* 21 (8): 984–998. doi:10.1080/13621025.2017.1377152.

Federal Court. 2015. "Galati V. Canada (Governor General)." Accessed 18 April 2017. https://decisions.fct-cf.gc.ca/fc-cf/decisions/en/item/108114/index.do

Fleras, A., and J. L. Kunz. 2001. *Media and Minorities: Representing Diversity in a Multicultural Canada*. Toronto: Thompson Educational Publishing .

Forcese, C. 2014. "A Tale of Two Citizenships: Citizenship Revocation for 'Traitors' and 'Terrorists." *Queen's Law Journal* 39 (2): 551–585. doi:10.2139/ssrn.2434594.

Gibney, M. 2017. "Denationalisation." In *The Oxford Handbook of Citizenship*, edited by A. Shachar, R. Bauböck, I. Bloemraad, and M. Vink, 360–379. Oxford: Oxford University Press.

Guillaumin, C. 1972. *L'idéologie Raciste: Genèse Et Langage Actuel*. La Haye: Mouton & .

Hailbronner, K. 2015. "Revocation of Citizenship of Terrorists: A Matter of Political Expediency." In *The Return of Banishment: Do the New Denationalisation Policies Weaken Citizenship?* edited by A. Macklin and R. Bauböck, 23–26. Florence: European University Institute.

Isin, E., and G. Nielsen, eds. 2008. *Acts of Citizenship*. London: Zed Books.

Joppke, C. 2010. *Citizenship and Immigration*. Cambridge: Polity.

Joppke, C. 2015. "Terrorists Repudiate Their Own Citizenship." In *The Return of Banishment: Do the New Denationalisation Policies Weaken Citizenship?* edited by A. Macklin and R. Bauböck, 11–14. Florence: European University Institute.

Joppke, C. 2016. "Terror and the Loss of Citizenship." *Citizenship Studies* 20 (6–7): 728–748. doi:10.1080/13621025.2016.1191435.

Korteweg, A., and G. Yurdakul. 2009. "Islam, Gender, and Immigrant Integration: Boundary Drawing in Discourses on Honour Killing in the Netherlands and Germany." *Ethnic and Racial Studies* 32 (2): 218–238. doi:10.1080/01419870802065218.

Lamont, M., and M. Virág. 2002. "The Study of Boundaries in the Social Sciences." *Annual Review of Sociology* 28 (1): 167–195. doi:10.1146/annurev.soc.28.110601.141107.

Lee, E.-J., and Y. J. Yang. 2010. "What Do Others' Reactions to News on Internet Portal Sites Tell Us? Effects of Presentation Format and Readers' Need for Cognition on Reality Perception." *Communication Research* 37 (6): 825–846. doi:10.1177/0093650210376189.

Lenard, P. 2016. "Democracies and the Power to Revoke Citizenship." *Ethics & International Affairs* 30 (1): 73–92. doi:10.1017/S089267941500063.

Lindekilde, L. 2014. "A Typology of Backfire Mechanism." In *Dynamics of Political Violence: A Process-Oriented Perspective on Radicalization and the Escalation of Political Conflict*, edited by L. Bosi, C. Demetriou, and S. Malthaner, 51–70. Farnham, UK: Ashgate Publishing.

Macklin, A. 2014. "Citizenship Revocation, the Privilege to Have Rights and the Production of the Alien." *Queen's Law Journal* 40 (1): 1–54.

Macklin, A. 2015. "Kick-Off Contribution." In *The Return of Banishment: Do the New Denationalisation Policies Weaken Citizenship?* edited by A. Macklin and R. Bauböck, 1–6. Florence: European University Institute.

Mahtani, M. 2001. "Representing Minorities: Canadian Media and Minority Identities." *Canadian Ethnic Studies* 33 (3): 99–133.

Mantu, S. 2018. ""'"Terrorist" Citizens and the Human Right to Nationality." *Journal of Contemporary European Studies* 26 (1): 28–41. doi:10.1080/14782804.2017.1397503.

Mills, B. 2016. "'A Privilege, Not a Right': Contemporary Debates on Citizenship Deprivation in Britain and France." *COMPAS Working Paper*, WP-16–130.

Montgomery, M. 2011. "The Accountability Interview, Politics and Change in UK Public Service Broadcasting." In *Talking Politics in Broadcast Media: Cross-Cultural Perspectives on Political Interviewing, Journalism and Accountability*, edited by M. Ekstrom and M. Patrona, 33–56. Amsterdam: John Benjamins Pub.

Nagra, B. 2017. *Securitized Citizens: Canadian Muslims' Experience of Race Relations and Identity Formation Post-9/11*. Toronto, ON: University of Toronto Press.

Parliament of Canada. 2012. "Bill C-425, an Act to Amend the Citizenship Act (Honouring the Canadian Armed Forces)." http://www.parl.gc.ca/HousePublications/Publication.aspx?Docid=5622699&file=4 doi:10.1094/PDIS-11-11-0999-PDN.

Parliament of Canada. 2013a. "Parliament. House of Commons. Standing Committee on Citizenship and Immigration. Minutes of Proceedings." (Meeting No. 74, March 26, 2013) 41st Parliament, 1st Session'. Ottawa: Parliament of Canada. March 26. http://www.parl.gc.ca/HousePublications/Publication.aspx?Language=e&Mode=1&Parl=41&Ses=1&DocId=6064385

Parliament of Canada. 2013b. "Parliament. House of Commons. Standing Committee on Citizenship and Immigration. Minutes of Proceedings." (Meeting No.75, April 16, 2013) 41st Parliament, 1st Session'. Ottawa: Parliament of Canada. April 16. http://www.parl.gc.ca/HousePublications/Publication.aspx?Language=e&Mode=1&Parl=41&Ses=1&DocId=6080563

Parliament of Canada. 2013c. "Parliament. House of Commons. Standing Committee on Citizenship and Immigration. Minutes of Proceedings." (Meeting No.77, April 23, 2013) 41st Parliament, 1st Session'. Ottawa: Parliament of Canada. April 23. http://www.parl.gc.ca/HousePublications/Publication.aspx?Language=e&Mode=1&Parl=41&Ses=1&DocId=6097654

Parliament of Canada. 2014a. "Parliament. House of Commons." *Debates, 41st Parliament, 2nd Session, 147* (053) Ottawa: Parliament of Canada. February 27. http://www.parl.gc.ca/HousePublications/Publication.aspx?Language=E&Mode=1&Parl=41&Ses=2&DocId=6445253

Parliament of Canada. 2014b. "Parliament. House of Commons. Standing Committee on Citizenship and Immigration. Minutes of Proceedings." (Meeting No.23, April 23, 2014) 41st Parliament, 2nd Session'. Ottawa: Parliament of Canada. April 30. http://www.parl.gc.ca/Committees/en/MeetingPublication?publicationId=6554507&parl=41&session=2

Parry, T. 2016. "Liberals Move to Overhaul Rules on Revoking, Granting Citizenship." *CBC News*, February 25. http://www.cbc.ca/news/politics/john-mccallum-citizenship-act-repealbill-1.3463471

Paskalev, V. 2015. "It's Not about Their Citizenship, It's about Ours." In *The Return of Banishment: Do the New Denationalisation Policies Weaken Citizenship?* edited by A. Macklin and R. Bauböck, 15–16. Florence: European University Institute.

Perigoe, R., and M. Eid. 2014. *Mission Invisible*. Vancouver: UBC Press.

Phillips, A. 2003. "When Culture Means Gender: Issues of Cultural Defence in the English Courts." *Modern Law Review* 66 (4): 510–531. doi:10.1111/1468-2230.6604002.

Pottie-Sherman, Y., and R. Wilkes. 2014. "Good Code Bad Code: Exploring the Immigration-Nation Dialectic through Media Coverage of the Hérouxville 'Code of Life Document'." *Migration Studies* 2 (2): 189–211. doi:10.1093/migration/mnt002.

Puddicombe, S. 2016. "Documents Shed a Little Light on What Spy Jeffrey Delisle Sold to Russians." *CBC News*, April 15. http://www.cbc.ca/news/canada/nova-scotia/jeffrey-delisle-navy-russia-espionage-documents-spying-1.3514194

Razack, S. 2008. *Casting Out: The Eviction of Muslims from Western Law and Politics*. Toronto, ON: University of Toronto Press.

Saldaña, J. 2013. *The Coding Manual for Qualitative Researchers*. London: Sage.

Santana, A. D. 2011. "Online Readers' Comments Represent New Opinion Pipeline." *Newspaper Research Journal* 32 (3): 66–81. doi:10.1177/073953291103200306.

Shaw, K. 2018. *The Court of Justice of the European Union Subsidiary and Proportionality*. Boston: BRILL.

Spiro, P. 2015. "Terrorist Expatriation: All Show, No Byte, No Future." In *The Return of Banishment: Do the New Denationalisation Policies Weaken Citizenship?* edited by A. Macklin and R. Bauböck, 7–8. Florence: European University Institute.

Statistics Canada. 2011. "Obtaining Canadian Citizenship." Accessed 16 February 2015. http://www12.statcan.gc.ca/nhs-enm/2011/as-sa/99-010-x/99-010-x2011003_1-eng.cfm

Vivadata. 2015. "Vividata Launches with Release of Fall 2015. Study Amalgamation of NADbank + PMB into Vividata Creates a Whole New Read on Readers." Accessed 16 February 2016. https://vividata.ca/news/press-release/

Wilkins-Laflamme, S. 2018. "Islamophobia in Canada: Measuring the Realities of Negative Attitudes toward Muslims and Religious Discrimination." *Canadian Review of Sociology* 55 (1): 86–110. doi:10.1111/cars.12180.

Yanow, D. 1996. *How Does a Policy Mean? Interpreting Policy and Organizational Actions*. Washington: Georgetown University Press.

Ziegler, R. (Ruvi). 2015. "Disowning Citizens." In *The Return of Banishment: Do the New Denationalisation Policies Weaken Citizenship?* edited by A. Macklin and R. Bauböck, 43–44. Florence: European University Institute.

Denaturalisation and conceptions of citizenship in the 'war on terror'

Patrick Sykes

ABSTRACT
The threat of American and British nationals returning home after fighting with ISIS sparked calls in 2014 for legislation to allow the revocation of terror suspects' citizenship. Using content analysis, this paper compares how citizenship was renegotiated during the debates that followed in both countries. For proponents of the new powers, acts considered prejudicial to national security did not simply constitute a 'bad' or dissenting citizen, but were incompatible with the status of citizenship itself. I find that republican discourses of citizenship conceived as loyalty to the state were used not as an alternative to liberal discourses that espouse individual rights and a more limited political arena, but precisely as means of discursively limiting of that arena, by selectively excluding particular undesirable or less desirable groups – terror suspects, naturalised citizens – from political life as we know it.

Introduction

In recent years, several Western governments have sought the power to deprive so-called foreign fighters of their citizenship. For a variety of reasons, which I discuss below, they consider the two categories irreconcilable. The 'foreign fighter' is thus presented as an inverse or negative image of the normatively desirable or acceptable citizen. The label of the 'foreign fighter' therefore invites study not only in itself or in order to understand its direct effects upon individuals, communities and policies, but because, through and in the course of its deployment as this inverse category, it reconfigures the 'centre' of citizenship, the (perceived) norms from which deviations are measured. This study analyses that process of reconfiguration in the cases of the UK and US, taking the debates over attempts to introduce denaturalisation powers for 'foreign fighters' as a lens through which to understand how citizenship is conceptualised by these two countries embroiled in their long 'war on terror'. Although conceptions of citizenship as loyalty to a state are usually contrasted with conceptions of citizenship as a body of individual rights, I find that, in the 'war on terror', the former is used to discursively delimit the bounds of the latter. The result is that citizenship is re-constructed as a privileged status that states are empowered to withdraw from 'undesirable' groups – terror suspects, naturalised citizens – in order to justify their exclusion from political life.

One must note from the outset that the figure of the 'foreign fighter' is by no means a distinct one. Various definitions have been proposed (Hegghammer 2010, 57–58; Malet 2013, 9), though none established in political science. As Kraehenmann notes, the phenomenon is neither uniquely Islamic nor even religious (2014, 5), and for Mustapha (2013), the concept conjures a spectrum of meanings from the 'terrorist' to the 'cosmopolitan citizen'.[1] Yet today it is a construct that is in practice used to refer to a group far smaller than its constituent terms suggest – namely those travelling abroad to fight with Islamic militant insurgencies. An individual or a non-state armed group fighting for a foreign government (rather than an insurgency), for instance, would qualify under the terminology but not the usage (Kraehenmann 2014, 6). Indeed the terminology is so loose that one can see how the initial invocation of the label to describe someone who leaves home to fight abroad can easily slide into the description of a fighter who becomes a de facto foreigner vis-à-vis the country they once called home – the state to which one is considered 'foreign' is undefined.

In 2014, politicians in both the UK and the US proposed new legislation that sought to empower the government to strip citizenship from terror suspects, explicitly in relation to the perceived threat of nationals who had joined jihadist groups abroad (particularly in Syria and Iraq) returning to their native countries. In the UK, it was passed as part of the Immigration Act, which enabled the government to revoke citizenship in some cases even if it results in statelessness; in the US, it was proposed first as the Terrorist Expatriation Act and later as the Expatriate Terrorists Act, but neither passed, and the government remains unable to revoke citizenship in lieu of proof of its affirmative renunciation by the citizen in question. This paper compares the conceptions of citizenship that were invoked in the two cases, and analyses the consequences of these conceptions for policy in the 'war on terror'.

Prior to 9/11, revocation powers had not been used in the UK since 1973 (Ross 2014). But since 2002, at least 27 people have been stripped of their nationality on the grounds that they were not conducive to the public good (Galey and Ross 2014).[2] The Bureau of Investigative Journalism's long-running 'Citizenship Revoked' investigation observed that 'The British [2010–15 coalition] government has dramatically escalated its use of secretive citizenship-stripping powers' (Ross and Galey 2013). Though the use of this power has grown, Herzog (2010) finds that it remains poorly understood among the publics of Western democracies, which more readily attribute such measures to far-away totalitarian regimes. The legitimacy of denaturalisation is indeed challenged in international law (League of Nations 1930; UN 1948, 1961), which enshrines nationality as a human right and explicitly prohibits its arbitrary deprivation.

The denaturalisation debate did not occur in a vacuum. In the UK in particular, this latest weapon in the 'war on terror' is emblematic of the rise of the 'homegrown terrorism' discourse that frames particular citizens as simultaneously 'at risk' (of radicalisation) and 'risky' (from the perspective of the state) (Heath-Kelly 2013, 411). In its violent othering of those deemed undesirable for their views, it also represents the continuation of the UK's move away from a multicultural policy towards one that expects or demands assimilation (Brighton 2007; Kundnani 2002) into a community normatively grounded in 'shared values' (Spalek and McDonald 2010), with all the exclusionary consequences that has for those who do not conform. This paper will provide further evidence of those two trends as manifested in this particular addition to states' legal armoury.

The literature engaging with denaturalisation and statelessness also encounters its fundamentally problematic nature. Following Arendt, Blitz and Lynch (2011, 4) argue that 'the very notion of statelessness exposes the essential weaknesses of the global political system, which relies on the state to act as the principal guarantor of human rights'.[3] Lavi holds up the mere possibility of denaturalisation to refute Aristotle's aphorism that human beings are political animals, since it shows that political 'nature' is only accessible to those endowed with the relevant civic status (2010, 405–6).

The more general condition of statelessness and the struggle to attain citizenship has received considerably more attention than its revocation, as exemplified in Blitz and Lynch's (2011) expansive volume of global case studies.[4] Waas (2008) and Walker (1981) offer thorough elucidations of the international legal architecture and the specific rights that can be invoked by those lacking a nationality. A dedicated issue of *Forced Migration Review* (Couldrey and Herson 2009) provides further background on statelessness through cases such as that of the Rohingya. Yet Kerber (2005) and Waas (2009) have shown that the problem is far from being limited to situations of overt political persecution in the underdeveloped world.

Even amid the 'crisis' of the nation state proclaimed by Benhabib (2005), or its 'inadequacy' according to Cooper and Yoder (1999), the state in which citizenship is anchored remains a meaningful category alongside transnational forces (Vertovec 2001). One example of this is the exponential rise in the number of countries allowing dual citizenship and in the number of individuals taking it up, as traced by Sejersen (2008). Rather than signalling the irrelevance of citizenship, then, the perceived 'decline' of the nation state's coherence suggests that citizenship is less and less a singular status befitting a zero-sum understanding of membership of or allegiance to a single political community.

Changing grounds for revocation: from loyalty to security

Appetites for denaturalisation are much increased in times of war (Herzog 2010, 7, Hooker 2005). In his history of the power's application in America, Aleinikoff (1986) notes that the loss of citizenship first emerged during the American Civil War as a question of expatriation (voluntary renunciation of citizenship by the citizen) rather than forcible withdrawal by the government. Later it was mostly used as a means of punishing deserters or those avoiding conscription during the world wars. In the Cold War period, it was wielded against suspected members of the Communist Party USA (CPUSA), whose organisation was perceived as an internal threat to national security.[5] Kerber's (2005) 'History of Statelessness in America' traces cases from the American Civil War up to PATRIOT II in our own time.

Whilst war has most often been the setting for denaturalisation, 'disloyalty' has historically been its most frequently evoked grounds, as discussed by Preuss (1942). The American precedent sharply deviated from this in the case of Trop v Dulles, in which Justice Warren, appearing to directly quote Arendt, ruled that:

> use of denationalization as a punishment is barred by the Eighth Amendment. There may be involved no physical mistreatment, nor primitive torture. There is instead the total destruction of the individual's status in organized society. It is a form of punishment more primitive than torture, for it destroys for the individual the political existence that was centuries in the development. The punishment strips the citizen of his status in the national and international political community. [...] In short, the expatriate has lost the right to have rights. (Trop v. Dulles 1958, 783).

This ruling epitomises what Abowitz and Harnish (2006, 653) would later describe as the 'liberal discourse' on denaturalisation, in their survey of 'the discourses that currently construct the meanings of citizenship in contemporary Western culture'. It emphasizes rights and protection for the individual, as opposed to the 'civic republican discourse', which stresses instead an implicit social contract that demands loyalty to the state. 'Whereas civic republican discourse values the common good of political communities, political liberalism envisions a more limited political arena, with greater focus on procedures that would ensure fair, inclusive deliberation about governance and policy' (662).

9/11 marked a turning point. Lavi (2010, 2011) recounts how some countries concluded that the notion of breach of allegiance was too vague a ground for denaturalisation in the context of the 'war on terror'. In the UK case, the government concluded that acts of perceived disloyalty

> have become dated and perhaps fail to reflect the full width of activity that might threaten our democratic institutions and our way of life. September 11th provides a horrific illustration of the sort of threat that we have in mind. (Lavi 2010, 407)

Hence the United Kingdom, the Netherlands, France, Denmark and Israel, all 'amended their laws to make it easier for the state to revoke the citizenship of both naturalized and born citizens' (Lavi 2011, 784). The US considered but ultimately rejected equivalent legislation, in the controversial USA PATRIOT II act and more recently in the Terrorist Expatriation Act and Expatriate Terrorists Act.[6] The question of what constitutes just denaturalisation and what the consequences are for citizenship is therefore very much contested.

Since then, denaturalisation has increasingly been discussed as a security measure. Whilst Aleinikoff (1986) proposed the preservation of public order as one justification almost 30 years ago, the decline of the citizenship-as-loyalty 'civic republican discourse' has left space for this securitisation discourse to flourish. For example, Lavi (2010, 410) conceives of contemporary citizenship as a right to reside, and by extension a mechanism for controlling migration. For some, such as Gross (2003), this security impulse is unproblematic. Once a citizen has been denaturalised, he writes, 'Deportation simply reflects the government's refusal to continue hosting people whom it does not want' (2003, 118). For others, the increasingly biometric management of citizenship, in which authenticated access takes precedence over identity, is ambiguously politicising and depoliticising (Muller 2004), with all the necessary exclusion that such a division entails. The denaturalised citizen is in this sense designed as a deterrent, 'throwing fear into the rest of us' (Kerber 2005, 745).

The existing literature is considerably weighted towards the US case. In the UK, Lord Goldsmith's (2008) report on citizenship for the British Government echoes the consensus that the notion of a duty of allegiance is outdated in a transnational world in which loyalties are increasingly blurred. Interestingly, he writes that terrorism might not necessarily constitute a breach of that allegiance, though he does not give further consideration to this. Groot De and Vink (2010) set the loss of citizenship in Europe in the legislative context, but do not discuss denaturalisation as a penal measure for behaviour that is deemed prejudicial to security.

Acknowledging that this once-clear link between individual and society has been weakened raises the question of how actors at the state level try to reconstitute it in the context of national security, both discursively and through legislation. A comparison of the UK and US cases, in which national security provided the impetus for a reconsideration of the law on citizenship's revocation, and in turn a debate on what citizenship *means*, can bring us some way towards an answer.

Methods

Research methods and design

My research was conducted using a combination of the three forms of content analysis outlined by Hsieh and Shannon (2005, 1277), namely conventional (in which 'coding categories are derived directly from the text data'), directed (in which 'analysis starts with a theory or relevant research findings as guidance for initial codes') and summative content analysis (which 'involves counting and comparisons, usually of keywords or content, followed by the interpretation of the underlying context'). I provided above a directed analysis of definitions of citizenship that emerged in relation to denaturalisation; conventional analysis allowed me to refine and code these conceptions through close reading of my textual data for each case; and I used summative analysis in comparing across the UK and US cases.

My research is based on a most similar systems design (MSSD), as described by Landman (2003, 29–34). My two cases, the UK and US, are on the same side in the 'war on terror', the same conflict that has caused decades-dormant debates over denaturalisation to resurface. Yet their policies on denaturalisation differ. Both cases saw denaturalisation debated at the highest political level in the same year (2014), with new powers proposed and successfully passed in the UK but blocked in the US. In each case, I collected data that cover the periods over which the new legislation was debated. In the US, this spans from May 2014; when then Senator Joe Lieberman announced his Terrorist Expatriation Act, to September 2014, when Senator Ted Cruz's Expatriate Terrorist Act (a modified form of Lieberman's earlier act) was blocked in the Senate. In the UK, this runs from January 2014, when the Home Office published its fact sheet on the proposed amendment to the Immigration Act that would grant the Home Secretary the power to revoke citizenship even if it made someone stateless, to May 2014, when the Immigration Act was passed.

Since I am particularly interested in contested definitions of citizenship, my data-set draws heavily on transcripts of debates in deliberative forums such as the House of Commons in the UK and Senate in the US. For both legislatures, transcripts are publically available online – Hansard in the UK and the Congressional Record in the US. But I also include published legal opinions, reports by rights organisations, speeches by individual politicians, press statements, newspaper articles and letters between politicians. These were selected on the basis of their relative capacity to influence the debate, either due to the prominence of the actor or their centrality to this particular debate. For example, in the US case I include all of Ted Cruz's public statements on the issue, because he was the person advocating legislation; in the UK, I include Guy Goodwin-Gill's paper because its influence on legislators was made clear by the frequency with which it was invoked in the Commons and Lords debates. All of these materials were produced either within the deliberative institutions (for example, the report of the Joint Committee on Human Rights (JCHR), commissioned by the Parliament) or from outside for lobbying purposes (for example, the letter by members of the Constitution Project to senators). Materials of both origins are often referenced in the more obviously deliberative environments, and I therefore take them to be part of a broader texture of deliberation in which meanings of citizenship were negotiated.

Analysis

The conceptions of citizenship that emerged during the course of both the UK and US debates fall under two categories that correspond to the nested but overlapping perspectives of the individual citizen, and the relationship between the citizen and the state. I call these, respectively, (1) citizenship as conduct and (2) citizenship as connection. In this section, I comparatively analyse how each one is articulated within the cases.

Citizenship as conduct

The phrase that epitomises the UK Government's position is 'Citizenship is a privilege, not a right'. It appeared in the Home Office's initial briefing fact sheet about the proposed change to the law (Home Office 2013), in the Home Secretary's speech to the House of Commons during the first Commons debate on 30 January 2014, and in official responses to press queries about the law, and became the potted justification for the policy. The phrase's main implication is that it extends the familiar expectation of loyalty to the state (usually only violated through treason or service with a foreign military), and makes citizenship more broadly conditional on good behaviour. By this logic, citizenship is not a default status to which everyone is entitled, but rather, to adopt the words of the new law, a privilege enjoyed only by those whose behaviour is not (deemed to be) 'seriously prejudicial to the vital interests' of the UK (Immigration Act 2014, [s40(4A)]). Deprivation therefore effectively functions here as a punishment for such behaviour – though, as I discuss in the next section, it bypasses the court system that dispenses punishment for criminal behaviour.

Though it forms the basis of the government's position, the phrase 'Citizenship is a privilege, not a right' seems to emerge from nowhere in its discourse, with no acknowledged source. In fact, it appears to have first been used not in the UK but in the US, in May 2010, by then Secretary of State Hillary Clinton. Speaking to the press following a meeting with former Lithuanian Prime Minister Andrius Kubilius, she used it in response to an off-topic press question regarding Lieberman's Terrorist Expatriation Act, which had been proposed the previous day. Furthermore, she was speaking not about citizenship in general (as the UK Home Office uses the phrase) but specifically about US citizenship. Aside from that one instance, it does not appear to have been used at all in the US case, except for once in Ted Cruz's speech to the Senate on 18 September 2014, when he was explicitly quoting Clinton. Either the UK Government came to the phrase independently, or it imported it from Clinton and turned what appears to have been an off-hand response to a surprise question into its guiding policy.

The UK's policy appears to have been developed in response to the case of Al-Jeddah, an Iraqi-born British man whose denaturalisation was overturned by the High Court, only to find that the government issued a second deprivation order shortly afterwards (BBC 2013). The government's argument was that 'it was his inaction, rather than her deprivation order, which had made him stateless' (Gower 2014, 19). This expands the familiar notion that citizenship can be lost due to a failure to act 'correctly' – or at least not to act 'incorrectly' – to the more radical one that it can be lost due to a failure to act full stop.

In the US, Ted Cruz also sought to frame citizenship as conditional on conduct. Since the case of Vance v. Terrazas in 1980, the US position has been that the government can revoke citizenship only where it is found to have been affirmatively renounced by the citizen. It is not enough to prove that a citizen did something that is considered deserving of denaturalisation; it must also be proven that the citizen did so with the intention of renouncing their citizenship. Cruz's argument rested on collapsing this distinction, specifically in the context of Americans who join jihadist groups in Iraq and Syria. For example, he insisted that 'Congress should make fighting for or supporting ISIS an affirmative renunciation of American citizenship' (*CNN*, 11 September 2014). When introducing his Expatriate Terrorists Act, he said: 'there can be no clearer renunciation of their citizenship' (Press release, 5 September 2014) than going to join the Islamic State of Iraq and the Levant (ISIS). And courting the Senate's support, he said: 'It is my hope that this body will stand together [...] to make clear in that any American that takes up arms with ISIS has, in doing so, constructively renounced his or her American citizenship' (Senate session, 8 September 2014). Taking up arms with ISIS, then, is taken to be at once the clearest possible renunciation of citizenship and an act whose import requires clarification.

Whilst Cruz claimed his bill was necessary to address new threats, his discourse is a well-established one. His argument relies on what I term 'zero-sum citizenship', in which loyalty to one's official country of citizenship is thought to be proportionally curbed by expressions of allegiance to foreign authorities. Cruz takes this to the extreme by declaring that such expressions of alternative allegiance do not simply dilute but in fact *eradicate* the original allegiance. Hence, he said: 'By fighting for ISIS, U.S. citizens have expressed their desire to become citizens of the Islamic state. And that cannot and will not peacefully coexist with remaining American citizens'. Similarly, 'By fighting for ISIS, U.S. citizens have expressed their desire to become citizens of the terrorist group, which calls itself the Islamic State' (Senate session, 8 September 2014). Whilst for the UK Government, the basis for revocation is a perceived act *against* the citizen's state, for Cruz it is a perceived allegiance *toward* an alternative authority. These two acts are of course one and the same – a UK/US national going to fight in Syria or Iraq – but the two discourses give different emphases. Whilst the UK appears to be framing revocation as a defensive measure against a perceived or potential aggressor, the US emphasises that defection *is* aggression.

Although on the one hand Cruz presents ISIS as a state-like authority that can admit 'citizens', he at the same time stresses ISIS's non-state status, calling it 'a nonstate terrorist group' (Congressional Record 18 September 2014, S5728), 'a grotesque parody of a nation state' (Senate Session, 8 September 2014), and one among many 'non-nation terrorist groups' (Congressional Record 18 September 2014, S5727). Joe Liebermann, the senator who in 2010 proposed a similar bill to Cruz's, drew the same distinction between the US's enemies during the Second World War and those it faces today – 'stateless actors who don't wear uniforms' (Quoted in Patterico 5 May 2014). Cruz and Libermann, then, both sought to present support for terrorism as an affirmative renunciation of American citizenship, but they did so by invoking the paradoxical possibility of a non-state *citizen*. The denaturalised terror suspect is lumbered with the incriminating loyalties of (enemy) citizenship, but furnished with none of its safeguards. The zero-sum logic is therefore not only fallacious in its structural suggestion of proportionate relationship between competing loyalties, but is also internally flawed, since the two loyalties are inconsistently presented as both equivalent and incompatible.

Citizenship as connection

'Citizenship as connection' refers to conceptualisations that present citizenship as constituting a particular relationship between the citizen and the state. From the perspective of the former, it mainly takes the form of claims to rights: citizenship as a status that entitles an individual to particular rights that can be invoked in particular circumstances. This is a familiar conception, but an interesting corollary emerged in the data-set from the perspective of the state, namely a conception of citizenship as a traceable link that allows a government to monitor its citizens – something that may not be possible, for example, in the case of a stateless person who has no legal status vis-à-vis the state in which they find themselves. This idea of citizenship was mainly found in the UK case, where it was presented as a threat-monitoring instrument. One example is Chris Bryant MP, who warned the Commons that revoking citizenship could create a population of stateless people who would present a greater threat than any citizen would.

> We would end up with people in this country who we would simply be keeping completely stateless, without any role or standing. We cannot simply banish them to France as we would have done in the middle ages. (Hansard, column 267WH).

In the Lords, Baroness Smith of Basildon also questioned the efficacy of creating a statelessness population.

> Does that not mean that we have people who are stuck here, whom we cannot deport and to whom we have obligations, but no charge has been brought against them? How does that help ensure that national security is protected? (Hansard, House of Lords Debate 17 March 2014, Column 44)

Her concerns were echoed by Baroness Hamwee (column 55) and Lord Pannick, who directly invited the government to consider the same criticism, saying:

> Does the Minister therefore accept that, far from contributing to national security, the exercise of Clause 60 against persons in this country will positively damage national security by making it more difficult to remove people who are a danger to the public good? (Column 48)

Even Liberty, the rights advocacy group, echoed this concern (2014, 13). Members of both houses thus tried to dispute the government's proposed legislation on its own terms, through the same discourse of national security that was used to justify the powers.

Though the proposed US legislation was intended to counter the same threat, this idea that a nation of citizens is more secure than a nation of stateless people did not feature at all in that case. Instead, the connection between the state and the citizen was predominantly conceived of as one of rights. Incredibly, the supposedly fundamental right *to* citizenship, enshrined in Article 15 of the UN Declaration of Human Rights, was not invoked by politicians in either data-set. This absence was only noted by Goodwin-Gill's (2014, 8) opinion paper on the UK law. But citizenship did feature – predominantly in the US case – as a body of rights, namely as a status that enabled access to them. Instead of international law, US contributors resorted to their Constitution. Writing to senators, David Cole of the Constitution Project stated explicitly that 'Citizenship is a constitutional right, and the Constitution prohibits the government from revoking a person's citizenship against his will under any circumstances' (Letter to Senators, 17 September 2014, 1). Laura Murphy and Arjun Sethil of the American Civil Liberties Union meanwhile said:

> S. 2779 is dangerous because it would attempt to dilute the rights and privileges of citizenship, one of the core principles of the Constitution [...] As the Supreme Court explained in 1967 in Afroyim v. Rusk, 'the Fourteenth Amendment was designed to, and does, protect every

> citizen of this Nation against a congressional forcible destruction of his citizenship, whatever his creed, color, or race.' (Letter to senators, 17 September 2014, 1)

Many speakers in the UK also opposed the law on rights grounds. Only one, the Government's Independent Reviewer of Terrorism Legislation, David Anderson QC, saw citizenship explicitly as the right to reside.

> The whole concept of citizenship is about the right of abode, and the right to come back to where you live. (Quoted in Gower 2014, 12)

But others, including the JCHR in their report and Simon Kirby MP in the Commons, indicated that this was the intended target of the new law.

> It appears from various statements by ministers that one of the principal purposes, and possibly the only purpose, of the new power is to enable the Secretary of State to remove from the UK individuals who are deemed to be dangerous and therefore a risk to national security. (JCHR 2014, 14)

> Is this not just about getting rid of very bad people and preventing them from coming back to our country? Is that not the nub of what we are discussing? (Hansard, House of Commons Debate, 30 January 2014, column 1049)

The majority of rights-related objections, however, were that denaturalisation might be used as an opaque alternative to established, transparent mechanisms of prosecution. According to Jacob Rees-Mogg MP,

> If people have committed an offence so serious, important and threatening to the life of the nation that their passport should be confiscated, surely they have committed some other crime for which they could be charged, dragged through the courts, perhaps found guilty by a jury and then sentenced accordingly, with the penalty handed down in the right and proper way and their rights and liberties as subjects being maintained. (Hansard HC, 30 January 2014, column 1086)

> His criticisms were echoed in the US.

> This provision would violate Americans' constitutional right to due process, including by depriving them of citizenship based on secret evidence, and without the right to a jury trial and accompanying protections enshrined in the Fifth and Sixth Amendments. (Murphy and Sethil 2014, 2)

> Anyone found to be aiding terrorist should be brought to swift justice. Our system already allows for that without the stripping away of Constitutional rights of the citizens we are trying to protect. (Rubens, quoted in DiStaso 29 August 2014)

> Rights were not only invoked by those opposed to the law, however. Describing the new powers he had proposed, Lieberman himself said:

> if a U.S. citizen travels to Somalia to train with and fight for alShabaab – as more than 20 young men have done over the past several years – the State Department will now have the authority to revoke their citizenship so that they cannot return here to carry out an attack. If, in some way, they do, and are then captured, they will not enjoy the rights and privileges of American citizenship in the legal proceedings against them. (Press statement, quoted in Patterico 5th May 2010)

Here citizenship is a body of rights that protects an individual during legal proceedings, ensuring a fair trial – or, more broadly, what Goodwin-Gill (2014, 1) means when he argues that 'Citizenship is not a "privilege"' reserved for those who swear, feel or perform allegiance, 'but a protected legal status'. Suspected militants are not considered deserving of these safeguards. Rather than refuting the rights contained in the Constitution, Lieberman sought to exclude people from eligibility to them, giving the supposedly undiscriminating document a distinctly discriminatory edge. The resulting vulnerable, extrajudicial zone sounds similar to that described in the JCHR's report in the context of a pair of denaturalised British citizens who were no longer able to avail themselves of the protection of their former state.

> The deprivation of citizenship removes the State's responsibility for the protection of the individuals concerned and exposes them to actions which lack due process. Two former UK citizens who have been deprived of their citizenship have subsequently been killed by US drone strikes, and others are reported to have been exposed to irregular treatment including rendition. (2014, 10).

Charges of discrimination were made in the UK, where politicians noted that Clause 60 of the Immigration Act would allow the government to strip naturalised citizens of their citizenship, whilst leaving British-born citizens immune from the new powers. Some, such as Jacob Rees-Mogg, used the argument to oppose the law.

> Once any one of us has a passport that says we are British, we are as British as anybody else, whether they were born here or got their passport five minutes ago. [...] I worry that if we give the Government the ability to take passports away from a certain category of British subject but not from others, it will create a potential unfairness and a second category of citizen. (Hansard HC, 30 January 2014, column 1086)

> Others, such as Alok Sharma MP, used it to argue for the powers' expansion.

> Perhaps my right hon. Friend should go even further [...] and introduce similar sanctions against anyone who is British, irrespective of how they got British citizenship, if they do something so heinous against the British state. (Hansard HC, 30 January 2014, column 1042)

Yasmin Qureshi MP challenged such a differentiation on grounds of fairness in terms of recourse to rights, whilst Jacob Rees-Mogg MP emphasised 'Britishness' as an equalising status.

> my hon. Friend the Member for Hackney North and Stoke Newington (Ms. Abbott) was born in England, but I was born in Pakistan. We are both British nationals, but if she was to commit murder, which I am sure she is not going to, she could not be deported, whereas if I did, I could be. Is that fair? (Qureshi, Hansard HC, 30 January 2014, column 1091–2).

> Anybody who is fortunate enough to be a subject of Her Majesty is an equal subject of Her Majesty with all others. (Rees-Mogg, Hansard HC, 30 January 2014, column 1087)

The same objection to 'two-tier citizenship', (Dr Julian Huppert MP, Hansard HC, 30 January 2014, column 1100) then, was mobilized on both liberal and nationalistic grounds. Diane Abbott MP best articulated the implications of such a differentiation:

> the fear will be that although this has started with suspected terrorists, where will it end, once the state decides that British citizenship is not indivisible? (Abbott, Hansard HC, 11 February 2014, column 255WH)

What these politicians were proposing was a conception of citizenship as an indiscriminate bond between the citizen and the state. Furthermore, unlike the US case, they largely did so not in explicit terms of the rights that might stem from that bond, but from its more structural quality as an equalising status.

Representing the Home Secretary in the Commons, Mark Brokenshire MP rejected their arguments, saying: 'The proposal merely reflects the fact that there are differing routes to citizenship' (Hansard HC, 11 February 2014, column 261WH). But it resurfaced in the Lords debate, where Baroness Smith of Basildon said: 'It would be helpful if the Minister could clarify whether there are any other areas of law in which we have different categories of citizens' (Hansard HL, 17 March 2014, column 40), adding: 'In most countries, if someone is a citizen then they are a citizen' (column 61). Whilst an international standard is here being invoked, it is a comparative one that seems to stoke pride in Britain as a leader, rather than a transcendent one of human rights or internationally accepted practices.

Ironically, 'equality between citizens' was the exact phrase used by Theresa May (2014) in a flagship speech on counterterrorism in September 2014 – 4 months after the Immigration Act became law. Referring to Islamic extremists, she said:

> The extremists believe in a clash of civilisations – a fundamental incompatibility between Islamic and Western values, an inevitable divide between 'them and us' [...] They utterly reject British and Western values, including democracy, the rule of law, and equality between citizens, regardless of their gender, ethnicity, religion or sexuality. They believe that it is impossible to be a good Muslim and a good British citizen.

The government at once appears to espouse equality among citizens whilst making some citizens' citizenship more precarious than others'. This brings us closer to the kind of contradiction championed by Cruz, a situation in which citizens are equal, but some are more equal than others.

Conclusion

In my section on citizenship as conduct, I showed that advocates of increased denaturalisation powers in both the UK and US tried to present citizenship on 'good' behaviour. Certain acts did not simply constitute a 'bad' or dissident citizen, but were re-framed as being incompatible with the status of citizenship itself – either through the UK's assertion that citizenship is a privilege rather than a right, or, in the US, through a fallacious zero-sum understanding of competing loyalties. In my section on citizenship as connection, I showed that these new powers effectively created a second class of citizens whose status is more precarious than others in the eyes of the state under whom they are supposedly equal. This precariousness in turn generated the possibility of exclusion from supposedly fundamental constitutional rights. In both cases, this discriminatory force was invoked in such a way as to delimit the bounds of the normatively 'good' citizen to whom the 'foreign fighter' was opposed by proponents of the new powers.

For all their rhetoric around behaviour that is conducive to the public good or behaviour that confirms an affirmative renunciation of citizenship, my analysis suggests that we are not simply seeing a resurgence of the 'civic republican discourse' (citizenship as loyalty to the state) over the 'liberal discourse' (citizenship as rights of the individual). Instead we are seeing elements of the former open up a space of exception in the latter. Citizenship is still conceived of as a body of individual rights, but they are conditional on loyalty to the state. The two discourses are in sequence, rather than competition. The civic republican discourse is being used not as an *alternative* to one that espouses a more limited political arena, but precisely as a tool designed *to effect the limitation of that arena*. This is not in the sense that liberalism espouses, i.e. through creating a small state that is content to assure the basic rights and freedoms of its citizens, but in the sense of selectively excluding particular 'undesirable' groups – terror suspects, naturalised citizens – from political life as we know it. This is in keeping with the accounts of Brighton (2007) and Kundnani (2002) on the broader shift in political culture away from multiculturalism and towards assimilation – and in turn the exclusion of those who do not or cannot assimilate.

If the American and British cases demonstrate the 'privileging' of citizenship through the exclusion of 'undesirables', the findings of this study could be further developed by considering further cases. Canada and Australia – both allied with the US and UK in the 'war on terror' – passed legislation similar to the UK's in 2015, and the number of denaturalisation cases has dramatically increased (Meurrens 2012). The Australian law in fact goes further than its UK equivalent. Offences such as 'damaging Commonwealth property' were also considered deserving of denaturalisation, and sole nationals were also considered (*The Guardian*, 24 June 2015). It appears that the space of exception analysed in this study is growing, at the expense of its corollary – the normative space of the 'acceptable' citizen.

Notes

1. See Jackson (2007) on the broader genealogy of the powerful 'Islamic terrorism' discourse as a whole, and its tendency towards orientalist tropes.
2. This does not include the 26 others who have been denaturalized on fraud grounds – i.e. they were found to have acquired British citizenship fraudulently, for example, by lying on their application form.
3. This specification of the state as guarantor demonstrates the limits of Arendt's definition, since a stateless person has rights under international law. What they lack is recourse to the (usually) state-level mechanism required to enforce them.
4. Article 1 of the 1954 *Convention Relating to the Status of Stateless Persons* defines a stateless person as someone 'who is not considered as a national by any State under the operation of its law'.
5. See, for instance, Lichtman (2012, 17) on the case of Stanislaw Nowak.
6. USA PATRIOT is an acronym for Uniting and Strengthening America by Providing Appropriate Tools Required to Intercept and Obstruct Terrorism.

Acknowledgements

The author would like to thank Professor Zeynep Kadirbeyoğlu for her invaluable comments during the writing of this paper.

Disclosure statement

No potential conflict of interest was reported by the author.

Funding

This research was supported by the Scientific and Technological Research Council of Turkey.

References

Abowitz, Kathleen Knight, and Jason Harnish. 2006. "Contemporary Discourses of Citizenship." *Review of Educational Research* 76 (4): 653–690.

Aleinikoff, T. Alexander. 1986. "Theories of Loss of Citizenship." *Michigan Law Review* 84: 1471–1503.

BBC. 2013. "Terror Suspect Loses UK Citizenship." December 2. http://www.bbc.co.uk/news/uk-25190305.

Benhabib, Seyla. 2005. "Borders, Boundaries, and Citizenship." *PS: Political Science and Politics* 38 (4): 673–677.

Blitz, Brad K., and Maureen Lynch, eds. 2011. *Statelessness and Citizenship: A Comparative Study on the Benefits of Nationality*. Cheltenham: Edward Elgar.

Brighton, Shane. 2007. "British Muslims, Multiculturalism and UK Foreign Policy: 'Integration' and 'Cohesion' in and beyond the State." *International Affairs* 83 (1): 1–17. doi:http://dx.doi.org/10.1111/j.1468-2346.2007.00600.x.

Cole, David. 2014. "Letter to Senators." September 17. http://www.constitutionproject.org/wp-content/uploads/2014/09/9-17_Letter_re_Terrorist_Expatriation_Act.pdf.

Congressional Record, 18 September 2014, S5726–28. https://www.congress.gov/congressional-record/2014/9/18/senate-section/article/S5726-2.

Cooper, Terry L., and Diane E. Yoder. 1999. "The Meaning and Significance of Citizenship in a Transnational World: Implications for Public Administration." *Administrative Theory & Praxis* 21 (2): 195–204.

Couldrey, Marion, and Maurice Herson, eds. 2009. *Statelessness: Forced Migration Review*. Vol. Issue 32. Oxford: Refugee Studies Centre.

Cruz, Ted. 2014. "Ted Cruz: How U.S. Can Stop ISIS." *CNN*, September 11. http://www.cnn.com/2014/09/10/opinion/ted-cruz-how-us-can-stop-isis/index.html.

DiStaso, John. 2014. "Brown Says It's 'Common Sense' to Revoke Citizenship of Americans Fighting alongside ISIS." *NH Journal*. http://nhjournal.com/brown-wants-to-strip-citizenship-from-americans-fighting-alongside-isis/.

Galey, P., and A. K. Ross. 2014, June 3. Interactive: The 53 Britons Stripped of their Nationality. *The Bureau of Investigative Journalism*. http://www.thebureauinvestigates.com/2014/06/03/interactive-the-53-britons-stripped-of-their-nationality/.

Goodwin-Gill, G. S. 2014, March 12. Deprivation of Citizenship Resulting in Statelessness and its Implications in International Law Opinion by Guy S. Goodwin-Gill. Immigration Law Practitioners' Association. http://www.ilpa.org.uk/resources.php/26308/professor-guy-goodwin-gill-deprivation-of-citizenship-statelessness-and-international-law-more-autho.

Gower, M. 2014, September 4. Deprivation of British Citizenship and Withdrawal of Passport Facilities - Commons Library Standard Note. http://www.parliament.uk/business/publications/research/briefing-papers/SN06820/deprivation-of-british-citizenship-and-withdrawal-of-passport-facilities.

Groot De, Gerard-René, and Maarten P. Vink. 2010. *Loss of Citizenship: Trends and Regulations in Europe*. SSRN Scholarly Paper. Rochester, NY: Social Science Research Network. http://papers.ssrn.com/abstract=1694701.

Gross, Emanuel. 2003. "Defensive Democracy: Is It Possible to Revoke the Citizenship, Deport, or Negate the Civil Rights of a Person Instigating Terrorist Action against His Own State." *UMKC Law Review* 72: 51–122.

Hansard. House of Lords Debate, 17 March 2014.

Heath-Kelly, Charlotte. 2013. "Counter-Terrorism and the Counterfactual: Producing the 'Radicalisation' Discourse and the UK PREVENT Strategy." *The British Journal of Politics & International Relations* 15 (3): 394–415. doi:http://dx.doi.org/10.1111/j.1467-856X.2011.00489.x.

Hegghammer, Thomas. 2010. "The Rise of Muslim Foreign Fighters Islam and the Globalization of Jihad." *International Security* 35 (3): 1–15.

Herzog, Ben. 2010. "Dual Citizenship and the Revocation of Citizenship." *Research in Political Sociology* 18: 87–106.

Home Office. "Immigration Bill: Overview Factsheet." October 2013. https://www.gov.uk/government/uploads/system/uploads/attachment_data/file/249251/Overview_Immigration_Bill_Factsheet.pdf.

Hooker, C. 2005. The Past as Prologue: Schniederman v. United States and Contemporary Questions of Citizenship and Denaturalization. 19 Emory Int'l L. Rev. 305.

Hsieh, H. -F., and S. E. Shannon. 2005. Three Approaches to Qualitative Content Analysis. *Qualitative Health Research* 15 (9): 1277–1288. http://doi.org/10.1177/1049732305276687.

Jackson, Richard. 2007. "Constructing Enemies: 'Islamic Terrorism' in Political and Academic Discourse." *Government and Opposition* 42 (3): 394–426. doi:http://dx.doi.org/10.1111/j.1477-7053.2007.00229.x.

JCHR (Joint Committee on Human Rights). *Legislative Scrutiny: Immigration Bill (Second Report)*, HL Paper 142 HC 1120, 3 March 2014.

Kerber, Linda K. 2005. "Toward a History of Statelessness in America." *American Quarterly* 57 (3): 727–749.

Kraehenmann, Sandra. 2014. *Foreign Fighters under International Law*. Vol. Academy Briefing No. 7. Geneva: Geneva Academy of International Humanitarian Law and Human Rights.

Kundnani, Arun. 2002. "The Death of Multiculturalism." *Race & Class* 43 (4): 67–72. doi:http://dx.doi.org/10.1177/030639680204300406.

Landman, Todd. 2003. *Issues and Methods in Comparative Politics: An Introduction*. London: Psychology Press.

Lavi, Shai. 2010. "Punishment and the Revocation of Citizenship in the United Kingdom, United States, and Israel." *New Criminal Law Review: An International and Interdisciplinary Journal* 13 (2): 404–426.

Lavi, Shai. 2011. "Citizenship Revocation as Punishment: On the Modern Bond of Citizenship and Its Criminal Breach." *The University of Toronto Law Journal* 61 (4): 783–810.

League of Nations. 1930. *Convention on Certain Questions Relating to the Conflict of Nationality Laws*. The Hague: League of Nations.

Liberty. 2014. *Liberty's Report Stage Briefing on Clause 64 of the Immigration Bill in the House of Lords*. Liberty. https://www.liberty-human-rights.org.uk/campaigning/other-campaigns/statelessness.

Lichtman, Robert M. 2012. *The Supreme Court and McCarthy-Era Repression: One Hundred Decisions*. Urbana: University of Illinois Press.

Lord Goldsmith, Q. C. 2008. *Citizenship: Our Common Bond*. http://image.guardian.co.uk/sys-files/Politics/documents/2008/03/11/citizenship-report-full.pdf.

Malet, David. 2013. *Foreign Fighters: Transnational Identity in Civic Conflicts*. New York: Oxford University Press.

May, Theresa. 2014. *Home Secretary Theresa May on Counter-Terrorism*. Speech, Royal United Services Institute, Whitehall, London. https://www.gov.uk/government/speeches/home-secretary-theresa-may-on-counter-terrorism

Meurrens, Stephen. 2012. "Understanding the Citizenship Revocation Process." *Meurrens on Immigration: Canadian Visas, Permits and Citizenship*. http://meurrensonimmigration.com/1800-people-poised-to-lose-citizenship/.

Muller, Benjamin J. 2004. "(Dis)Qualified Bodies: Securitization, Citizenship and 'Identity Management'." *Citizenship Studies* 8 (3): 279–294.

Murphy, Laura, and Arjun Sethi. 2014. "Oppose Cruz Bill S. 2779, Expatriate Terrorists Act; S. 2779 is Unnecessary and Dangerous." September 17. https://www.aclu.org/sites/default/files/assets/140917_citizenship_stripping_letter.pdf.

Mustapha, Jennifer. 2013. "The Mujahideen in Bosnia: The Foreign Fighter as Cosmopolitan Citizen and/or Terrorist." *Citizenship Studies* 17 (6–7): 742–755.

Office of Senator Ted Cruz. 2014. "Cruz to Introduce Bill to Stop Americans Who Join ISIS from Returning to United States." September 5. https://www.cruz.senate.gov/?p=press_release&id=1678.

Patriot Act. 2001. http://www.gpo.gov/fdsys/pkg/BILLS-107hr3162enr/pdf/BILLS-107hr3162enr.pdf.

Preuss, Lawrence. 1942. "Denaturalization on the Ground of Disloyalty." *The American Political Science Review* 36 (4): 701–710.

Ross, Alice K. 2014. "Interview by Author. via Skype." November 28.

Ross, Alice K., and Patrick Galey. 2013. "Rise in Citizenship-Stripping as Government Cracks down on UK Fighters in Syria." *Citizenship Revoked*. December 23. http://www.thebureauinvestigates.com/2013/12/23/rise-in-citizenship-stripping-as-government-cracks-down-on-uk-fighters-in-syria/.

Sejersen, Tanja Brøndsted. 2008. "'I Vow to Thee My Countries': The Expansion of Dual Citizenship in the 21st Century." *International Migration Review* 42 (3): 523–549.

Spalek, Basia, and Laura Zahra McDonald. 2010. "Terror Crime Prevention: Constructing Muslim Practices and Beliefs as 'Anti-Social' and 'Extreme' through CONTEST 2." *Social Policy and Society* 9 (01): 123–132. doi:http://dx.doi.org/10.1017/S147474640999025X.

Taylor, L. (2015). "Citizenship Could Be Stripped for Damaging Commonwealth Property." *The Guardian*, June 24. http://www.theguardian.com/australia-news/2015/jun/24/new-laws-dual-nationals-lose-citizenship-for-damaging-commonwealth-property.

Trop v. Dulles. 1958. 52: 777–784.

UN (United Nations). 1948. *Universal Declaration of Human Rights*. 217 A (III). Accessed May 23 2016. http://www.refworld.org/docid/3ae6b3712c.html.

UN (United Nations). 1954. *Convention Relating to the Status of Stateless Persons*. United Nations, Treaty Series, Vol. 360, p. 117. Accessed 23 May 2016. http://www.refworld.org/docid/3ae6b3840.html.

UN (United Nations). 1961. *Convention on the Reduction of Statelessness*. United Nations, Treaty Series, Vol. 989, p. 175. Accessed 23 May 2016. http://www.refworld.org/docid/3ae6b39620.html.

U.S. Senate: Morning Business. 2014. *C-SPAN.Org*. Accessed December 28. http://www.c-span.org/video/?320891-1/us-senate-morning-business&live

Vertovec, Steven. 2001. "Transnational Challenges to the 'New' Multiculturalism." Paper Presented to the ASA Conference Held at the University of Sussex, March30–April 2, 2001.

Waas, Laura van. 2008. *Nationality Matters: Statelessness under International Law*. School of Human Rights Research Series, V. 29. Antwerp: Intersentia.

Waas, Laura van. 2009. "Statelessness: A 21st Century Challenge for Europe." *Security and Human Rights* 20: 133–146.

Walker, Dorothy Jean. 1981. "Statelessness: Violation or Conduit for Violation of Human Rights?" *Human Rights Quarterly* 3 (1): 106–123.

Simply a matter of compliance with the rules? The moralising and responsibilising function of fraud-based citizenship deprivation in France and the UK

Émilien Fargues

ABSTRACT

Scholarship largely sees fraud-based citizenship stripping as a tool for guaranteeing the consistency of the naturalisation process against applicants who do not respect the rules. This implies that the line between 'desirable' and 'undesirable' citizens is drawn in accordance with procedural norms. In contrast, this article argues that deprivation on grounds of fraud aims to create a virtuous and responsible political subject. Drawing on the cases of France and the UK, the paper shows how government officials and judges understand citizenship deprivation not simply as a means to safeguard the procedural integrity of naturalisation, but as a mechanism for the moralisation and responsibilisation of applicants. The article further contends that not everyone is made the subject of 'renationalisation'. British and French deprivation policies reproduce suspicions and stereotypes against specific categories of migrants, constructing them as second-class citizens.

Introduction

The power to revoke the citizenship of individuals convicted or merely suspected of terrorism is back on the political agenda in Europe and elsewhere. By contemplating or enacting changes in citizenship law in response to 'terrorists', governments draw upon citizenship as a mechanism for managing 'undesirable citizens'. As Nyers (2009, 1) puts it, 'while citizenship is credited for being the political category that brings people together within a political community, [it] also serves an exclusionary function'. Citizenship law sets forth the criteria for national membership according to a principle of 'exclusive inclusion' that allows for the inclusion of some and the exclusion of others (Turner 2014). It not only formally distinguishes between citizens and non-citizens, but also constructs a normative ideal of what a 'good' citizen should be and draws a line between 'desirable' and 'undesirable citizens' (Byrne 2014). Citizenship policies play a crucial role in how the line is actually drawn. In fact, they can be seen as an on-going negotiation process between bureaucrats and applicants rooted in the 'state's desire for desirable citizens' (Fortier 2016, 5).

In the literature, the revival of citizenship deprivation has raised questions about the governing strategy that states pursue in citizenship policies.[1] One view of contemporary citizenship policies (not only those pertaining to deprivation) is that states have considerably 'lightened' their exclusive character over the last 60 years (Joppke 2010). Though citizenship still differentiates between citizens and foreigners, the difference has become less relevant in terms of rights and the process of acquisition is less demanding for individuals wishing to join the national community (Soysal 1994; Jacobson 1995).[2] In addition, according to some commentators, the symbolic boundaries of citizenship are being reduced to 'thin and procedural' forms (Joppke 2010, 12). In this view, states follow a liberal strategy of governing in their citizenship policies: there is no obstacle to membership as long as one abides by the rules of the host society. The revival of deprivation is part of the same strategy. It enables states to cut the bond of citizenship based on the individual's actions and can thus be seen as a new expression of the liberal 'contractarian logic' that drives citizenship policies (Joppke 2016, 736).

A divergent view maintains that under the pretence of liberal principles the exclusive character of citizenship is actually being strengthened.[3] With the introduction of language and citizenship tests in particular, states emphasise that joining the political community requires compliance with a common understanding of what binds their citizens together (a shared language, shared values or even a shared way of life), and not simply with the law alone (Goodman 2012). They enhance the conditionality of citizenship and link it to a 'thick' vision of national membership (Kostakopoulou 2010; Orgad 2015). They also reaffirm the significance of citizenship in terms of individuals' rights and duties, against the idea that there is no difference between nationals and foreigners in this respect anymore (Hansen 2009). Therefore, by making inclusion harder and exclusion easier – including through deprivation –, states renationalise citizenship (Mouritsen 2012; Fargues 2017). The renationalisation of citizenship relies upon the injunction to assimilate the values or way of life of the national community. In this respect, it denotes a communitarian rationale that aims to produce political subjects that are committed to 'virtue' and the 'common good', rather than simply being law-abiding.[4] However, as Schinkel and Van Houdt (2010, 699) argue, this strategy of 'governing through community' is intertwined with a 'neo-liberal emphasis on the responsibilization of the individual' in citizenship and migration policies. Newcomers are asked to conform to all aspects that make the host society a community *and* to demonstrate that they behave as fully autonomous and self-sufficient subjects. The renationalisation of citizenship thus combines both communitarian and neo-liberal features.

While these debates address the revival of citizenship deprivation, they have so far exclusively focused on citizenship deprivation based on public good grounds, that is, on the use of deprivation against alleged terrorists. Citizenship deprivation based on grounds of fraud has been largely neglected in academia (Macklin and Bauböck 2015). Where grounds of fraud are mentioned, they are presented as a rather uncontroversial mode of involuntary loss of citizenship (Lavi 2011; Bauböck and Paskalev 2015; Gibney 2017). Deprivation based on fraud is seen purely as a means to guarantee the consistency of the naturalisation process against applicants who do not respect the rules.[5] This tends to reinforce the idea that the line between 'desirable' and 'undesirable' citizens is drawn in accordance with 'thin and procedural' norms, which supports the general thesis of a 'lightening' of citizenship policies (Joppke 2010). This paper calls into question this view of fraud-induced citizenship deprivation in order to establish to what extent it forms part of the renationalisation of citizenship, and what this means for its 'exclusionary function' (Nyers 2009, 1).

France and the UK represent two interesting case studies.[6] In both countries, citizenship policies have been at the forefront of political debates. In the UK, the New Labour government introduced new naturalisation and deprivation provisions in order to attach greater 'importance' to citizenship (Gibney 2013). While scholars have usually emphasised the communitarian character of the new provisions (Kostakopoulou 2010; Anderson 2013), recent research has shed light on their neoliberal underpinnings. In particular, the injunction to become 'super citizens' – compelling applicants to prove that they will be an asset to the host society – has been identified as a mechanism for individualisation and responsibilisation (Badenhoop 2017). In France, the recent introduction of instruments such as integration contracts or citizenship ceremonies has reinforced the idea that acquiring citizenship should be a reward for 'good' integration (Hajjat 2012; Hachimi-Alaoui 2016). In the area of deprivation, the notion that citizenship should be reserved for individuals who truly deserve it has also been used to justify an expansion of the executive's power to take citizenship away (Beauchamps 2016). As in the UK, recent changes in French citizenship policies have thus conditioned the admission of migrants into the citizenry on their capacity to be 'élite citizens', showing that they are politically, economically and culturally integrated (Mazouz 2017).[7] This suggests a convergence between the British and French citizenship regimes along similar neo-liberal/communitarian lines. Though fraud has been a key concern of the British and French governments in citizenship and migration policies in recent years (Ferré 2010; Anderson 2013), its relevance for testing the convergence of governing strategies in the two countries has not yet been investigated. This paper will do so by focusing on fraud-based deprivation policies, more specifically the *décrets rapportant* (Art. 27–2 of the Civil Code) and *annulations* (Art. 26–4) in France, and deprivation on grounds of fraud/concealment (British Nationality Act: 40 (3) and 40 (6)) and nullity in the UK (Table 1).

This paper will look at the underlying bureaucratic practices for citizenship deprivation due to alleged fraud, which have not yet been specifically examined. Focusing on these practices not only makes it possible to question potential discrepancies with the political rhetoric that justifies these policy changes, but also to test the impact of said rhetoric on the

Table 1. Legal background of citizenship deprivation based on fraud in France and the UK.

France	UK
Article 27–2, Civil Code – *décret rapportant* • Naturalisation by decree • Fraud (within two years after the fraud has been signalled) • Failure to satisfy a legal condition of naturalisation (within two years after naturalisation) • A court decision is required • Statutory appeal	**British Nationality Act: 40 (3) and 40 (6) – deprivation** • Citizens by acquisition • Fraud/concealment of a material fact • No time limit • No court decision is required • Statutory right of appeal
Article 26–4, Civil Code – *annulations* • Registration through marriage • Fraud (within two years after the fraud has been signalled) • Failure to satisfy a legal condition of registration (two years after registration) • 'Fraud presumption' (12 months after registration) • Within two years after naturalisation • Requires a court decision • Statutory appeal	**Nullity** • Citizens by acquisition • False identity • No time limit • No court decision is required • No statutory right of appeal (judicial review)

way bureaucratic institutions negotiate national boundaries (Bertossi 2016). So far, discussions on the lightening vs. renationalising trends in citizenship policies have not looked at how officials and judges justify the decisions they take. Following scholars who have emphasised the role that these intermediaries play in the implementation of citizenship policies (Hajjat 2012; Mazouz, 2017), this paper will concentrate on the justifications they provide about their work to explore the 'moral economy' of fraud-based deprivation in France and the UK. Fassin (2013, 23) defines 'moral economy' as the processes of production, circulation and appropriation of norms and emotions within specific social contexts such as institutions. In the context of citizenship deprivation policies, it is through such processes that laws and regulations are negotiated and become effective.[8] More specifically, analysing the norms and emotions behind the decision-making process is crucial for understanding how the selection between 'desirable' and 'undesirable' citizens is made and how citizenship functions as a mechanism of 'exclusive inclusion' (Turner 2014). To this end, the paper draws on analyses of public discourses and case law concerning citizenship fraud from the 1990s onwards, as well as on observations and semi-structured interviews with judges, lawyers and officials at the local and national levels. More precisely, in the case of France, I rely on interviews with two officials working on citizenship deprivation at the Directorate on Access to French Citizenship (*Sous-direction de l'accès à la nationalité française* – hereafter SDANF), two Council of State judges who take part in the decision-making process leading to citizenship deprivation, and a lawyer who has defended people targeted by citizenship deprivation orders. I also use materials I collected during ethnographic fieldwork in French prefectural boards between 2016 and 2017. In the case of the UK, my argument is based on two meetings with officials from the United Kingdom Visas and Immigration (UKVI) agency: one official who deals with fraud-based deprivation policies and another who works on the implementation of citizenship regulations. I also draw on interviews with two lawyers who specialise in UK citizenship deprivation law.

The first part of the paper will address the politicisation of fraud in the two countries' immigration policies over the last 30 years to highlight that similar securitised approaches are at work, aimed at tightening the controls and sanctions against alleged fraudsters. The second section will examine if and how this approach affects the way officials and judges understand citizenship deprivation on both sides of the Channel. It will show that the procedural dimension of citizenship stripping (ensuring the consistency of naturalisation law) serves a moralising and responsibilising function vis-à-vis the applicants. The naturalisation process stipulates a standard of virtuous behaviour that applicants have no choice but to adopt for fear of the sanctions they would otherwise face. This proves that the deprivation policies in both countries produce citizens that are not abstract and legal subjects in the sense of citizenship liberalisation – instead, the renationalisation of citizenship aims to create virtuous and responsible subjects. Finally, the last part of the paper will explore the targeting of citizenship deprivation to show that not all migrants are subject to renationalisation. In fact, this section will illustrate how citizenship deprivation reproduces suspicions and stereotypes against African migrants in France and asylum seekers in the UK. This demonstrates that the moralising and responsibilising function of deprivation is applied to specific categories of migrants, which turns them into second-class citizens.

Fraud and the securitisation of citizenship and migration policies

Politicisation can be broadly understood as a process that redefines all sorts of social practices into political activities (Lagroye 2003, 11). The construction of a social practice into a public problem therefore represents a key component of politicisation (Gusfield 1981). This section compares the politicisation of fraud in France and the UK to reflect upon the type of public problem it is said to represent in citizenship and migration policies. This is particularly important given the influence that such framing may have on how officials and judges put citizenship deprivation into practice. Fraud has been framed as a security problem in both France and the UK, and the notion that fraudsters threaten the integrity of the immigration system has served to justify tighter controls and sanctions. The politicisation of fraud can thus be seen as a securitisation process. Drawing upon Wæver (1995), I define securitisation as the framing of a social issue in security terms, as a social issue that represents an existential threat and requires action.[9] Scholars have noted that securitisation legitimates the conferment of a threatening character to the social issue in question (Balzacq, 2005) and that public debates over legislative changes play a key function in this respect (Perret 2018). Following this approach, this section will examine public discussions over changes to British and French citizenship and migration policies over the last 30 years and how fraud concerns have contributed to their securitisation.

Though there is no instance of a public debate around citizenship fraud in the British case, the politicisation of fraud in migration policies has been intense and one may wonder to what extent this has affected citizenship. From the end of the 1990s onwards, the British government made the need to 'tackle fraud' one of its priorities in the field of migration. This has most notably affected the asylum system and marriage migration. In 2002, the White Paper *Secure Borders, Safe Haven* revealed the government's desire to avoid the image of a country 'open to abuse' (Home Office 2002, 5). It thus proposed the introduction of application registration cards for asylum seekers, including digital footprints, tighter controls of immigration advisers suspected of 'smuggling' people into the UK, and new sanctions against employers of 'illegal migrants'. In 2008, another White Paper entitled *The Path to Citizenship* emphasised the same government intention to 'make it harder for those people who are here illegally' to remain in the UK, in order to prevent 'fraudulent access to benefits and services' (Home Office 2008, 45). 'Marriages of convenience' have also been singled out as attempts to circumvent the immigration system. These suspicions have resulted in stricter controls, including assessments of couples' 'intention to live together' (Wray 2013). The notion that 'failed asylum seekers' and 'illegal migrants' more generally are 'cheaters' or 'scroungers' who should be punished and eventually removed from the UK has been at the heart of the British immigration policy since the 2000s (Anderson 2013). The 'hostile environment' strategy that Theresa May has pursued since 2012 follows the same rationale. Though concerns about fraudsters have not been most forcefully voiced in discussions about citizenship policies, they have nevertheless found a clear echo in the ten-year naturalisation ban that the Home Office introduced against applicants who had been 'staying illegally' in the UK. The change was implemented in 2014 in response to an Independent Chief Inspector's report that called for sanctions against people 'absconding from immigration control' (Independent Chief Inspector 2014, 24–25).

The same securitised approach to fraud has been present in French debates about immigration policies since the 2000s. Irregularly entering or staying on French territory is also seen as a subversion of the immigration system. This led to the introduction of tougher controls and sanctions, including against people suspected of 'helping' irregular migrants (Henriot 2013). Contrary to the UK, the discussions of fraud have been more narrowly connected to citizenship. As early as the 1980s, marriages of convenience (*mariages blancs*) and the provision of false information on civil status documents (or even the forgery of such documents) were presented as the two main practices whereby migrants fraudulently seek French citizenship. This was evident in the discussions within the Marceau Long Commission on citizenship in 1988. The Commission's report underlined that some migrants were instrumentalising French nationality law to escape immigration controls (Long 1988, 73). Officials from the SDANF cited growing public concerns on the 'fraud question' to push the Commission towards firm responses (Long 1988, 138).[10] During the 2000s, changes in the registration process for spouses of French citizens made citizenship acquisition harder and cancellation easier.[11] More specifically, the 2011 changes to Article 26–4 on *annulations* were connected to debates about the fight against 'marriages of convenience' (Salcedo 2011).

Though fraud and citizenship have not been directly linked in the British immigration discourse, and the legal framework for fraud-based citizenship deprivation has been more stable than in France,[12] since the 2000s the politicisation of fraud has followed a similar securitised approach. The idea that suspected fraudsters should be more strictly controlled and, if found guilty, sanctioned has driven policy changes on both sides of the Channel. According to Nyers (2009, 3), 'bring[ing] security to the forefront of political debate and calculations has profound implications for what it means to be a political subject'. However, an analysis of public discourses alone does not clarify what the implications might be. More specifically, the emphasis on more sanctions may well strengthen the view of the political subject as a law-abiding citizen or as a virtuous individual who should know that citizenship acquisition entails moral obligations. The following section will thus examine how officials and judges understand fraud-based citizenship deprivation to identify what exactly the political implications of these securitising discourses might be.

Enforcing naturalisation rules, sanctioning unworthy applicants

To get a sense of how citizenship deprivation is conceived by those who put it into practice, it is important to understand the institutional framework within which it is embedded. In both France and the UK, the agencies responsible for citizenship policies play a key role in deprivation. As of 2017, two officials from the SDANF were in charge of investigating whether fraud played a role in any of the naturalisation cases they were reviewing. As regards nullifications, the office dealing with acquisition through marriage is responsible for investigating the cases before passing them on to another office within the Ministry of Justice. The SDANF usually receives such information from various institutions (registry officials from the *Service central de l'état civil*, prefectural boards, French consulates abroad) and occasionally from private individuals denouncing someone they know.[13] The system works in a similar way in the UK: in 2017, the Citizenship Deprivation Team at the UKVI consisted of five people from the Status

Review Unit.[14] This team collects reports from other institutions (the Passport Office, Border Force, Visas Services) or from private individuals, verifying if the legal conditions for citizenship deprivation apply and then investigating whether any such allegations are credible or not.[15]

The application of the provisions relating to fraud is not subject to the same legal scrutiny in the two countries. Indeed, in the UK, there is no need to receive the approval of any court before issuing a deprivation order or deciding that a naturalisation is null and void (see Table 1). The officials only have to ensure that the satisfaction of the Secretary of State is established (Home Office 2017, chapter 55.8.2). In France meanwhile, they either have to go through a local court to obtain nullifications, or appear before the Interior Section of the Council of State to defend any deprivation order they have been preparing. In France, a deprivation order can only be issued if a judge confirms the decision as appropriate, which translates into direct control over the government's deprivation cases. To assess a proposed deprivation on grounds of fraud, judges from the Council of State will consider a set of individual circumstances such as the length of residence in France, whether the applicant is employed, has children living with her/him in France, and also whether the deprivation order would result in statelessness. Although statelessness is not an insuperable obstacle to fraud-based deprivation (as it is allowed by international law), it is nevertheless one of the factors against which decisions are balanced. French officials anticipate the control exercised by the Council of State: if it appears that a case would not pass the test of the Interior Section – that is, if the deprivation decision appears too far outside the current case law – they will abandon it. This represents the majority of fraud cases: of the 500 cases investigated each year, only 30 result in deprivation orders (see Table 2).[16]

In the UK, even though judges do not systematically scrutinise their decisions, officials also need to balance their decisions against the circumstances of each case, and guidance from the Home Office specifies the situations when the Secretary of State will normally not consider deprivation appropriate (if the fraud postdates naturalisation; if the person was a minor at the time of naturalisation – see Home Office 2017, chapter 55.7.5). However, the set of circumstances differs from that in France. For instance, statelessness is not something that the British Deprivation Team cares about. When asked whether she knew the number of individuals whose British citizenship was stripped on grounds of fraud and who were left stateless as a result, one UKVI official underlined that this was of no interest to her and her team since deprivation resulting in statelessness is legal (field notes, UKVI, 23/02/2017). As in France though, a significant number of the investigated cases do not result in citizenship deprivation orders: of the 400 investigations each year, only around 15 lead to deprivation and 100 to nullity (Independent Chief Inspector 2014, 34).

Table 2. Proposed and actual deprivation orders in accordance with Art. 27–2 of the French Civil Code (*décrets rapportant*) between 2002 and 2015 (sources: Ministère de l'Emploi, de la Cohésion sociale et du Logement, 2006; personal communication from the SDANF).

	2002	2003	2004	2005	2006	2007	2008	2009	2010	2011	2012	2013	2014	2015
Investigations	580	644	579	755	817	651	716	747	767	791	588	463	427	567
Cases presented to the Council of State	30	29	42	44	32	16	27	31	36	42	33	28	34	26
Positive verdict	30	27	42	35	27	13	25	27	14	17	30	17	25	22
Negative verdict	0	2	0	0	3	1	0	3	1	1	1	1	0	0

Although citizenship deprivation on grounds of fraud is not subject to the same degree of judicial review, it relies on the same 'police logic' (Spire 2005) in both France and the UK. Citizenship deprivation is understood as a tool for identifying potential cheaters. Significantly, one French official referred to the investigative part of her job as 'fraud hunting' (field notes, SDANF, 13/04/2017). The referral system on which deprivation decisions are based (as in deprivation on public good grounds) places officials in a position where they have to act on suspicions. In both countries, investigations will involve exchanging correspondence with the individuals being targeted in order to obtain information and get a sense of whether citizenship was obtained by fraudulent means. Since this is the only direct contact with the people being targeted, these exchanges are crucial to start the deprivation process (field notes, UKVI, 23/02/2017; field notes, SDANF, 13/04/2017). Officials will sometimes act tactically in order to obtain information that may be important for establishing sufficient grounds for a potential deprivation decision. They may, for instance, decide not to disclose the exact nature of the evidence against an individual if they believe that this would aid the collection of information.

Rather than being merely a legal issue, the uncovering of fraud is invested with moral meaning in both countries. This is evident in the legal categories that officials use to identify alleged fraudsters at the naturalisation stage: 'good conduct and behaviour' for naturalisation by decree and 'unworthiness' for registration through marriage in France, and 'good character' in the UK. This moral dimension is also perceptible in the statements of the officials in charge of deprivation in both countries, as well as in the relevant case law. The French officials referred to the individuals they deprived of citizenship as 'dissemblers' and presented the purpose of their work as deterring people from 'lying', 'dissimulating' or 'misbehaving' (field notes, SDANF, 13/04/2017). In fact, they suggested that by maintaining the procedural integrity of the naturalisation process they are also protecting its moral value. In the UK, cheating and lying were similarly presented as wrong for threatening the very purpose of naturalisation, namely to celebrate citizenship as a 'high standard', a 'very important step' that only those who are worthy deserve to take (field notes, UKVI, 23/02/2017). The same discourse can be found in British case law, as this excerpt from a judgment shows:

> *British citizenship carries with it important rights and privileges. There is an important public interest in maintaining the integrity of the status which citizenship confers on an individual and the process by which it is obtained. Removal of citizenship where that integrity is infringed is an important factor in maintaining public confidence and providing a deterrent against fraud and deception* (Upper Tribunal, Immigration and Asylum Chamber, Appeal Number: DC/00003/2014, §21)

On both sides of the Channel, deprivation on grounds of fraud functions as a sanction to safeguard the 'logic of honour' of naturalisation, that is, the idea that naturalisation comes as a reward or privilege for those who have shown themselves to be deserving (Sayad 1999). Citizenship deprivation is seen as serving this important objective, with serious (and legitimate) consequences for the targeted individuals. The judge cited above insisted on the deterrent function of citizenship deprivation, as did the French deprivation officials. They explained that the intended purpose of deprivation is to make people aware that they will be sanctioned and that the consequences are serious.

They also indicated that people talk about deprivation decisions on Internet forums and that they encourage these discussions because of their deterrent effect (interview with an official dealing with citizenship deprivation at the SDANF, 24/04/2017). The deterrent function of deprivation proves that the aim is to transform the applicants' behaviour by means of fear. In fact, citizenship deprivation has very serious consequences anywhere, though they differ from one country to the next.

In France, *décrets rapportant* affect the individuals being targeted and may result in loss of citizenship for their children (if it was acquired collectively), of their name (if they had chosen to 'Frenchify' it), and of their jobs if they are working in public services. Nullifications may similarly affect the persons being targeted and their children (unless they are adults at the time of the nullification).[17] Although there is no right to a residence permit and prefectural boards will consider applications on their own merits, people stripped of their citizenship on grounds of fraud will usually be allowed to stay on French territory.[18] There is no attempt on the part of the French authorities to make deprivation on grounds of fraud result in removal, in contrast with deprivation on public good grounds.

The opposite is the case in the UK, where the UKVI tries to deport people who are subject to deprivation on grounds of fraud, just as it does in case of deprivation on public good grounds. UKVI officials from the Deprivation Team were quite clear that removal was systematically considered (field notes, UKVI, 23/02/2017). The only exceptions are cases where British children would be separated from their parent, in order to comply with Article 8 of the European Convention on Human Rights. Even in such cases, individuals who have lost their citizenship will not be able to receive indefinite leave to remain (ILR), as the Home Office will only grant them temporary leave to remain. To date, there has been a major difference between nullity and deprivation decisions (see Table 1) on this matter. People whose citizenship has been considered null normally retrieve the ILR and the Home Office will not seek to remove them from the UK. However, at the time of fieldwork, there were discussions as to whether the affected individuals should also have their ILR revoked (field notes, UKVI, 23/02/2017).

Hence, the British and French policies diverge on the question of whether or not removal is the objective of citizenship deprivation on grounds of fraud. However, the institutional configuration of the process and its implementation in both countries show that it serves both as a means to protect the integrity of the naturalisation process and as a sanction with significant consequences for individuals deemed unworthy. More specifically, all applicants are expected to responsibilise themselves for fear of deprivation and to adopt the virtuous behaviour set forth by the naturalisation process as a condition for national membership. What implications does this have on the meaning of being a political subject (Nyers 2009, 3)? British and French deprivation policies reveal a vision of the citizen not as a purely formal, legal subject and member of a juridico-political order. In other words, this is not the vision put forward by advocates of the 'lightening' theory of citizenship policies (Joppke 2010). On the contrary, it produces a vision of a virtuous and responsible subject that is in line with the renationalisation of citizenship. By combining moralising (communitarian) and responsibilising (neoliberal) features, British and French deprivations policies follow a governing strategy that renationalises citizenship.

But who exactly is the target of renationalisation? In order to reflect on the type of exclusion that deprivation entails, the last part of the paper will examine whether its moralising and responsibilising function is directed at specific categories of people.

The targets of citizenship stripping

The notion that citizenship entails the duty to behave as a virtuous and responsible individual, which serves to justify deprivation in France and the UK, may seem sociologically neutral as it may apply equally to all. On the contrary, this section demonstrates that the moralising and responsibilising function that civil servants and judges subscribe to draws upon and perpetuates stereotypes against specific categories of migrants in both countries.

In France, the vast majority of fraud-based deprivations involve people who failed to mention the name of a spouse/a child living abroad and who apply for family reunification (see Table 3) afterwards.

Family reunification is a condition for acquiring French citizenship: applicants are required to have established their 'centre of family interests' in France at the time of application. This is linked to the idea that family members should be present in France, and eventually should all apply for French citizenship if the process of integration is to work correctly.[19] The people targeted in fraud-based citizenship deprivation are, in fact, accused of deflecting the family reunification process because once someone becomes French, they do not need to satisfy the same requirements (basically, conditions related to sufficient income and floor space to host family members).

Although the number of decisions taken is small, fraud-based citizenship deprivation is part of a system of control over civil status documents that can also be found at the naturalisation stage and is directed against the figure of the family migrant. In public discourses, this figure has been constructed as a category of 'endured migrant', as opposed to the category of 'chosen migrant', and is commonly associated with African migrants (Hachimi-Alaoui 2016).[20] Suspicions of fraud vis-à-vis these migrants were already expressed by the Marceau Long Commission. Members of the Commission notably argued that 'serious doubts' existed on the civil status documents of African migrants and that they should all be examined with greater care and caution given their rising numbers (Long 1988, 55). More recent public pronouncement by representatives of the French government also pointed towards the 'former French possessions', especially in Africa, as the countries where civil status fraud is most common (Mariani 2007, 16). These discourses are based on the vision that African migrants may present a risk of mass migration due to them having larger families. Such stereotypes find echoes in the explanations that officials and judges give about the targets of fraud-based deprivation. For example, a civil servant responsible for citizenship

Table 3. Motivations for deprivation orders issued in accordance with Art. 27–2 of the French Civil Code (*décrets rapportant*) between 2007 and 2015 (source: personal communication from the SDANF).

	2007	2008	2009	2010	2011	2012	2013	2014	2015
Good character	2	0	1	1	0	4	1	4	1
Residence in France	0	2	1	0	0	0	2	1	0
Fraud	12	23	28	14	18	27	15	20	21

deprivation at the SDANF explained that as EU citizens and their partners are allowed to settle in France, there is nothing suspicious if they do not have declaration of a marriage from their country of origin when applying for French citizenship. However, she justified her suspicions over naturalised French citizens originating from Cameroon by saying 'it is well-known that Cameroonian women often obtain the right to stay in France by having a French father acknowledge their children' (field notes, SDANF, 13/04/2017). Put differently, the same action – not declaring one's spouse or one's child in the naturalisation process – may not be regarded as fraudulent, depending on nationality. This example suggests that suspicions of fraud stem both from existing legal differentiations between categories of migrants (EU citizens vs. others) and from specific stereotypes (African migrants as more likely to attempt to deflect the family reunification process).

British fraud-based citizenship deprivation policies do not target the same category of migrants as in France, but they also perpetuate similar suspicions. In the UK, a large number of the cases under investigation involved former asylum seekers who are accused of providing false information about where they came from or who they are. Between October 2012 and February 2014, such cases counted for 13 of the 14 nullity decisions taken (Independent Chief Inspector 2014, 35). Albanian citizens make up the single largest group of cases. The case law shows that 6 out of 16 appeals or judicial reviews dealing with fraud-based deprivation and nullification decisions between 2009 and 2017 involved Albanian nationals accused of having provided false information in their applications for asylum.[21] This is largely due to concerns made public in the late 2000s about the large number of fraudulent applications from Albanians pretending to have fled Kosovo when the country was at war with Serbia. This has resulted in the re-examination of a large number of naturalisation applications from Albanians and has sometimes led to deprivation (the exact number of cases is unknown). The UKVI teams working on naturalisation applications and citizenship deprivation frequently share the suspicions about asylum seekers being 'bogus migrants' or 'fake' asylum seekers. Officials from the Nationality Casework Team (the service responsible for the processing of British naturalisation applications) explained that if applicants apply as Kosovan refugees, they systematically contact the Albanian authorities to check their birth records (field notes, UKVI, 23/02/2017). Moreover, beyond the issue of fraud, the Nationality Casework Team operates an automatic referral mechanism for naturalisation applications made by former asylum seekers from countries with a high risk of involvement in 'war crimes' – a Screening Team will then assess whether this was the case or not (field notes, UKVI, 23/02/2017). In other words, asylum seekers are not only suspected of cheating, but also of being war criminals. It should also be noted that the Citizenship Deprivation Team is part of the Status Review Unit, which includes a specific team dealing with the potential removal of 'failed asylum seekers'. There are thus institutional explanations for the targeting of asylum seekers in British citizenship deprivation policies on grounds of fraud. Though the stereotyping is not cultural as is the case with African migrants in France, fraud also tends to be seen as a problem posed by a specific category of migrants.

Conclusion

In both France and the UK, the threat that fraud poses to the immigration system has been a key argument for the securitisation of citizenship and migration policies over the last 30 years. Citizenship deprivation has been one of the principal instruments that the British and French authorities have used against alleged fraudsters in the naturalisation process. This paper has focused on how government officials and judges understand citizenship deprivation on both sides of the Channel. It has shown that the instrument is not merely seen as a means to safeguard the procedural integrity of naturalisation – contrary to a view commonly expressed in the literature (Lavi 2011; Bauböck and Paskalev 2015; Gibney 2017).[22] Citizenship is conceived by those who put it into practice (officials and judges) as a mechanism for the moralisation and responsibilisation of applicants. They are expected to responsibilise themselves for fear of deprivation and to adopt the virtuous behaviour that the naturalisation process sets forth as a condition for national membership. This implies that the political subject produced by citizenship deprivation policies is not a liberal and abstract legal subject, but that it aims instead to create a virtuous and responsible subject in the spirit of citizenship renationalisation.

The paper has identified important differences between British and French deprivation policies. The French government does not attempt to make deprivation orders result in removal, while the opposite is the case in the UK. Moreover, French courts have greater powers to review the decisions of the Ministry of the Interior than their British counterparts (most notably on statelessness). However, despite these differences, the policies for deprivation on grounds of fraud reveal a convergent governing strategy of renationalising citizenship. This paper has further argued that this governing strategy does not target all migrants equally. To put it differently, not everyone is made the subject of citizenship renationalisation. African migrants in France and asylum seekers in the UK are singled out for citizenship deprivation. Nyers argues that one potential outcome of the practices of unmaking citizenship is the production of 'accidental' citizens as 'nominal (not necessary), ephemeral (not essential), and dangerous (not desirable)' citizens (Nyers 2006, 24). In applying suspicions of fraud to some naturalised citizens, in particular, British and French deprivation policies give a 'nominal' and 'ephemeral' character to their membership. This is justified on the grounds that they pose a danger not simply to the procedural consistency of the naturalisation process, but also to its 'logic of honour' (Sayad 1999). Such an outcome may not be specific to fraud-based citizenship deprivation, as the evidence from deprivation orders on public good grounds in both countries shows that Muslims are frequently targeted (Fargues 2017). The extent through which the affirmation of a renationalised vision of citizenship strengthens the division between 'accidental' and 'essential' citizens – those whose membership is never called into question – should thus be further explored in policy fields other than citizenship deprivation and in jurisdictions beyond France and the UK.

Notes

1. In keeping with British law, I will use the term 'deprivation' to refer broadly to the government's power to revoke citizenship and will specify the relevant distinctions with other processes such as nullity or cancellation of citizenship.
2. Although Joppke acknowledges an 'indisputable truth' in these postnational theses (Joppke 2010, 12), he also criticises them for ignoring the 'high variability of differently developed alien rights across countries' and the 'possibility of regression' (Joppke 2007b, 42).

3. Joppke (2007a) acknowledges that liberalism has been given a 'repressive' character in recent years. He nevertheless argues that this does not disprove the 'lightening' of citizenship policies.
4. Schinkel (2008) explains that a republican/communitarian conception of citizenship gives more weight to moral commitments towards the 'common good' while a liberal conception is more attached to a formal vision of the subject as a 'member of a juridico-political order'.
5. Deprivation on grounds of fraud is indeed restricted to naturalised citizens. The difference – as Gibney (2013) points out – is that it targets individual behaviour in the naturalisation application, which is not the case for deprivation on public good grounds.
6. The importance of long-established institutional configurations for analysing contemporary citizenship policies should not be underestimated (Goodman 2012). However, to avoid taking pre-existing distinctions for granted and presenting France and the UK as two *a priori* opposing 'models' (Bertossi and Duyvendak 2012), the paper highlights specific institutional legacies, rather than enumerating how the traditions differ.
7. All translations from French are the author's own, unless otherwise stated.
8. Notwithstanding the role of intermediaries for negotiating the rules and regulations, nationality law retains an important function for structuring citizenship deprivation.
9. Though scholars have been interested in the securitisation of citizenship and migration (Bigo 2002; Nyers 2009), the role that fraud plays in this process has been relatively neglected.
10. The Commission finally chose to underline that instruments for fighting citizenship fraud were already available, including citizenship deprivation.
11. The condition of residence for registering as a French citizen was extended from one to four years in 2003 and 2006. The French government has also made two successive changes to the cancellation/*annulation* provisions. Since 2003, the government can revisit its decision if the legal conditions for registration were not met. In 2006, the period for reconsidering citizenship registrations was extended to two years.
12. The only change to the legal framework in the UK has been the extension of citizenship deprivation provisions from naturalisation to acquisition of British citizenship through registration in 1981 (Gibney 2013).
13. Although private individuals may contact the SDANF directly, the prefectural boards usually serve as a filter for reviewing the credibility of denunciations before passing them on to the SDANF. They may also launch a police investigation to verify any such allegations (interview with the chief assistant of a prefectural office for foreigners in the Paris area, 12/01/2017).
14. The creation of this team dates back to 2012. It also deals with the revocation of indefinite leave to remain and the potential removal of failed asylum seekers (field notes, UKVI, 23/02/2017).
15. In France, deprivation on public good and on grounds of fraud are processed by the same administrative team, whereas in the UK, a 'Special Cases Unit' with a high level of security clearance is in charge of deprivation on public good grounds (field notes, UKVI, 23/02/2017).
16. As far as nullity is concerned, around 100 orders are issued each year, compared to 400 investigated cases. See Ministère de l'Intérieur, 'Contestation des decisions d'acquisition de la nationalité française', 09/11/2016, URL: https://www.immigration.interieur.gouv.fr/Accueil-et-accompagnement/La-nationalite-francaise/Contestation-des-decisions-d-acquisition-de-la-nationalite-francaise, consulted on 29/08/2018.
17. See Cour de Cassation, Chambre civile 1, 17/02/2004, 01–10.060, Publié au bulletin.
18. However small, the prefectural management staffs enjoy a margin for manoeuvre in the implementation of deprivation orders and, more specifically, in the seizure of the documents related to French citizenship. Depending on how they evaluate the circumstances of each case (the motivation for the deprivation decision, the consequences of deprivation), they may decide to hasten or to delay the seizure of these documents (field notes, Prefectural board located in Paris area, 10/01/2017).

19. Until the end of the 1980s, the French authorities held that foreign couples should apply together for French citizenship and that application would be processed jointly. Applications for French citizenship were not treated individually, but based on the notion of 'familial unity of citizenship' ('unité familiale de nationalité'). The Council of State changed this approach to citizenship acquisition for couples in 1986 (Conseil d'Etat, 26/09/1986, 'Ministère des Affaires sociales et de la solidarité nationale c/Epoux Vo Ngoc Que, n° 54,518) See Spire (2005, 348).
20. 'Chosen migration' is an expression coined in the 1980s by Alain Griotteray, a member of the far-right Club de l'Horloge, which was then popularised by Nicolas Sarkozy at the time he was Minister of the Interior.
21. Cases of deprivation include Deliallisi [2013] UKUT 00439(IAC); Arusha and Demushi Albania [2012] UKUT [80] and KB Albania [2009] UKAIT 00043. Cases of nullity include Hysaj & Ors, R. (On the Application of) v Secretary of State for the Home Department [2015] EWCA Civ 1195; Kaziu & Ors v Secretary of State for the Home Department [2014] EWHC 832 (Admin); R (Kadria) and R (Krasniqi) v SSHD [2010] EWHC 3405 (Admin).
22. A parallel can be drawn with a recent paper by Mantu (2018) who argues that framing citizenship deprivation (though in the case of 'alleged' terrorists) as a purely administrative measure tends to obscure the broader political implications of the process.

Acknowledgments

I would like to thank the guest co-editors, Elke Winter and Matthew Gibney, the anonymous reviewers, my two PhD supervisors, Janie Pélabay and Réjane Sénac, and all the participants in the 2018 IPSA panel "When States Take Rights Back: Questioning the Public Justifications of Citizenship Revocation" (RC14.34), for their helpful comments. I am also grateful to Christoph Gottstein and Maja Spanu who helped me to sharpen my argument.

Disclosure statement

No potential conflict of interest was reported by the author.

References

Anderson, B. 2013. *Us and Them? the Dangerous Politics of Immigration Control.* Oxford: Oxford University Press.

Badenhoop, E. 2017. "Calling for the Super Citizen: Citizenship Ceremonies in the UK and Germany as Techniques of Subject-Formation." *Migration Studies* 5(3): 409–427. doi:10.1093/migration/mnx053

Balzacq, T. 2005. "The Three Faces of Securitization: Political Agency, Audience and Context." *European Journal of International Relations* 11 (2): 171–201. doi:10.1177/1354066105052960

Bauböck, R., and V. Paskalev. 2015. "Citizenship Deprivation: A Normative Analysis." *CEPS Paper in Liberty and Security in Europe*, n° 82. https://www.ceps.eu/publications/citizenship-deprivation-normative-analysis

Beauchamps, M. 2016. "The Forfeiture of Nationality in France: Discursive Ambiguity, Borders and Identities." *Space and Culture* 19 (1): 31–42. doi:10.1177/1206331214560091

Bertossi, C. 2016. *La Citoyenneté À La Française. Valeurs Et Réalités.* Paris: CNRS Éditions

Bertossi, C., and J. W. Duyvendak. 2012. "National Models of Immigrant Integration: The Cost for Comparative Research." *Comparative European Politics* 10 (3): 237–247. doi:10.1057/cep.2012.10

Bigo, D. 2002. "Security and Immigration: Toward a Critique of the Governmentality of Unease." *Alternatives* 27 (1): 63–92. doi:10.1177/03043754020270S105

Byrne, B. 2014. *Making Citizens. Public Rituals and Personal Journeys to Citizenship*. Basingstoke: Palgrave Macmillan.

Fargues, É. 2017. "The Revival of Citizenship Deprivation in France and the UK as an Instance of Citizenship Renationalisation." *Citizenship Studies* 21 (8): 984–998. doi:10.1080/13621025.2017.1377152

Fassin, D., ed. 2013. *Juger, Réprimer, Accompagner. Essai Sur La Morale De L'état*. Paris: Seuil.

Ferré, N. 2010. "Soupçon Systématique De Fraude." *Plein Droit* 85: 3–6. doi:10.3917/pld.085.0003

Fortier, A.-M. 2016. "The Psychic Life of Policy: Desire, Anxiety and 'Citizenisation' in Britain." *Critical Social Policy* 36 (4): 1–19.

Gibney, M. 2013. "'A Very Transcendental Power'. Denaturalisation and the Liberalisation of Citizenship in the United Kingdom." *Political Studies* 61: 637–655. doi:10.1111/j.1467-9248.2012.00980.x

Gibney, M. 2017. "Denationalization." In *The Oxford Handbook of Citizenship*, edited by A. Shachar, R. Bauböck, I. Blœmraad, and M. Vink, 358–383. Oxford: Oxford University Press.

Goodman, S. W. 2012. "Fortifying Citizenship: Policy Strategies for Civic Integration in Europe." *World Politics* 64 (4): 659–698. doi:10.1017/S0043887112000184

Gusfield, J. R. 1981. *The Culture of Public Problems. Drinking-Driving and the Symbolic Order*. Chicago: University of Chicago Press.

Hachimi-Alaoui, M. 2016. "L'immigration Familiale: Une Obligation D'« *Intégration Républicaine* ». Le Cas Du Contrat D'accueil Et D'intégration." *Recherches Familiales* 13 (1): 79–93. doi:10.3917/rf.013.0079

Hajjat, A. 2012. *Les Frontières De L'identité Nationale. L'injonction À L'assimilation En France Métropolitaine Et Coloniale*. Paris: La Découverte.

Hansen, R. 2009. "The Poverty of Postnationalism: Citizenship, Immigration and the New Europe." *Theory and Society* 38 (1): 1–24. doi:10.1007/s11186-008-9074-0

Henriot, P. 2013. "Dépénalisation Du Séjour Irrégulier Des Étrangers: L'opiniâtre Résistance Des Autorités Françaises." *La Revue Des Droits De L'homme* 3. https://journals.openedition.org/revdh/426

Home Office. 2002. *Secure Borders, Safe Haven: integration with diversity in modern Britain*.

Home Office. 2008. *The Path to Citizenship: Next Steps in Reforming the Immigration System*.

Home Office. 2017. *Nationality Policy Guidance, Chapter 55: Deprivation and Nullity of British Citizenship*. https://www.gov.uk/government/publications/deprivation-and-nullity-of-british-citizenship-nationality-policy-guidance

Independent Chief Inspector. 2014. *An Inspection of Nationality Casework*.

Jacobson, D. 1995. *Rights across Borders. Immigration and the Decline of Citizenship*. Baltimore, MD: John Hopkins University Press.

Joppke, C. 2007a. "Beyond National Models: Civic Integration Policies for Immigrants in Western Europe." *West European Politics* 30 (1): 1–22. doi:10.1080/01402380601019613

Joppke, C. 2007b. "Transformation of Citizenship: Status, Rights, Identity." *Citizenship Studies* 11 (1): 37–48. doi:10.1080/13621020601099831

Joppke, C. 2010. "The Inevitable Lightening of Citizenship." *European Journal of Sociology* 51 (1)" 9–32. doi:10.1017/S0003975610000019

Joppke, C. 2016. "Terror and the Loss of Citizenship." *Citizenship Studies* 20 (6–7): 728–748. doi:10.1080/13621025.2016.1191435

Kostakopoulou, D. 2010. "The Anatomy of Civic Integration." *The Modern Law Review* 73 (6): 933–958. doi:10.1111/mlr.2010.73.issue-6

Lagroye, J., ed. 2003. *La Politisation*. Paris: Belin.

Lavi, S. 2011. "Citizenship Revocation as Punishment." *University of Toronto Law Journal* 61 (4): 783–810. doi:10.3138/utlj.61.4.783

Long, M. 1988. *Être Français Aujourd'hui Et Demain, T. 2: Conclusions Et Propositions De La Commission De La Nationalité.* Paris, La Documentation française.

Macklin, A., and R. Bauböck, eds. 2015. *The Return of Banishment: Do the New Denationalisation Policies Weaken Citizenship?* Florence: EUDO Observatory on Citizenship.

Mantu, S. 2018. "'Terrorist' Citizens and the Human Right to Nationality." *Journal of Contemporary European Studies* 26 (1): 28–41. doi:10.1080/14782804.2017.1397503

Mariani, T. 2007. *Rapport Législatif N° 160.*

Mazouz, S. 2017. *La République et Ses Autres: Politiques De L'altérité Dans La France Des Années 2000.* Lyon: ENS éditions. doi:10.4000/books.enseditions.7513.

Mouritsen, P. 2012. "Beyond Postnational Citizenship. Access, Consequence, Conditionality." In *European Multiculturalisms: Cultural, Religious and Ethnic Challenges*, edited by A. Triandafyllidou, T. Modood, and N. Meer, 88–115. Edinburgh: Edinburgh University Press.

Nyers, P. 2006. "The Accidental Citizen: Acts of Sovereignty and (Un)Making Citizenship." *Economy and Society* 35 (1): 22–41. doi:10.1080/03085140500465824

Nyers, P., ed. 2009. *Securitizations of Citizenship.* London: Routledge.

Orgad, L. 2015. *The Cultural Defence of Nations.* Oxford: Oxford University Press.

Perret, S. 2018. "L'écrit Comme Pratique De Sécuritisation: Analyse Des Évolutions Législatives Sur La Nationalité Française." *Études Internationales* 49 (1): 57–82. doi:10.7202/1050544ar

Salcedo, M. 2011. "Bleu, Blanc, Gris… La Couleur Des Mariages." *L'Espace Politique* 13 (1). http://journals.openedition.org/espacepolitique/1869

Sayad, A. 1999. "La Naturalisation." In *La Double Absence- Des Illusions De L'émigré Aux Souffrances De L'immigré*, edited by A. Sayad, 393–459. Paris: Seuil.

Schinkel, W. 2008. "The Moralisation of Citizenship in Dutch Integration Discourse." *Amsterdam Law Forum* 1 (1): 15–26.

Schinkel, W., and F. Van Houdt. 2010. "The Double Helix of Cultural Assimilation and Neo-Liberalism: Citizenship in Contemporary Governmentality." *The British Journal of Sociology* 61 (4): 696–715. doi:10.1111/j.1468-4446.2010.01337.x

Soysal, Y. 1994. *Limits of Citizenship. Migrants and Postnational Membership in Europe.* Chicago, IL: University of Chicago.

Spire, A., 2005. *Étrangers À La Carte. L'administration De L'immigration En France (1945-1975).* Paris: Grasset.

Turner, J. 2014. "Testing the Liberal Subject: (In)Security, Responsibility and 'Self-Improvement' in the UK Citizenship Test." *Citizenship Studies* 18 (3–4): 332–348. doi:10.1080/13621025.2014.905273

Wæver, O. 1995. "Securitization and Desecuritization." In *On Security*, edited by R. D. Lipschutz, 46–86. New York: Columbia University Press.

Wray, H. 2013. "An Ideal Husband? Marriages of Convenience, Moral Gate-Keeping and Immigration to the UK." *European Journal of Migration and Law* 8, 303–320. doi:10.1163/157181606778882582

The concept of allegiance in citizenship law and revocation: an Australian study

Helen Irving

ABSTRACT

The idea that the citizen owes allegiance to his or her state has long historical roots, and has been repeatedly affirmed in theory and in law. Revocation of citizenship has a long history, too. The most recent Australian example is the 2015 amendment to the *Australian Citizenship Act* (2007) which provides for the citizenship revocation of terrorists who have demonstrably 'repudiated their allegiance to Australia.' Further Australian examples include the constitutional disqualification from parliament of MPs who hold dual citizenship, and proposed tightening of the eligibility criteria for naturalisation to include enhanced affirmations of allegiance, and to associate allegiance with national 'values'. The meaning of allegiance remains, nevertheless elusive, but such examples reveal that the core idea that allegiance to the state must be single and undivided has endured, despite the modern tolerance of dual citizenship. Similarly, the idea that conduct is relevant to citizenship is not new. It is, furthermore, encouraged by many normative theories of citizenship. This paper discusses Australian law as a case-study of allegiance in the conceptualisation of citizenship.

Introduction

The idea that allegiance is the core attribute or character of citizenship[1] is an ancient one, and the notion that the relationship between the citizen and the state is marked by allegiance is commonplace and enduring. We find it in legal history, in common law, in legislation and case law, in legal and political theory, and in many other contexts. Allegiance is central to legal schemes for the revocation of citizenship, and particularly relevant to such schemes in recent years in which terrorism is the principal ground for revocation.

Many modern commentators identify allegiance as fundamental to citizenship (see contributions to Macklin and Bauböck 2015; also Pillai and Williams 2017a for examples of political assertions of the centrality of allegiance to citizenship). Breach of allegiance or disloyalty are also frequently identified as the animating principle behind revocation schemes. Christian Joppke, for example, describes religiously inspired terrorism as privileging allegiance 'to the community of believers' over 'the community of political citizens' and argues that revocation is a proportionate response to a terrorist's acts (Joppke 2016, 732). A 2018 British 'think-tank' report describes citizenship as 'entail[ing] a duty of allegiance' (Ekins et al. 2018, 11) and foregrounds modern terrorism as a betrayal of that duty. Even theorists who reject the legitimacy of revocation locate allegiance in the concept of citizenship; Audrey Macklin, for example, writes that 'social solidarity, belonging and allegiance have a place in conceptions of citizenship and deserve to be promoted' (Macklin 2015, 6).

Citizenship revocation, however, is not a modern phenomenon, although the specific grounds for revocation have evolved over time (see Gibney 2013; Miller 2016; Barry and Ferracioli 2016). Revocation for terrorism is also unsurprising, given the normative weight that has been attached to individual conduct in much citizenship theory. This paper concentrates on the concept of allegiance in Australian citizenship law and policy, but suggests that Australia, notwithstanding some specific constitutional peculiarities (see Arcioni 2018), may serve as a case study of a wider phenomenon (at least in the 'Western' world). It concludes with a reflection on theoretical conceptions of citizenship and on the risks in associating citizenship with allegiance and in conceptualising citizenship in terms of personal conduct.

The historical background

The language of allegiance (or 'ligeance') as a legal term for nationality emerged in English law in feudal times. Most famously, it was central to the reasoning in the so-called *Calvin's Case* of 1608, in which Chief Justice Coke affirmed that English nationality was acquired by birth in the 'ligeance' (that is, territory) regardless of the nationality or status of the child's parents,[2] and declared that 'ligeance or obedience of the subject to the sovereign is due by the law of nature.'[3] Ligeance, Coke affirmed, 'is immutable and cannot be changed'. This common law principle of perpetual, indelible and indivisible allegiance – inhering, organically, by and from birth – endured until the mid-nineteenth century.

Deriving from these origins, and associated with the British (monarchical) concept of 'subject' (as opposed to the republican 'citizen'), the language of allegiance occupies a particular place in the common law world. It is, nevertheless, a concept that resonates in other legal systems (see Orgad 2014), as well as in legal and political theory. It (or its analogues 'loyalty' or 'commitment') is increasingly valorised in political movements around the world, in particular in its association with nationalism.[4]

The common law rule of perpetual allegiance was abandoned in the mid-nineteenth century. The prohibition on multiple citizenship was lifted or eased in many countries and by the international community in the second half of the twentieth century. There is little likelihood of a return to the old formulations. Still, the suspicion endures that dual nationals, or persons who acquire citizenship by naturalisation, or those with foreign family antecedents, may not be fully or single-mindedly allegiant. It is a long-standing part of Australia's history (albeit far from exclusive to Australia: see Brundage 2016), flaring up in particular in time of war and directed at those with 'enemy alien' lineages. Having grown relatively quiet in the post-WWII decades (the term was dropped from 1948 UK and Australian citizenship legislation), it has recently experienced a resurgence, stimulated by the apprehension of terrorism and by concerns that divided loyalties may pose a threat to the national interest. As Sandra Mantu writes of Britain's modern citizenship laws, 'allegiance has made a comeback ... [L]oyalty occupies an important discursive space in political imaginaries about what it means to be a citizen... [H]olding dual nationality is suspect and invites questions as to one's loyalty' (Mantu 2015, 10).

For all this, as is apparent from the legal initiatives discussed below, the meaning of 'allegiance' itself remains unclear and elusive. Despite the frequent and increasing use of the term in Australian law and policy, the concept has not acquired a clear modern meaning. The historical understanding in which allegiance (or 'ligeance') had, essentially, a territorial reference was clearer. But the modern use of the term suggests something more substantive. However, none of the 'definitions' that have been tackled in Australian law provides a distinct sense of content; nor have other countries' perspectives on Australia's law (see Ekins et al. 2018).

In a leading constitutional case (*Singh v Commonwealth of Australia*, 2014) regarding the legislative repeal in 1986 of citizenship acquisition by simple fact of birth in Australia, the High Court of Australia traversed historical understandings, foregrounding the feudal origins of the concept and its legislative evolution. Despite more than 200 references to 'allegiance' in the judgment, the Court failed to identify a modern definition. Indeed, as three of the judges commented:

> Using the concept 'allegiance' to distinguish between [citizens] and aliens invites attention to what is meant by 'allegiance'. Pointing to its root in the feudal idea of a personal duty of fealty to a lord ... does little to identify the content of the term. Plainly it is a term which connotes duty or obligation, but what exactly are the duties or obligations embraced by the word? ... The content of those duties or obligations is not spelled out. That may be because 'allegiance' and 'loyalty' are terms that point to a political or social relationship yet in this context are being used to describe a legal status.

However, despite the lack of clarity about the content of allegiance, what emerges from the political or social discussion is that 'allegiance' connotes a citizen-state relationship of singularity. Dual citizenship, while legally permitted sits uncomfortably with the idea that citizenship is defined by 'allegiance'. This, then, is the modern conundrum at the heart of schemes for citizenship revocation.

Citizenship revocation

In 1870, with the passage of Britain's Naturalization Act, the centuries-old common law rule that allegiance was perpetual and inalienable was abandoned. With this Act, it was recognised for the first time that a British-born subject could lawfully transfer allegiance to a foreign sovereign by naturalisation in a foreign country. Once this occurred, it was also accepted that British nationality could be revoked by the British sovereign/state; revocation happened initially through the Act's provision for loss of British nationality upon either a British person's foreign naturalisation[5] or a British woman's marriage to a foreigner. The status of British subject was, thus, no longer inviolable. The law and the policy that underpinned it were followed throughout the Empire, including in Australia, which has consistently provided for the revocation of birthright citizenship, as well as that of naturalised citizens.

Under Australia's Nationality Act 1920, a person who acquired British subject status by naturalisation could be denaturalised for, among other things, showing himself (or herself) 'by act or speech to be disaffected or disloyal to His Majesty.'[6] Australia's 1948 Nationality and Citizenship Act removed this provision, but provided that any citizen (dual national) who served in the armed forces of a country at war with Australia would 'cease to be an Australian citizen'. Subsequent versions of the Act have repeated this provision.[7] Numerically, these particular revocation grounds had little impact. They were, however, just the tip of the iceberg.

Until 2002, Australia also revoked the citizenship of any natural-born Australian citizen who had been (voluntarily) naturalised in a foreign citizenship; large numbers are likely to have lost their citizenship this way. More drastically, but often overlooked in the literature on revocation, between 1870 and 1948, Australia (as virtually everywhere else in the world over a comparable period: see Irving 2016) revoked the citizenship of women – native-born or naturalised – who married foreign men.[8] In doing so, Australia followed the provision of Britain's Naturalization Act of 1870 that 'deemed' a woman with a foreign husband to be the subject or citizen of her husband's country, and – as dual citizenship was not permitted under British law – thus, automatically, and without exception, revoked her British citizenship. The provision was reaffirmed in subsequent British legislation[9] and duplicated in Australia, enduring in both countries until 1948. Over time, probably hundreds of thousands of British and Australian women (not to mention countless numbers around the world) were affected, losing their premarital 'birthright' citizenship.

Under what principle was it assumed that loss of citizenship was appropriate, indeed proportionate, in either of these cases – a citizen's foreign naturalisation, or a woman's foreign marriage? The assumption was that each act represented a transfer of allegiance, a voluntary withdrawal of allegiance from the state/sovereign under which citizenship had been granted, and an attachment of that allegiance to another state/sovereign (in the woman's case, via allegiance to her husband, and thus his country[10]). These were not active expressions of *disallegiance*, in the sense of fighting for, or assisting the enemy, but the underlying idea was similar. Allegiance could not be divided or multiplied; it had to be singular. In the act of foreign naturalisation or foreign marriage, the full quantum of allegiance, it was thought, was withdrawn and transferred. The idea has endured, despite the repeal of these particular laws. Undivided allegiance and citizenship revocation remain two sides of the same coin.

In 2015, following the United Kingdom and Canada (see Pillai and Williams 2017a), Australia amended its Citizenship Act to establish new grounds under which Australian citizenship could be revoked. The Act, entitled *The Australian Citizenship Amendment (Allegiance to Australia) Act*, unequivocally signalled its normative framework by the words in brackets. The emphasis on allegiance in the Act's title was repeated in its statement of purpose[11]:

> This Act is enacted because the Parliament recognises that Australian citizenship is a common bond, involving reciprocal rights and obligations, and that citizens may, through certain conduct incompatible with the shared values of the Australian community, demonstrate that they have severed that bond and repudiated their allegiance to Australia.

The Act provides specifically for revocation, by executive act of the relevant government minister, of the Australian citizenship of persons (dual citizens) convicted of terrorist acts or acts supporting terrorism,[12] as well as automatic revocation for such acts committed in foreign countries. Such persons, in the Act's words, have demonstrably 'repudiated their allegiance to Australia.'[13] Notably, revocation only applies to persons with a citizenship additional to their Australian citizenship. This fact, however, does not challenge the underlying principle of single allegiance; it is purely a concession to the international rule against creating statelessness[14] (and a source of frustration to the Minister responsible for the law[15]).

The Allegiance to Australia Act was greeted with general public approval in Australia. Although its constitutional validity has been questioned, as has its conformity to the rule of law principle of equality before the law in distinguishing in its revocation scheme between sole and dual citizens, the Act has become relatively settled[16]; no constitutional challenge so far has been mounted against it.

In 2017 the Australian government sought to amend the Citizenship Act further, to make citizenship by naturalisation ('by conferral') significantly more difficult than it currently is. The Australian Citizenship Legislation Amendment (Strengthening the Requirements for Australian Citizenship and Other Measures) Bill 2017 was expressly conceptualised as a companion to the 2015 Allegiance to Australia Act. The proposed amendments included tightening naturalisation eligibility criteria by lengthening the (pre-application) period of legal residence in Australia, and toughening both the existing citizenship 'knowledge' test and the English language competency test. Additionally, the current naturalisation oath – the Citizenship Pledge[17] – in which 'loyalty' is pledged, was to be changed, to restore the pledge of *allegiance* (as it had been named until 1986). The word 'loyalty' in the preamble to the Citizenship Act would also be replaced with the word 'allegiance', and, as stated in the Explanatory Memorandum to the Bill, the preamble would otherwise be amended to 'make it clear that part of the common bond of Australian citizenship is allegiance to Australia and its people' (Commonwealth of Australia 2017b, 9). It failed, however, to offer any substantive distinction between 'loyalty' and 'allegiance', merely implying that 'allegiance' was a stronger term.

Introducing the Bill to the House of Representatives in June 2017, the then Minister for Immigration explained that the tightened eligibility measures would contribute to Australian security through the strengthening of 'Australian values': applicants for naturalisation would be required to sign an Australian Values Statement.[18] Furthermore, in addition to existing police background checks, the Minister said, 'an applicant [would] be assessed for specified conduct that is inconsistent with Australian values'.[19] The reworded pledge 'of allegiance' would be extended to 'all streams of citizenship by application'. The proposed changes, the Minister claimed, would reflect the expectation of the Australian community 'that aspiring citizens demonstrate their allegiance to our country, their commitment to live in accordance with Australian laws and values, and be willing to integrate into and become contributing members of the Australian community.'[20]

It quickly became clear that the animating idea behind these proposals was to prevent non-citizens who might be seen to have a weak or compromised allegiance to Australia from acquiring citizenship and with it the shield against deportation (which the revocation provisions of the 2015 Act are designed to combat, but are not effective against dual citizens). It was equally clear that the unspoken target of these initiatives was Islamic fundamentalism.

The proposed changes followed recommendations of the government's 2015 'National Consultation on Citizenship'. The Consultation's Final Report, *Australian Citizenship: Your Right, Your Responsibility*, speaks of citizenship as having a 'deeper sense' than its 'formal privileges', and it noted concerns that citizenship was 'undervalued by some in our community … most acute[ly] in the cases of Australians who by their conduct have chosen to break with the values inherent in being an Australian with a commitment to Australia first most and fore most' (Commonwealth of Australia 2015b, 3). Among other things, the Consultation recommended that the citizenship pledge 'should be updated to include language on allegiance to Australia', and that consideration should be given to expanding the 'usage' of the pledge to the broader community (for example, in the process for renewing a passport). It also recommended that the Citizenship Test for naturalisation should be 'updated' to include 'questions about allegiance and more questions about the rule of law, values and democratic rights and responsibilities' (8).

Much in these recommendations appears as a repeat of ideas that have been under discussion and debate for many years. But, what is significant here, is the idea (in tandem with the 2015 Allegiance to Australia Act) of identifying allegiance and national values as counterparts, and giving this legal recognition. Tying allegiance to values opens further space in thinking about the nature of both allegiance and disallegiance, and about revocation. It explains how it is possible, for instance, for an Australian citizen to be regarded under the 2015 Act as acting disallegiantly to Australia and repudiating the bond of Australian citizenship through allegiance to a non-state actor (such as ISIS), in a foreign country with which Australia is not at war, when legal sanctions against active disloyalty or treason have always previously presupposed a context of war or hostility between states. The repudiation of allegiance to Australia, in other words, could be evidenced in the embrace of 'un-Australian' values, regardless of their context. There was little ambiguity in the reasoning between the lines. Religiously inspired 'allegiance' – specifically Islamic extremism – was incompatible with Australian values and thus with undivided allegiance to Australia.

In the event, the 2017 Bill was defeated, but, notably, the primary objection raised in the parliamentary debate was to the proposed language and residency tests, and almost no concern was expressed about the allegiance provisions. Before its introduction to parliament, the Bill had been reviewed by a parliamentary committee. More than 600 public submissions were received; almost all opposed the Bill. But, again, while some raised the allegiance issue, the great majority addressed proposed changes to eligibility, and almost none tackled allegiance as a concept. The Committee's Report took note, briefly, of the objection that the term 'allegiance' was an outdated concept and that terms such as 'loyalty' and 'commitment' were 'more accessible and more widely understood'. It declined, however, to make any comments on such submissions, adding simply and blandly that it agreed that 'the civic literacy of many existing Australian citizens could do with some improvement.'[21]

The proposed Australian 'values' test attracted a few more reflections in submissions. The Muslim Legal Network (NSW) commented:

> [T]he proposals to introduce a ... 'values statement' (which references matters contrary to Australian law and is superfluous to the existing loyalty pledge) add no value to the citizenship application or process. Amendments in this regard will simply aid in marginalizing immigrants who were not schooled in Australia or born into an English speaking country or family. Furthermore, vulnerable residents such as refugees will likely feel added pressures regardless of their levels of integration or how much they may have contributed to the Australian social fabric.

It also pointed out the obvious disconnect between the desire to become an Australian citizen by naturalisation and the rejection of Australian values, noting the unlikelihood that an applicant would formally reject the values suggested in the proposal. It commented, further, albeit without elaboration, that values are vague and relative concepts.

Overall, however, the Bill's privileging of allegiance and values in its language of citizenship was accepted without protest. The lack of clarity surrounding the term 'allegiance' and the generic character of examples of Australian values[22] were (with rare exceptions) un-remarked.

Dual citizenship

An understanding of these initiatives must factor-in the historical repudiation of multiple citizenship and its decline over time. The conceptualisation of citizenship as an indivisible and inalienable relationship of allegiance between the citizen and the state meant that multiple citizenship was conceptually incoherent. Even after citizenship became alienable, the rule of single allegiance endured; dual nationality/citizenship was considered to be anathema (comparable to bigamy). Although it was acknowledged that it occurred as a regrettable accident of conflicting laws (see Boll 2007), it was treated as something to be reduced if not eliminated. Since the Second World War, however, the international community and many countries have gradually come to accept that dual citizenship is a growing reality, not necessarily desirable, but irreversible (see Spiro 2016). This acceptance took longer in Australia than in most comparable countries. In 2002, dual citizenship for Australian-born citizens was finally permitted, following the repeal of the section of the Australian Citizenship Act under which natural-born Australians who voluntarily acquired another citizenship would cease to be Australian. Its repeal followed much reflection on the nature of allegiance.

Over many years, official inquiries had considered proposals for repeal. In 1994, for example, the parliamentary Joint Standing Committee on Migration prepared a report, *Australians All: Enhancing Australian Citizenship*, in which, among other things, repeal was recommended. The 'overwhelming view' in public submissions to the Committee, it reported, was that 'Australia's insistence on single citizenship for those born in Australia [was] outmoded and discriminatory.' The Committee rejected 'the argument that a person could not owe allegiance or commitment to more than one country.' Several million Australians, it noted, were dual nationals (most by virtue of retaining a previous citizenship, having acquired Australian citizenship by naturalisation), and there was no evidence 'to suggest that these persons [were] disloyal or lack a commitment to Australia' (Commonwealth of Australia 1994, 206).

Significantly, and consistently with other reports, however, the Committee went on to recommend that the preamble to the Citizenship Act should be amended, to include a statement of 'obligation that all Australians should have an overriding and unifying commitment to Australia, to its interests and future first and foremost' (Commonwealth of Australia 1994, xxv). The suspicion conveyed in this view would prevail. Notwithstanding the end of citizenship revocation for foreign naturalisation eight years later, concerns about divided allegiance intensified over the following decades. It can reasonably be surmised that repeal of the provision, and tolerance for Australian dual citizenship, would find fewer supporters today. Singular, undivided allegiance – the historical legacy – is increasingly validated in social and political discourse and conceptually implied in the legal developments discussed. Constitutional jurisprudence has also contributed to this movement.

'Spilt' allegiance and eligibility for parliament

Despite its common and powerful use in other legal contexts, the term 'allegiance' does not appear in the Australian Constitution with reference to Australian citizens.[23] It is found, however, with reference to foreign citizenship. Section 44(i) of the Constitution states that:

> Any person who – ... Is under any acknowledgement of allegiance, obedience, or adherence to a foreign power, or is a subject or a citizen or entitled to the rights or privileges of a subject or citizen of a foreign power ... shall be incapable of being chosen or of sitting as a senator or a member of the House of Representatives.

Notwithstanding several official inquiries into this section over the years, and recommendations that it should be the subject of constitutional amendment (see Commonwealth of Australia 2018a), it slumbered, largely undisturbed, for most of the life of the Constitution. Over the decades, probably hundreds of Members of Parliament with dual citizenship have sat unchallenged and – to all appearances – fully allegiant to Australia. In 2017, however, the provision dramatically awoke, with the revelation that a number of sitting MPs held, or might hold, a foreign citizenship in addition to Australian, bringing their constitutional eligibility to serve in parliament into question. This revelation – publicised initially and opportunistically by party political opponents – set in train an exploration of the Constitution's section, attracting major public and media attention as well as extensive legal analysis, and leading to several High Court cases.

In the first and most significant of the recent cases (*Re Canavan,* 2017), the High Court ruled unanimously on the status of seven individual MPs. Acting as the Court of Disputed Returns, it had first to determine whether each was, in fact, under the law of another country, a foreign citizen (five were found to be) and secondly, whether the section should be interpreted in such a way as to render them ineligible to sit. Allegiance was at the heart of this question. The Court had, thus, the opportunity to explore modern meanings of the concept. But, as in the 2004 case of *Singh*, it failed to coherently identify substantive content. Indeed, it further muddied the conceptual waters. Again, what emerged was simply an affirmation of the singularity of allegiance.

The term 'allegiance,' we note, appears only in the first clause of the Constitution's section; in none of the instances where eligibility was at issue did the question of whether an MP was 'under any acknowledgement of allegiance … to a foreign power' arise. Despite this, allegiance was much discussed both in the case and in public commentary. The purpose of the section, the Court agreed – that which the Constitution's framers (in the late 1890s) appeared to have intended – was to avoid 'split allegiance.' The matter revolved around, essentially, two questions. First, what sort of obligations or commitments might a person who was a citizen of another country be bound by, or might undertake, by virtue of their foreign citizenship potentially against Australia's interests, either by choice or because the law of that country required it? In other words, might foreign citizenship lead a member of the Australian parliament into disallegiance? Secondly – a related question – how might an MP have a split allegiance if he or she was ignorant of being a citizen of a foreign power (as, quite reasonably on the facts, almost all the MPs in this case claimed to be)?

The first question was answered by the Court in the abstract: citizenship of a foreign country, it suggested, always carried with it the potential for obligations of allegiance (such as military service) to be imposed by that country upon the citizen. Whether these obligations amounted to, or could be characterised as, acts of disallegiance to Australia was not addressed. Again, beyond the hypothetical (and incomplete) example of military service, 'the duties or obligations embraced by the word' were not spelled out.

The second question – the knowledge question – was considered more closely, particularly in response to the government's vigorous submission to the Court that allegiance could not be engaged if an individual was unaware of his or her citizenship. Notably, the government did not claim that dual citizenship was compatible with undivided allegiance to Australia, but, rather, that the threat of split allegiance could not arise when foreign citizenship was not acknowledged. The Court disagreed, unequivocally rejecting what it called the 'mental element' argument, concluding that subjective allegiance (either to Australia or the country of foreign citizenship) was not relevant to the inquiry, and that a test of knowledge would create uncertainties and might invite 'wilful blindness' on the part of individuals about the possibility that they might hold foreign citizenship.

Here, the High Court advanced a formalistic understanding of allegiance – namely, that if the law of a foreign country deemed a person to be a citizen of that country, that fact alone was a sufficient affirmation of foreign allegiance. It was not consistent, however. The Court identified certain exceptions to the principle that foreign citizenship was incompatible with service in the Australian parliament, illustrated by hypothetical examples: foreign law that prohibited the renunciation of citizenship; or that required an unreasonable, excessive or dangerous procedure for renunciation; or, more wildly, that mischievously purported to confer automatic citizenship upon all Australian MPs, thus rendering the whole parliament ineligible. Foreign law, the Court added, should not 'irremediably' prevent an Australian citizen from enjoying his or her (implied) constitutional right to take part in Australia's representative democracy.

The idea that allegiance meant something more substantive than mere entitlement to legal citizenship – something inhering in citizenship, beyond the formal law – did not go away. Still, it remained unresolved.

What the Court's decision meant, in practice, however, was (apart from the enforced resignation of the MPs in question) that any dual citizen who henceforth wished to nominate as a candidate for the federal parliament must renounce his or her non-Australian citizenship(s), even if the foreign citizenship has never been activated. Furthermore, the renunciation, so the Court held in a subsequent case (*Re Gallagher*, 2018) in which lengthy delays in the foreign country's administration of renunciation applications were at issue, must be acknowledged and authorised by the foreign country, or the foreign country's refusal to accept an application for renunciation must be certified, regardless of how long this takes. In reaching this conclusion, the Court's apparent tolerance for dual allegiance in exceptional cases was seriously diminished.

Renunciation is often difficult, complicated and costly. It does not directly equal revocation, but its effect is not dissimilar. Rights, including the core right to live in the country of one's (former) citizenship, are similarly lost. Family and cultural connections may be severed. Nomination as a candidate for parliament is, of course, voluntary, but this fact does not as such distinguish it from the acts that have been counted as pre-conditions for revocation. The law has always treated the acts justifying revocation – foreign military service, foreign naturalisation, foreign marriage, terrorism – as voluntary.

The price a dual citizen must pay for nominating for the Australian parliament is high. The Court's decision is likely to have a chilling effect on potential candidates (in particular, as minor party candidates), especially immigrants or the children of immigrants. The broader message, again, is one of single allegiance as an indicator of true citizenship. In the public debate surrounding the constitutional eligibility cases, it was even suggested by some that failure to investigate possible dual citizenship might be evidence in itself of 'split allegiance', a breach of trust with the Australian people (Finlay 2017).

The sudden and dramatic burst of interest in the previously dormant provision of the Australian Constitution (in a national culture marked by low levels of public knowledge about, or interest in, the Constitution) was not an isolated event. It coincided with heightened political and public perception of foreign allegiance as a threat and with the new legislative scheme for citizenship revocation for terrorist acts. It emerged in a context of growing suspicion of dual and foreign citizenship generally. Although the major political parties and most of the media were careful to avoid targeting any particular sector of the community, the persistent, underlying inference in these developments was that Islamic 'allegiance' was the concern.

To at least one minor party politician, Senator Pauline Hanson (leader of the 'One Nation' party), the connection was indisputable. Australia, Hanson said in a speech to the Senate in September 2016, was 'in danger of being swamped by Muslims, who bear a culture and ideology that is incompatible with our own'; among other defects, she claimed, Muslims were 'not prepared to become Australian and give this country [their] undivided loyalty'.

Hanson's speech (and her stunt of wearing a burqa in the Senate chamber) was roundly denounced by major party leaders and mainstream media. However, the discourse of undivided allegiance, and its resurgence in Australian law and government initiatives in the same period, cannot be isolated from the cultural context in which this speech was given. Notably, a 2017 opinion poll found that, while a majority of Australians supported a multicultural intake in immigration, the percentage of respondents who reported a positive attitude to Muslims had fallen since 2010 from 31.9% to 28.3%, albeit with a smaller rise in 'negative attitude' to Muslims, from 23.5% to 25%. Commentators attributed these shifts to, among other things, Senator Hanson's campaign.[24]

Conclusion

Notwithstanding changes over many decades in Australia's citizenship law, the idea that allegiance is the core element of citizenship and, as such, must be undivided, never disappeared. This idea, as well as the view that certain acts on the part of individual citizens in which allegiance is implicated merit revocation, can be found in what may appear to be disparate developments. Far from disparate, they are intermeshed. We note that, in the past, two types of justification for citizenship revocation have presented themselves: active disallegiance, and transfer of allegiance. Transfer of allegiance was not necessarily threatening, but was in conflict with the rule against dual citizenship. Revocation laws, past and present (and the disqualification of dual citizens from parliament) were built upon the principle that allegiance must be singular.

In short, while Australian law now permits Australian-born citizens to hold dual citizenship, at key moments it reveals its apprehension of that which it permits, and draws back from its apparent tolerance for divided allegiance. Although the new regime for revocation has been cast as a retreat from the common law principle that citizenship is not conditioned upon conduct, and signalling now that citizens 'are no longer able to expect that their membership of the community will be retained irrespective of their actions' (Pillai and Williams 2017b, 554), the picture is more complex than this.

With the abandonment of the doctrine of inalienability of allegiance, individual conduct became directly relevant to the concept of citizenship; that is to say, 'allegiance' (and thus, nationality) was no longer ascribed to the whole class of persons born in the relevant territory, but could be removed following measures or tests that applied to individuals (a person's foreign naturalisation; a woman's foreign marriage; a man's military service to an enemy state). Still, the principle of allegiance remained central. The degree to which this idea was expressed in law has waxed and waned over time. In the decades immediately after the Second World War, it appeared to wane. In 1946, one international law scholar, indeed, concluded that the term 'allegiance' to describe the relationship of citizen to state was inapt and 'archaic' (Koessler 1946, 68). Its current waxing is evident in recent legal developments in which allegiance is given a heightened role in conceptualising the right to retain citizenship, and is specifically associated with the idea that Islamic terrorism represents a form of repudiation and transfer of allegiance.

A person may, under law, hold dual citizenship, but 'dualism', these developments suggest, cannot extend to allegiance. The feudal idea of indivisible allegiance to a single sovereign has not been exhausted by changes in the law. Allegiance, we find repeatedly affirmed, must be singular. To reject Australian values by actively extending allegiance to a foreign 'sovereign' (whether another state or some other power) – one that represents alternative 'values' – is accordingly thought to sever the common bond of allegiance that unites all Australian citizens.

This is not just an Australian view,[25] although Australian law has gone a good distance in manifesting it. It is a view that has been intensifying around the world in the last two decades, both in law and in resurgent nationalist political movements. It is also a view that has its seeds in, and has been encouraged by, the heavily normative understandings of citizenship that have been advanced in political theory since the 1980s. In short, if citizenship, as argued by many theorists, represents (or should represent) qualities in the individual of civic virtue, commitment to the polity, and 'republican' values (see Dagger 1997; also Irving 2016 for a critique), it is not surprising or inconsistent for law-makers to pick up this idea, and to invest citizenship with their version of similar qualities, including with the conclusion that persons who actively reject the norms or values that nourish these qualities are not entitled to the status of citizen.

Schemes for the revocation of citizenship encourage the idea that the allegiance of citizens should be fostered, or even tested by the state.[26] They sit alongside a conceptualisation of citizenship as a relationship of attachment between the citizen and his or her country, an attachment that is necessarily single and undivided. This notion appears both anti-cosmopolitan and illiberal (see Gibney 2013; Orgad 2014). It also denies the global reality of multiple citizenship. The assumption of allegiance as an attribute that entails a positive, unidirectional affect fosters a discourse of unwelcome to non-citizens. Paradoxically, it also encourages suspicion of fellow citizens.

This is not to say that there can be no justification for revocation of citizenship on allegiance grounds, but reasoned argument for revocation will focus on the wider social or public value, rather than the motivation or mentality of the individual. For some theorists, revocation sends a positive social message that the state will protect its members (see Finnis 2008; also Joppke 2016; Miller 2016). Others reach a contrary conclusion about the likely wider impact. Macklin, for example, argues that revocation 'only enhances discretionary and arbitrary power of the executive, at the expense of all citizens, and of citizenship itself' (Macklin 2015, 6). Sociological evidence over time will be needed if any of these propositions are to be conclusive. But official initiatives in countries like Australia, adopted in the name of securing the 'common bond' by enhancing allegiance and rooting out disallegiance, would suggest that Macklin's warning has cautionary force. The adoption of new executive powers over revocation has had, it appears, a 'multiplier' effect, leading to further and more generalised initiatives in which distrust of dual citizens is signalled.

The Australian case is not unique, either historically or comparatively; the legal and political narrative in other comparable countries follows not-dissimilar lines. Undivided allegiance has never been absent from the concept and discourse of citizenship. In recent times, however, it has been newly energised, and has found a new object.

Notes

1. For economy and simplicity, I use the term 'citizenship' generically, to refer to the legal concepts of nationality or subject status, as well as to the status of citizenship itself, unless otherwise required by context.
2. Known in law as the *jus soli* principle: its exceptions applied to children born to diplomatic representatives of foreign countries, or fathered by men from invading armies. The fathers in these cases were said to owe allegiance to a foreign sovereign.
3. The sovereign's protection was the other side of what was conceptualised as a reciprocal relationship. Protection is not the subject of this paper, but also deserves attention with regard to a country's legal obligations to its own citizens. For a modern analysis see Pillai and Williams 2017b.
4. In Denmark, for example, recent laws designed to instil 'Danish values' in immigrant communities have been promoted as a means of protecting the traditional national culture and fostering a 'commitment' to Denmark. See Prime Minister Lars Lokke Rasmussen's 2018 New Year Address, http://stm.dk/_p_14611.html.
5. The Act, however, provided for such a person who was 'desirous of remaining a British subject' to make a declaration of that desire, subject to taking the oath of allegiance, and with the restriction that British nationality could not be held in the foreign state in which the person had been naturalised. This declaration right was dropped in the British Nationality and Status of Aliens Act 1914. Foreign naturalisation ceased to be a ground for revocation of British nationality in 1948.
6. The expression, with the substitution of the pronoun 'Her' after the ascension of Elizabeth II, endured in British citizenship legislation until 2002.
7. The Citizenship Act, as amended in 2015, restates it as '[s]ervice outside Australia in armed forces of an enemy country or a declared terrorist organisation.'
8. In 1936 (following the Hague Nationality Convention of 1930) Australia's Nationality Act was amended so that Australian wives of foreign men would retain their citizenship in the event that they did not, upon marriage, acquire the citizenship of their husband. Britain's law had been amended similarly in 1933.
9. Although, in 1914, under the British Nationality and Status of Aliens Act, the wording was changed: the woman married to an alien was deemed to be an alien. In 1918, the Act was amended to permit British-born women who had lost their British nationality through foreign marriage to apply for its restoration in the event of widowhood or divorce; that is, when the marriage ceased to 'subsist' under law. Many other countries adopted similar exceptions to their marital denationalisation laws (see Irving 2016).
10. It was assumed, although not investigated by the revoking country, that the woman would automatically acquire her husband's nationality under his country's law. Automatic naturalisation of all women who married citizens did occur in many countries, including Britain (after 1844), but not all, and not for all classes of women (notably, the USA: see Aleinikoff 1986; Volpp 2005).
11. The Preamble to the Australian Citizenship Act (2007) itself, however, currently uses the term 'loyalty': http://www.austlii.edu.au/cgibin/viewdoc/au/legis/cth/consol_act/aca2007254/preamble.html .
12. Terrorism is defined in the Commonwealth (Federal) Criminal Code, as 'an action or threat of action where: ... (b) the action is done or the threat is made with the intention of advancing a political, religious or ideological cause; and (c) the action is done or the threat is made with the intention of: (i) coercing, or influencing by intimidation, the government of the Commonwealth [of Australia] or a State, Territory or foreign country, or of part of a State, Territory or foreign country; or (ii) intimidating the public or a section of the public.
13. Neither the amending Act nor the principal Citizenship Act, however, define 'allegiance'.
14. The UN Convention on the Reduction of Statelessness (1961) does permit revocation leading to statelessness for conduct that is 'inconsistent[] with [a person's] duty of loyalty to the Contracting State' (the state that grants citizenship) (as well as for misrepresentation

or fraud in the application for citizenship). The 'loyalty' exception, however, has limitations that would make it difficult for Australia to rely on in its revocation scheme.

15. See the speech by the Minister for Home Affairs, Peter Dutton, on 21 February 2018: https://minister.homeaffairs.gov.au/peterdutton/Pages/Address-to-the-National-Press-Club-of-Australia.aspx.
16. Legally, the Act was much less controversial than its first version (as a Bill), which was subject to an inquiry by the Parliamentary Joint Committee on Intelligence and Security. The Committee, after receiving many public submissions and holding hearings with witnesses, made multiple recommendations for amendment, and these were incorporated in the Bill before its passage through parliament. See Commonwealth of Australia 2015a.
17. 'From this time forward I pledge my loyalty to Australia and its people, whose democratic beliefs I share, whose rights and liberties I respect, and whose laws I will uphold and obey.'
18. It is already required of individuals applying for non-temporary visas; they are required to sign a statement: *I confirm that I have read, or had explained to me, information provided by the Australian Government on Australian society and values.* A list of values and commitments follows. The list, as provided in an official booklet, describes Australian values as including: 'respect for equal worth, and the dignity and freedom of the individual; freedom of speech; freedom of religion and secular government; freedom of association; support for parliamentary democracy and the rule of law; equality under the law; equality of men and women; equality of opportunity; peacefulness; a spirit of egalitarianism that embraces tolerance, mutual respect and compassion for those in need.' The booklet explains that 'these values may be expressed in different ways by different people while still maintaining the same meaning. They are not unique to Australia, but have broad community agreement and underpin Australian society and culture.' (Commonwealth of Australia 2016).
19. Note the statement of purpose to the 2015 Allegiance to Australia Act, which speaks of 'conduct incompatible with the shared values of the Australian community'.
20. In the Prime Minister's 'National Security Statement' to parliament, 13 June 2017, which outlined the various measures taken by the government to combat terrorism and enhance security, including the proposed changes to the Citizenship Act, the then PM, Malcolm Turnbull, used the language of 'patriotism': '[W]e should make no apologies for asking those who seek to join our Australian family [as citizens] to join us as Australian patriots – committed to the values that define us, committed to the values that unite us.' https://www.pm.gov.au/media/national-security-statement.
21. Senate Standing Committee on Legal and Constitutional Affairs, Final Report (Commonwealth of Australia 2017a, 29).
22. See note 18.
23. Except in a Schedule reciting the Oath or Affirmation that all federal MPs are required to make before taking office.
24. https://www.smh.com.au/politics/federal/fairfax-ipsos-poll-australians-split-on-muslim-migration-ahead-of-new-population-policy-20181118-p50gt0.html.
25. Note the 2008 UK Goldsmith Report for the Ministry of Justice, entitled 'Citizenship: Our Common Bond', which is echoed (without reference) in Australia's 2018 'booklet' for intending or newly-naturalised Australians: 'Australian Citizenship: Our Common Bond' (Commonwealth of Australia 2018b).
26. The type of inquisition carried out by the United States House Committee on Un-American Activities in the Cold War years may now appear obsolete, but its justification, in its time (rooting out subversive influence in public life, with a particular focus on communism) was cast in terms not-dissimilar to the rationale for modern citizenship revocation schemes, and in associated citizenship theory.

Acknowledgments

Research for this paper has been generously supported by an Australian Research Council Discovery Grant, and the invaluable assistance of Kristin Macintosh.

Disclosure statement

No potential conflict of interest was reported by the author.

References

Aleinikoff, T. A. 1986. "Theories of Loss of Citizenship." *Michigan Law Review* 84 (7): 1471–1503. doi:10.2307/1288994.

Arcioni, E. 2018. "Citizenship." In *The Oxford Handbook of the Australian Constitution*, edited by C. Saunders and A. Stone, Part III, 14. Oxford: Oxford University Press.

Barry, C., and L. Ferracioli. 2016. "Can Withdrawing Citizenship Be Justified?" *Political Studies* 64 (4): 1055–1070. doi:10.1177/0032321715606569.

Boll, A. M. 2007. *Multiple Nationality and International Law*. Leiden/Boston: Martinus Nijhoff.

Brundage, D. 2016. "Allegiance, Dual Citizenship, and the Ethnic Influence on U.S. Foreign Policy." In *The Oxford Handbook of American Immigration and Ethnicity*, edited by R. H. Bayor. Oxford University Press. Online edition https://www-oxfordhandbooks-com.ezproxy1.library.usyd.edu.au/view/10.1093/oxfordhb/9780199766031.001.0001/oxfordhb-9780199766031-e-022

Commonwealth of Australia. 1994. *Australians All: Enhancing Australian Citizenship*. Joint Standing Committee on Migration. Canberra: AGPS.

Commonwealth of Australia. 2015a. *Advisory Report on the Australian Citizenship Amendment (Allegiance to Australia) Bill 2015*. Canberra: Parliamentary Joint Committee on Intelligence and Security. www.aph.gov.au/Parliamentary_Business/Committees/Joint/Intelligence_and_Security/Citizenship_Bill/Report

Commonwealth of Australia. 2015b. *Final Report: Australian Citizenship: Your Right, Your Responsibility*. Canberra: National Consultation on Citizenship. https://www.homeaffairs.gov.au/Citizenship/Documents/australian-citizenship-report.

Commonwealth of Australia. 2016. *Life in Australia: Australian Values and Principles*. Canberra: Department of Immigration and Border Protìtion. https://www.homeaffairs.gov.au/LifeinAustralia/Documents/lia_english_full.pdf.

Commonwealth of Australia. 2017a. *Final Report. The Senate Legal and Constitutional Affairs Legislation Committee, Australian Citizenship Legislation Amendment (Strengthening the Requirements for Australian Citizenship and Other Measures) Bill 2017*. https://www.aph.gov.au/Parliamentary_Business/Committees/Senate/Legal_and_Constitutional_Affairs/CitizenshipBill2017/Report

Commonwealth of Australia. 2017b. *Explanatory Memorandum to Australian Citizenship Legislation Amendment (Strengthening the Requirements for Australian Citizenship and Other Measures) Bill*

2017. http://parlinfo.aph.gov.au/parlInfo/search/display/display.w3p;query=Id%3A%22legislation%2Fems%2Fr5914_ems_93402f76-ce95-4678-928f-9d18e6de4fda%22.

Commonwealth of Australia. 2018a. *Excluded: The Impact of Section 44 on Australian Democracy.* Canberra: Parliamentary Joint Committee on Electoral Matters. www.aph.gov.au/Parliamentary_Business/Committees/Joint/Electoral_Matters/Inquiry_into_matters_relating_to_Section_44_of_the_Constitution/Report_1.

Commonwealth of Australia. 2018b. *Australian Citizenship: Our Common Bond.* Canberra: Department of Home Affairs. https://www.homeaffairs.gov.au/Citizenship/Documents/our-common-bond.PDF.

Dagger, R. 1997. *Civic Virtues: Rights, Citizenship, and Republican Liberalism.* New York: Oxford University Press.

Ekins, R., P. Hennessey, K. Mahmood, and T. Tugendhat. 2018. *Aiding the Enemy: How and Why to Restore the Law of Treason.* London: Policy Exchange.

Finlay, L. 2017. "Near Enough May Not Be Good Enough as Parliament's Dual Citizenship Crisis Deepens." *The Conversation* 6 (December). https://theconversation.com/near-enough-may-not-be-good-enough-as-parliaments-dual-citizenship-crisis-deepens-88565.

Finnis, J. 2008. "Nationality, Alienage and Constitutional Principle." *University of Oxford Faculty of Law Legal Studies Research Paper Series. Working Paper no. 08/2008.*

Gibney, M. 2013. "Should Citizenship Be Conditional? the Ethics of Denationalization." *The Journal of Politics* 75 (3): 646–658.

Irving, H. 2016. *Citizenship, Alienage and the Modern Constitutional State: A Gendered History.* Cambridge: Cambridge University Press.

Joppke, C. 2016. "Terror and the Loss of Citizenship." *Citizenship Studies* 20 (6–7): 728–748. doi:10.1080/13621025.2016.1191435.

Koessler, M. 1946. "'Subject,' 'Citizen,' 'National,' and 'Permanent Allegiance'." *Yale Law Journal* 56: 58–76. doi:10.2307/793250.

Macklin, A. 2015. "Kick-Off Contribution." In *The Return of Banishment: Do the New Denationalisation Policies Weaken Citizenship?* edited by A. Macklin and R. Bauböck. Florence: EUI Working Paper RSCAS 2015/14. http://cadmus.eui.eu/handle/1814/34617

Macklin, A., and R. Bauböck, eds. 2015. *The Return of Banishment: Do the New Denationalisation Policies Weaken Citizenship?* Florence: EUI Working Paper, RSCAS 2015/14.

Mantu, S. 2015. "Citizenship in Times of Terror: Citizenship Deprivation in the UK." Paper prepared for ECPR Standing Groups, Warsaw, March 29–April 2.

Miller, D. 2016. "Democracy, Exile, and Revocation." *Ethics & International Affairs* 30 (2): 265–270. doi:10.1017/S0892679416000137.

Orgad, L. 2014. "Liberalism, Allegiance, and Obedience: The Inappropriateness of Loyalty Oaths in a Liberal Democracy." *Canadian Journal of Law and Jurisprudence* 27: 99. doi:10.1017/S084182090000624X.

Pillai, S., and G. Williams. 2017a. "The Utility of Citizenship Stripping Laws in the UK, Canada and Australia." *Melbourne University Law Review* 41 (2): 845.

Pillai, S., and G. Williams. 2017b. "Twenty-First Century Banishment: Citizenship Stripping In Common Law Nations." *International Comparative Law Quarterly* 66: 521. doi:10.1017/S0020589317000021.

Spiro, P. J. 2016. *At Home in Two Countries: The past and Future of Dual Citizenship.* New York: New York University Press.

Volpp, L. 2005. "Divesting Citizenship: On Asian American History and the Loss of Citizenship through Marriage." *UCLA Law Review* 53: 357.

Citizenship revocation: a stress test for liberal democracy

Janie Pélabay and Réjane Sénac

Abstract

This chapter sheds some light on why and how citizenship revocation currently acts as a borderline case with regard to liberal democracy. On the basis of the case studies of Australia, Canada, France, the Netherlands, the UK and the US collected in this edited volume, we analyse what is philosophically at stake in public discourses and policies about citizenship revocation, and how the latter questions and even destabilises liberal democracy. Firstly, we ask whether such destabilising effects consist not only in intensifying some internal tensions but in conjuring up dilemmas which imply a possible exit from liberal democracy or, at least, a decoupling between liberalism and democracy. Investigating this possible shift from tensions to dilemmas, we underline that the liberal dimension of citizenship, based on individual rights, have lost importance in setting out the conditions of access to the political 'us'. Conversely, both the republican and communitarian claims, based on civic virtue and collective identity respectively, have gained prominence and have converged on a primary interest in a 'thick' common bond. Finally, we examine two specific issues the book shows to be of key interest in understanding how citizenship revocation puts liberal democracy to the test: on the one hand, the challenge to cosmopolitanism as posed by the return of patriotism and, on the other hand, the state promotion of shared values as a means to secure national identity, thus expressing an ethicisation-cum-ethnicisation of citizenship.

Introduction

Promoted by public authorities as a means to ensure the primary good of security and to fight against Islamist terrorism, citizenship revocation appears to be both 'exceptional' and 'pragmatic' since it is part and parcel of the discourse and practice of an emergency regime in search of effective and lasting solutions. It is worth taking some distance from this 'framework of exception, suggesting a practice reserved for the most dangerous and undesirable of citizens' (Troy, *this volume*, 10) and of political pragmatism (Fargues; Boekestein and de Groot, *this volume*), as all the chapters collected in this edited volume invite us to do. Based on a variety of combined approaches – legal, political, sociological and historical – and of case studies – Australia, Canada, France, the Netherlands, the United Kingdom and the the United States of America – they all highlight the depoliticisation process of the narrative of emergency policies and, more specifically, of counter-terrorism which is used in support of denationalisation measures. Operating in the name of national security, such a process makes it difficult or illegitimate to debate citizenship revocation as a matter of political choice among different visions of justice. With a view to unveiling what is obscured by these depoliticising effects, the chapters in this volume explore the historical continuity and socio-political frames underpinning what is investigated here as the 'revival' (Fargues; Winter and Previsic, *this volume*) of citizenship revocation.

In the same vein, and with a similar purpose, our contribution in this volume belongs within a field of enquiry explicitly focused on the theoretical issues raised by the current controversy surrounding deprivation of citizenship. While the chapters all provide a fascinating glimpse of these issues, we will address them more directly by clarifying what is philosophically at stake in the controversial revival of denationalisation. More precisely, we will analyse what this renewed interest in citizenship revocation suggests about the challenges posed to liberal democracy. As shown by the chapters in this volume, the contemporary public and academic debate over the deprivation of citizenship reveals how the latter questions, and indeed destabilises, liberal democracy. The core ideals of liberal democracy as well as the public institutions and policies dedicated to putting these ideals into practice are the principal objects of such destabilisation. All of these elements are being tested for internal consistency and for relevance to citizens and the larger society.

In the remainder of this afterword, our aim is to shed some light on why and how citizenship revocation currently acts as a borderline case with regard to liberal democracy. On the basis of the contributions in this edited volume, we will first consider how citizenship revocation affects liberal democracy both from within and from without. We will look at whether it results not only in the intensification of a number of internal tensions but also in the creation of dilemmas which imply a possible exit from liberal democracy or, at the very least, a decoupling of liberalism and democracy. To analyse this potential shift from tensions to dilemmas, we will return to the three dimensions of citizenship – namely: rights, participation, identity – mentioned in the editors' introduction to this volume (Fargues and Winter) and investigated by Winter and Previsic in relation to Canada. We will then examine how these dimensions relate to each other in terms of a normative priority for setting out the conditions of access to citizenship. Finally, we will focus on two specific issues which the chapters in this volume show to be of key interest in investigating such a possible shift: on the one hand, the challenge to cosmopolitanism as posed by the return of patriotism and, on the other hand, the promotion of common values as a means to ensure national security and, by the same token, strengthen the ethical-cum-cultural integrity of national identity.

Citizenship revocation as a borderline case

In their introduction, the editors of this edited volume refer to Brubaker (1992) and Nyers (2009), respectively, in order to remind us that citizenship as such can be approached 'as a mechanism of "social closure"' which provides an 'exclusionary function' (Fargues and Winter, 3). In this view, citizenship is about delineating the boundaries of the political 'us' by defining who is – and who is not –subject of the benefits and burdens, the rights and duties attached to being a citizen, what conditions must be satisfied to this end, and by what procedure this is achieved. These are pillars of any concept and practice of citizenship which justify analysing deprivation of citizenship through the prism of exclusion, as all the contributions to this volume do brilliantly. At the same time, two elements of reflection must be added and considered in order to better understand why and how citizenship revocation acts as a borderline case which puts liberal democracy to the test.

To begin with, it is worth emphasising that the debate on denaturalisation and the national cases investigated in this volume do not deal with just any form of citizenship but with liberal-democratic citizenship. Nor do they deal with any reading of the 'closure' and 'exclusionary' dimension pertaining to citizenship generally speaking: instead, what is at stake is a variant of exclusion specific to liberal democracy. As a consequence, this form of exclusion must meet the basic moral, legal and political standards of liberal citizenship. This raises the issue of a particular version of citizenship through which democracy as the government of the people, by the people and for the people is conceptually and practically imbued with, and constrained by, the liberal principles and norms of the rule of law and the constitutional state. In that respect, when Patti Lenard (2016, 73) is questioned (Cohen 2016; Herzog 2016; Miller 2016) on her thesis that 'the claimed power to revoke citizenship in democratic states [...] is incompatible with democracy', her concept of democracy equates, in fact, with liberalism, and even with justificatory liberalism. She indeed concludes that citizenship revocation is 'undemocratic' on the basis of a liberal principle of non-discrimination and equal treatment as well as procedural norms of justice such as transparent justification and proportionality of penalties. Such a form of liberal citizenship is informed by strong expectations that individual liberties and the fundamental rights of all human beings will be respected, regardless of their different and competing visions of the good and of the world. Liberal citizenship is – at least in principle – governed by a logic of openness and pluralism which is both universalistic and individualistic in nature. Democracy, on the other hand, focuses on collective autonomy and self-government, thus prioritising the will and the sovereignty of the people, the pursuit of the common good and the flourishing of the political community as a whole. Consequently, liberal democracy, from the outset, is fuelled by a variety of diverging foundations, requirements and purposes which still need to be reconciled (Bobbio 1990; Graham 1992; Habermas 1996). Therefore, while embodying at its best the exclusionary aspect of any model of citizenship, deprivation of *liberal* citizenship is likely to exacerbate the inner tensions constitutive of liberal democracy. In a liberal state, citizenship revocation takes a paradoxical turn. Hence the widely debated question (Fargues 2017; Joppke 2016; Macklin 2018), to which we will return below, as to whether denationalisation can be liberal at all, if it is at odds with the liberal principles of justice or if it represents a legitimate 'illiberal' means to secure a liberal regime. In the context of the 'war on terror', such securitisation is analysed by Sykes (*this volume*, 72) as operating through a 'civic republican discourse', based on loyalty of the good citizen, which 'open[s] up a space of exception in' a liberal discourse that defines citizenship as a body of individual rights. The republican conception of citizenship acts here as a 'tool designed to effect the limitation' of the political arena such as delineated by liberal norms, thus justifying the exclusion of 'undesirable' groups – terror suspects, naturalised citizens – from political life (Sykes, *this volume*, 72).

This is all the more important now that the above 'paradox of liberal citizenship revocation' has emerged in a context where '9/11 marked a turning point' (Sykes, *this volume*, 65). In such a context, this paradox is being intensified by various forms of resurgent nationalism which manifests itself in worldwide pleas for a robust patriotism and in the public promotion of common values as a precondition of inclusion within the citizenry. The electoral successes of 'populist' parties in many parts of the world over the last decade illustrate a strengthening of the moral and cultural boundaries of citizenship. Similarly, the discourse of an 'open society', proud of its 'diversity' and in search of 'global justice', is dramatically declining and losing its political attractiveness. What is more, the formal requirement – even in a superficial, purely rhetorical manner – to justify state action in the liberal language of basic rights has also been dropped. As this decline in 'justificatory liberalism' increases, it may well be the case that the test of a liberal democracy, as reflected by the contemporary discourse on and practice of citizenship revocation, will go beyond the limited scope (and, as it were, conventional framework) of internal tensions. It may turn into a series of far-reaching dilemmas: universalism *vs* particularism, cosmopolitanism *vs* patriotism, pluralism *vs* homogeneity, neutrality *vs* partiality, etc., and of course inclusiveness *vs* exclusion.

Talking about dilemmas rather than mere tensions that liberal democracies are used to managing implies that a choice has to be made between one of two alternatives. This is the second and ultimate reason why citizenship revocation should be considered as currently acting as a borderline case: the manner in which it is defended by some particular governments rightly or wrongly labelled as 'populist' (Freeden 2017; Müller 2016) possibly means a resolute choice for 'illiberal democracy'. At this point, the question becomes one of determined illiberalism, and not of still emerging or indeed failed reconciliation between liberalism and democracy.

In sum, the above two considerations, once put together, contribute to making deprivation of liberal-democratic citizenship a borderline case in the sense that it raises the question as to whether a transition from tensions to dilemmas is taking place within liberal democracy. In what follows, we will focus on how such a possible shift presents itself within the concept of 'conditional citizenship' (Gibney 2013), thus analysing what citizenship revocation as investigated in this volume tells us about the (re)definition of the conditions for becoming and remaining a member of the political community.

Setting out the conditions: The common bond first and foremost

As previously stated, the tensions expressed by public and academic debate on citizenship revocation is particularly revealing of the multifaceted nature of citizenship writ large. Following a number of social and political theorists (Joppke 2007; Bellamy and Castiglione 2008; Bauböck 1994), the concept of citizenship is composed of three main dimensions around which the inclusion/exclusion dichotomy revolves.

The first one concerns the legal status with a focus on individual rights. From this perspective representative of political liberalism such as defended by Rawls (1971, 1993), Dworkin (1978), Larmore (1990) and Ackerman (1994), citizenship is defined by the following features: a universalist-cum-individualist conception of the 'self'; moral and political egalitarianism based on the principle of equal concern for each human being; a contractualist approach to political society; and a politics of basic rights focused on both fundamental and distributive justice, whose aims are to guarantee equal liberties to each citizen, to prevent their infringement from the state or any particular group, and to reduce inequalities due to morally irrelevant differences among citizens. All of these features contribute to giving priority to the right over the good, and to the individual over the community (Rawls 1971, 1993). This liberal vision of citizenship is marked by what Walzer (1984) qualified as an 'art of separation'. The individual's beliefs and values cultivated in the private sphere are separated from the institutionalised range of norms and principles of justice according to which citizens are urged to act in the public sphere. A principle of state neutrality, which requires public institutions to be neutral or impartial towards the competing visions of the good and of the world, follows from this; it also requires them not to endorse any of the controversial values in justifying state action and public policy.

The second dimension of citizenship consists in emphasising political participation as a civic virtue. It goes hand in hand with a (neo)republican approach which opposes a purely rights-based, procedural conception of citizenship for being too atomistic, passive and selfish. With a view to promoting an active vision of citizenship, civic republicans prioritise the exercise of the popular will over the individual defence of 'negative liberty', the pursuit of the public good over that of private interests, and the fulfilment of duties and responsibilities over that of individual rights and preferences. Be it granted an intrinsic (Pocock 1992) or instrumental (Skinner 1992) value, civic participation is here considered as a virtue, thus attributing moral strength and authority to active citizenship and the duties attached to it.

The third dimension, focused on collective identity, can be philosophically associated with a communitarian approach to citizenship. Despite their differences, communitarian thinkers (MacIntyre 1981; Sandel 1982; Taylor 1989a; Walzer 1983) assert that the identity of the self is inevitably situated and embedded in a framework of 'shared meanings' and 'common values' inherited from the community the self belongs to. In their view, it is neither possible nor desirable for any democratic state (even a liberal one) to be ethically and culturally neutral. On the contrary, the state cannot but be 'perfectionist': to be considered legitimate by the citizenry, its institutions and policies should express, promote and protect a core of 'thick'[1] values regarded as constitutive of 'our' collective identity. Taken in this third dimension, citizenship is a matter of providing visions of the good which give the political 'us' its cultural-cum-ethical authenticity and, as a consequence, its *raison d'être*. As Etzioni (2007, 359) asserts against the 'liberal view', a citizen 'has responsibilities not merely toward the political entity (e.g. obeying the state's laws), but also toward the national community (e.g. supporting its core of shared values)'.

The above three-fold philosophical outline, albeit sketchy, allows for a better understanding of the role each of these dimensions of citizenship is playing in the tensions, or indeed the dilemmas of liberal democracy such as revealed by the controversial revival of citizenship revocation. This is because it helps to identify a change of emphasis in the very definition of the conditions posed by citizenship to become and remain a member of the political 'us'.

In their diagnosis of a 'return of the citizen' in the mid-1990s, Kymlicka and Norman (1994, 353) observed that two previously neglected claims, pertaining to the republican and communitarian dimensions of citizenship, respectively, have been placed at the forefront of the theoretical literature on citizenship: 'namely, civic virtues and citizenship identity'. What is theoretically sound proves to be confirmed practically speaking, as far as citizenship revocation is concerned. The manner in which the latter is currently debated and enforced shows that the republican and communitarian claims have gained prominence. Furthermore, they have converged on a primary interest in a thick common bond, which would be robust enough to ensure the moral and cultural preconditions for the political community's survival. Conversely, as demonstrated by Boekestein and de Groot (*this volume*), this means the weakening of the liberal dimension of citizenship and of the practical importance of respect for individuals' rights regardless of their personal beliefs, values and allegiances.

From a philosophical point of view, this convergence can be illustrated by Taylor's account of the liberal-communitarian debate on citizenship (Taylor 1989b) where the republican and communitarian dimensions come together in an emphasis on the need to foster a sense of belonging and loyalty to a genuine community of citizens (Schnapper 1998), rather than a mere 'social union' *à la* Rawls. Sharing the language of the common good, they converge on the importance for all citizens to be committed to the political community's values and identity, for liberal democracy to overcome its viability problem. On both sides, priority is given to membership of a body of citizens whose sovereignty is anchored in a particular territory and whose collective identity is shaped by a particular way of life and historical legacy. This is where the republican and communitarian approaches intersect, thus promoting versions of patriotism that are more or less supportive of nationalism, and more or less hostile to rights-based liberalism (from Viroli 1995 to Miller 1995 and to MacIntyre 2002).

This underlines why two, and not three, dimensions of citizenship are indeed at stake in the controversy over citizenship revocation, and why the republican-cum-communitarian dimension not only conflicts with the liberal one but also prevails over it in setting out the conditions for having political rights (and obligations). As we shall see now, the public justifications put forward in support of deprivation of citizenship as an anti-terrorist measure are in line with the promotion of a thick concept of membership, whether republican or communitarian, which originates in a critical stance towards the primacy of individual rights, denounced for its fragmentary effects on the political community as a whole. On that point, Irving (104) rightly argues in this edited volume that 'the heavily normative understandings of citizenship that have been advanced in political theory since the 1980s' have greatly contributed to spreading the idea among law-markers that citizenship should be invested with thick 'qualities', such as the country's values and a sense of civic commitment to the polity. As Sykes (*this volume*) points out in his study on the US and the UK, the emphasis on 'good behaviour' and 'loyalty to the state' has played a historical role in the justifications made by decision makers to put new provisions on denaturalisation into the political agenda. In a context of the 'war on terror', the ground of disloyalty has been incorporated into a flourishing 'securitisation discourse' (Sykes, *this volume*, 65). Thus, the primary focus has been placed on preserving the unity and indeed integrity, if not homogeneity, of 'our' political community, notably through protecting the shared meanings and conceptions of the good publicly declared to unite the citizenry. Very interestingly, the cultural and ethical thickening of citizenship is not unique to revocation for anti-terrorist purposes. This is the key point made by Fargues (*this volume*): such a process has proven to be so prevalent that it occurs even in revocation measures based on fraud grounds that appear highly procedural, i.e. culturally and ethically neutral, at least at first glance. As demonstrated by this author, the neoliberal standards, pertaining to individual performance and merits, can easily combine with communitarian – and here we add: republican – conditions for citizenship. The (very republican-style) 'duty to behave as a virtuous and responsible political subject' – Fargues argues (86) – serves as a rationale for a 'governing strategy of renationalising citizenship' that culminates in 'the moralising and responsibilising function of deprivation'. As a result of its exclusionary and homogenising effects, such a thickening of citizenship has paved the way to 'the idea that the allegiance of citizens should be fostered, or even tested by the state', and that the 'attachment between the citizen and his or her country' must be 'single and undivided', a notion which appears to Irving (*this volume*, 104) 'both anti-cosmopolitan and illiberal'.

This is where the tensions within liberal-democratic citizenship could evolve into dilemmas: once conceived of and endorsed as a prerequisite for being included in (and not at risk of being excluded from) the political 'us', do commitment to national community and compliance with its so-called 'common values' still play in favour of the fostering of liberal-democratic citizenship at a time when it proves to be highly vulnerable, or do they translate into its being subverted by another vision of citizenship?

The return of patriotism: Cosmopolitanism under challenge

The above question is of topical resonance in light of the widespread calls for patriotism that are currently being made. In a great number of democratic societies – including those usually considered as champions of liberalism – and from all sides of the political spectrum, both the concept and the practice of patriotism is reviving. After decades of disgrace due to the fact that patriotism has been associated with nationalism as well as the wars and crimes perpetrated in its name (Tolstoy 1987), patriotism is undergoing a dual rehabilitation. The idea of patriotism, defined as a 'special concern for our country and compatriots' (Primoratz 2001, 10), has benefitted from renewed interest among a variety of political theorists and philosophers since the 2000s, with a view to demonstrating its moral relevance. The political reinstatement of patriotism through explicitly patriotic policies manifests the practical side of such renewal. From both perspectives, the current return of patriotism is justified by its proponents as a way to remedy the ills of liberal democracy, especially in terms of fragmentation, disaffiliation and disengagement towards the common good and the citizenry. In this regard, the converging communitarian and republican emphasis on a thick political bond goes hand in hand with a weakening of cosmopolitanism.

In the aftermath of World War II, the development of the international order was structured around the aims of universalising human rights and realising global justice and peace. These purposes were almost inescapable if states were to be recognised as legitimate both internally and externally. As shown by electoral results in the USA, Brazil, Italy and Hungary, or by the debate on Brexit, this apparent consensus has declined with the rise in patriotism. In many other countries, nationalist movements have gained ground among the electorate and in public discourse, and have unsettled traditional political arrangements, in particular with regard to immigration policy and acquisition/revocation of citizenship. As illustrated by the chapters in this edited volume, naturalisation and revocation policies epitomise the return of patriotism and the related undermining of cosmopolitan calls for human rights and global justice. Public justifications and the legal treatment of denationalisation, particularly when it comes to ensuring national security and fighting terrorism, tend to show that little remains of the imperative that the rule of human rights and humanitarian law be strictly observed. As explained by Boekenstein and de Groot (*this volume*, 27), what remains is 'the well-accepted prohibition of statelessness'. Nevertheless, the strength of this support should not be overestimated. Indeed, the British case, analysed by Fargues (*this volume*, 83), gives an example of how public authorities consider that 'deprivation resulting in statelessness is legal'. For their part, in this volume Boekenstein and de Groot, together with Irving, warn about a deflationary (and somewhat self-defeating) interpretation of the prohibition of statelessness. As prescribed by the 1961 UN Convention, the reduction of statelessness currently has the effect of limiting the application of denationalisation measures to dual nationals. In contrast with Joppke's defence of citizenship revocation and his idea that the creation of two classes of citizens by such measures is merely an 'unavoidable consequence of abiding by international law' (Joppke 2016, 745), Boekenstein and de Groot point out in this volume (32) that 'the prohibition of statelessness does not justify either form of discrimination [since] it is simply a legal limitation on the personal scope of denationalisation'. Instead of being 'invoked as an excuse' (Boekenstein and de Groot, 27) which allows to distinguish between citizens, the avoidance of statelessness should be replaced within its normative framework: the international protection of human rights, and its key principle of equality. The authors bemoan the undermining of the force of equality which 'not only constitutes a fundamental principle of citizenship, but a binding *human right* guaranteed through the prohibition of discrimination' (27).

Similarly, in relation to the Australian case, Irving (*this volume*, 105–106, note 14) notices that 'the "loyalty" exception' to the prohibition of statelessness, as provided for in the 1961 Convention, 'has limitations that would make it difficult for Australia to rely on its revocation scheme'. And yet, the fact that 'revocation only applies to persons with a citizenship additional to their Australian citizenship' – as Irving underlines (97) – has been considered by the authorities as a mere 'concession to the international rule against creating statelessness (and a source of frustration to the Minister responsible for the law)', thus having no challenging effects on the 'principle of single allegiance' that underlies the very conception of Australian citizenship. On the contrary, what is challenged by this discourse of undivided loyalty is the cosmopolitan promotion of multiple identities, that is, in Waldron's words, 'a way of being in the world, a way of constructing an identity for oneself that is different from, and arguably opposed to, the idea of belonging to or devotion to or immersion in a particular culture' (Waldron 2000, 227).

In sum, these two contributions illustrate that what has been lost with the decreasing importance of legal cosmopolitanism, as manifested by patriotic discourse in support of revocation laws, is the value attached to non-discrimination and the founding principle of equal concern and treatment at the core of moral universalism.

At the same time, Irving (*this volume*, 94) emphasises that the language of allegiance has deep historical roots and 'resonates in other legal systems'. And indeed, the image of a golden age of human rights and universalism that no longer exists because of the irruption of exclusionary forms of patriotism into liberal democracy is misleading and should be made much more complex. It suffices to consider the slavery system, colonialism or the past use of 'cruder technologies such as convict transportation' (Troy, *this volume*, 14) to acknowledge how fragile, and indeed questionable, is the normative coherence of many democratic regimes which have availed themselves of their charters of human rights, and have exported them to the rest of the world. Therefore, the above diagnosis has to be replaced, as Troy (11) does in her chapter in this volume regarding the UK, in the longer history of a practice – i.e. revocation – which is not independent of citizenship but 'a part of it'. And she elaborates (11): 'Tracing a narrative that extends beyond the nation-state and into Empire' allows to 'position revocation not as an exception to citizenship, but as a practice that represents the logic of citizenship – a logic that divides and codes subjects, categorising them as desirable or undesirable'. Hence the historical link analysed by Troy (11) between 'an imperial strategy of governing subject mobility' and the contemporary 'technology of national security' embodied by current revocation policies. In the light of this history (which may apply to the other national cases investigated in this volume), the transversal question as to whether the tensions of liberal democracy are shifting into dilemmas proves to be even more significant since such imperial echoes, and indeed continuity, aggravate the exclusionary effects of contemporary forms of renascent patriotism.

Here again, a philosophical detour clarifies what is at stake in the two hypotheses – i.e. mere tensions or real dilemmas, respectively – raised by the conflicting relations between cosmopolitanism and patriotism, which current debate and citizenship revocation policies have made explicit. From a theoretical point of view, the scenario that these are mere tensions opens a series of innovative combinations that aim to overcome the opposition between, on the one hand, the cosmopolitan openness, egalitarianism and impartiality attached to universalist morality and, on the other hand, patriotic concern and partiality underpinned by particularist rootedness. The literature of the last three decades is rich in formulas for reconciliation. Among them: the notions of 'cosmopolitan patriot' and of 'rooted cosmopolitanism' put forward by Appiah (1997); the tentative definition of a patriotism that respects liberal norms as illustrated by Nathanson's (1989) defence of 'moderate patriotism'; the strategy advanced by Richard Miller (1998) to make room for 'the duties of patriotic bias' in a reconceptualised cosmopolitanism based on a version of Kantian morality that focuses on 'equal respect', rather than 'equal concern'.

From a practical point of view, the tensions between cosmopolitanism and patriotism have nourished a philosophical debate on which one of these should have priority over the other in terms of moral and, more importantly, political obligations. At the core of this issue is the balance to be found between 'global duties' – i.e. what we owe to individual human beings – and 'special duties' – i.e. what we owe to our fellow citizens as compatriots and co-nationals. Here again, a variety of arrangements have been developed and discussed. Some of them state the unconditional priority of fundamental rights and/or global justice, while recognising that the associative ties and collective commitments pertaining to patriotism are worth cultivating. For instance, according to Tan (2004), it is not cosmopolitanism which should be 'restricted' by the moral and political strength attributed to patriotic ties, but patriotism which must be 'limited' and 'constrained' by the impartial principles of global justice. David Miller's strategy takes the opposite point of view. His starting point is what Tan (2004, 145) labels 'conventional patriotism', that is, the common-sense idea that 'nationality', including patriotic allegiance and partiality towards compatriots, has an 'intrinsic value' and 'is *one* of the human goods' (Miller 2005, 69). Based on this premise, he advocates 'patriotic partiality', which can be 'reasonable' provided it is 'balanced against recognition of the duties of global justice' (Miller 2005, 63).

This balance is achieved by 'weight[ing] duties according to whether they are local or global in scope' (Miller 2005, 72). The result of this exercise is as follows: only 'the negative duty to refrain from infringing basic rights by our own actions' has priority over local duties towards compatriots; the 'positive duty to secure the basic rights of the people we are responsible for protecting' depends on the degree of responsibility; local duties take precedence over the two global positive duties 'to prevent rights violations by other parties' and 'to secure the basic rights of people when others have failed in their responsibility' (Miller 2005, 74). In this weighting, the crucial factor is to determine how far local standards in a particular state are met – notably, its 'national sovereignty', the implementation of 'a scheme of social justice among its citizens', and 'economic growth' (Miller 2005, 76–78). It is remarkable that Miller himself, a proponent of 'liberal nationalism', who is also considered to be a 'moderate anti-cosmopolitan' (Tan 2004), acknowledges that the enterprise of weighting leads to 'a genuine ethical dilemma' (Miller 2005, 78). This is confirmed by the application of Miller's position to the issue of citizenship revocation. The more limited 'citizenship rights' related to 'reasonable human rights standards' (Miller 2016, 269) and global duties are, the more decisive is patriotic priority and the state's responsibility to secure the national identity. 'For liberal states' – Miller (2016, 270) asserts – 'this is an opportunity to inculcate values and national loyalty'.

Ensuring national security though the protection of 'shared values'

As universal concern has weakened, patriotic concern has taken major precedence, thus emphasising the political bond and collective identity. Such focus expresses a loss in legitimacy of two principles largely considered as constitutive of liberal democracy: pluralism and state neutrality. As pointed out above, the debate over citizenship revocation and the moral and political anxieties it voices have reinforced the communitarian and republican need to inculcate and promote the values declared to be at the core of the ties that bind us together. The process of assigning a crucial value to 'shared values' has taken place in the context of a 'retreat from multiculturalism' (Joppke 2004). Indeed, multicultural policies have been criticised for aggravating division in society and suspected of perverting the sense of national belonging. With a view to answering these perceived threats and consolidating national identity, thicker integration and naturalisation policies have developed under the label of a 'civic turn' (Borevi, Jensen and Mouritsen 2017; Mouritsen and Jørgensen 2008; Mouritsen, Kriegbaum and Larin 2019). The revival of citizenship revocation is part of this process through which states renationalise citizenship 'by making inclusion harder and exclusion easier' (Fargues, *this volume*, 78). In this respect, as shown by Winter and Previsic (*this volume*, 47), it 'challenges the thesis of increasing citizenship liberalization' defended by Joppke (2010). This is a similar view that upholds Sykes who underlines in his chapter on the UK and the US that the othering and indeed exclusion of the 'undesirable groups' are to be understood in light of a 'broader shift in political culture away from multiculturalism and towards assimilation – and in turn the exclusion of those who do not or cannot assimilate' (Sykes, *this volume*, 72).

Such a framework marked by the 'return of assimilation' (Brubaker 2001) raises the question of what is left of the theoretical endeavours to accommodate ethno-cultural diversity. Indeed, large sections of the literature on citizenship in the 1990s and 2000s have focused on discussion of tentative reconciliations between integration and pluralism. The latter include Kymlicka's liberal multiculturalism (2000) and Laborde's critical republicanism (2008), both of which aim to overcome the tensions between the individual and the community, personal belonging and political membership, differentiated treatment and respect for equality, private beliefs and public norms. Beyond these tensions, they put forward a genuinely pluralistic model of integration which takes the fight against discrimination seriously, while aiming at building a common political culture that would be more hospitable to differences. However, echoing the public statements about the failure of multiculturalism and the dangers created by the politics of difference, such as those made by Angela Merkel, Nicolas Sarkozy and David Cameron from October 2010 to February 2011, academic debate has moved on to the conditions required to ensure unity. From the stability of public institutions to the survival of national identity, more or less robust conceptions of the commonalities to be fostered have been discussed.

Initiated by Barry (2001) and by Alesina, Glaeser and Sacerdote (2001) in the philosophical and political economy literature, respectively, debate on the conflicting relations between multiculturalism and the welfare state (Banting and Kymlicka 2006) has culminated in what has been qualified as a 'progressive dilemma' (Ascherson 2006; Goodhart 2004; Pathak 2007, 2008). In academia and in the public sphere, calls for pluralism and recognition of differences have been criticised for clashing with the very possibility of equality in terms of social and distributive justice. This clash exposes different concepts of equality and places the issue of categorisation at its core. Within this framework, the paradoxical question of for and to whom equality should primarily be applied holds centre stage. From that perspective, the specific constraints created by the economic crisis and its moral and political repercussions justify the precedence of social justice over ethno-cultural recognition and antidiscrimination policies. More often than not, this line of thought is complemented by the assertion that identity insecurities among the majority group must be taken into account (Bouvet 2015; Orgad 2015). These two arguments have fuelled nationalist discourses which demand that the benefits of distributive justice be limited to the national community, thus stigmatising the 'non-national' as the source of danger to equality and its implementation. From this viewpoint, a certain degree of cultural homogeneity is deemed to be necessary to ensure trust and solidarity among citizens (Putnam 2007). Such analysis of the responsibility of multiculturalism for increasing inequalities in a neoliberal context can paradoxically conjoin with recommendations to use neoliberal tools – public management, performance indicators, conditionality of public assistance – as a means of rescuing the welfare state or at least its redistributive aims. As the ideal of an open society recedes, and the divide between majority and minority groups grows, inequality becomes the object of various managerial strategies which, in lieu of examining its systemic causes, engage in various quick fixes and 'band-aid solutions'. In this edited volume, Fargues's analysis of fraud-induced citizenship deprivation significantly illustrates this combination of neoliberal rationality and communitarian closure.

The dilemma between unity and diversity occurs through the demand to preserve not only the implementation of equality within the welfare state but also the pursuit of a core set of liberal values and virtues declared to be vital to a healthy liberal democracy. The issue then addressed is the possibility and desirability for the liberal-democratic state to be neutral or impartial in terms of visions of the good life and worldviews. Considered a 'mirage' by Stephen Macedo (1992, 209), the principle of state neutrality is criticised by liberal perfectionists (Raz 1986; Sher 1997; Wall 1998) for undermining the moral foundations of liberalism, and thus the political stability of liberal-democratic regimes. According to them, there is no 'value-blind' state action (Raz 1986, 136) and 'the liberal must, in the end, defend his partisanship and not evade it' (Macedo 1990, 298). Following a perfectionist approach, it should be recognised that liberalism, far from being neutral, has on its own visions of the good life and of the good citizen. In this approach, the liberal values and virtues do shape a particular ethical life, and their public promotion, inculcation and reproduction are a legitimate and indeed crucial purpose of any liberal democracy. For, beyond 'reasonable disagreements', pluralism – these thinkers underline – may occur through some morally 'ugly' and publicly 'unreasonable' forms which are incompatible with the liberal morality and culture based on individual rationality, autonomy and liberty. If diversity is to 'remain a blessing rather than a curse' (Macedo 2000, 6), then what Macedo (2000, 34) significantly qualifies as the 'liberal Republic' should adopt a forceful attitude towards illiberal beliefs in order to discredit them. If the liberal goods and their underlying culture are to survive – the argument goes – liberals must reject the idea that fundamental rights be balanced by group rights, as expressed through Okin's well-known 'dilemma' in relation to the debate on whether 'multiculturalism is bad for women' (Cohen, Howard and Nussbaum 1999). Obviously, no liberal would deny the priority given to basic rights, including individual liberty and gender equality. But the perfectionist approach goes beyond this priority; it claims that, instead of supporting a politics of neutrality designed to respect pluralism, liberal democrats must enter the cultural battle of values, and assume 'a certain boldness in the defense of liberalism' (Macedo 1990, 294). 'Confronting fanatics and grappling with divisiveness' should remind us – Macedo (1990, 294) continues – that we, as liberal democrats, need to 'preserve our ability to recognize and fight the good fight'. This is the meaning of Cameron's plea for a 'muscular liberalism'.[2]

As illustrated by the case studies analysed in this edited volume, citizenship revocation constitutes a borderline case of the above dilemma between unity and diversity, and of the opposition between perfectionist and neutral state action. Citizenship revocation policies and their public justifications have contributed to establishing this dilemma as inescapable. What is more, they have also established the idea that the only way out of this dilemma is to opt for one side as opposed to the other. This is to say that the 'good fight' aims at nothing less than securing liberal democracy, and that this aim entails reaching thick unity through state partiality towards 'our' values. The chapters in this book here make it clear that such a choice does not only have homogenising effects; it also has exclusionary ones. Those citizens whose beliefs and behaviours are suspected of being incompatible with the values deemed to be the cornerstone of national identity are perceived as endangering social cohesion and political unity. In a context of terrorist threats, concrete security pertaining to the safety of people and property, evidently is a public concern of primary importance. What the collected contributions reveal is that security as a public good has expanded into symbolic, identity-based security protected by means of perfectionist discourse and politics of shared values and good citizenship.

This dual process of homogenisation and exclusion, such as manifested by contemporary policies of revocation, result from both the ethicisation and the ethnicisation of citizenship. By ethicisation, we refer to a concept of integration consisting in the stabilisation and reproduction of 'the basic ethical orientations of the cultural form of life dominant in [a particular] country', which contrasts with 'political integration' based on respect of the legal norms institutionalised through citizenship (Habermas 1998, 225–228). The case studies on citizenship revocation analysed in this volume demonstrate how strong the link between belonging to the citizenry and allegiance to national values is. Full and complete adherence to the nation's value system thus constitutes a necessary condition for being legally and socially recognised as a citizen. As shown by Irving (*this volume*, 99), this ethicisation lies in 'the conceptualisation of citizenship as an indivisible and inalienable relationship of allegiance between the citizen and the state', and this makes 'multiple citizenship [...] conceptually incoherent'. In practice, this conception of 'undivided loyalty' has exclusionary effects, even towards citizens who are not guilty of active disloyalty or treason. A very telling example of this is provided by the resignation of Australian MPs who hold dual citizenship. On a similar note, Sykes (*this volume*, 68) also underlines that the recent bills supporting new denaturalisation powers in the US have been relying on what he calls '"zero-sum citizenship", in which loyalty to one's official country of citizenship is thought to be proportionally curbed by expressions of allegiance to foreign authorities'.

While being obvious in policies explicitly based on the promotion of shared values, the ethicisation of citizenship is also part of seemingly thin and procedural measures, such as fraud-based revocation. This process of ethicisation is carried out through 'the moralising and responsibilising function of deprivation applied to specific categories of migrants, which turns them into second-class citizens' (Fargues, *this volume*, 80). Thus, ethicisation of citizenship goes hand in hand with a process of ethnicisation. The line drawn between desirable and undesirable citizens overlaps 'the division between "accidental" and "essential" citizens' (Fargues, *this volume*, 88), thus involving ethno-cultural categories in the definition of good citizenship. As underlined by Troy (*this volume*, 19–21), not only is class at play in government policies of citizenship revocation but 'the revoked citizens' ethnicity' is also a key aspect. And indeed, it is significant that 'suspicions of fraud stem both from existing legal differentiations between categories of migrants (EU citizens vs. others) and from specific stereotypes (African migrants as more likely to attempt to deflect the family reunification process)' (Fargues, *this volume*, 87).

Fuelled by such ethicisation/ethnicisation dynamics, the closure function of citizenship proceeds not only by excluding revoked citizens from the national community but also by producing 'others' within it. As stated by Winter and Previsic (*this volume*, 45), it 'is, above all, an official act of legally *and* symbolically "un-belonging"'. Moreover, the extension of exclusion applies not only to its scope but also to its target:

> While the legal effects only apply to (potentially few) dual nationals, the symbolic boundaries drawn by legislating citizenship revocation extend to broader social categories associated – in political and public discourse – with these individuals, such as dual nationals, immigrants, and members of certain ethno-religious minorities.
>
> (Winter and Previsic, *this volume*, 48)

As for which individuals and groups are the most affected by such exclusionary effects, the chapters in this volume conclude that Muslims are the main target. With respect to Canada, Winter and Previsic (49) show how they are the most likely to be 'associated with' those deserving of citizenship revocation and then how they 'become guilty by association'. In a context of fundamentalist Islamic terrorism, Muslims pay the price of ascriptive membership of a group suspected of endangering national security. Examining how public discourse interprets and interacts with government policies, Winter and Previsic (55–56) explain that 'placing the "real" next to the "hypothetical" – and the frequent enumeration of Muslim individuals, groups, and events in the context of terrorism – contributes to the popular suspicion that Canadian Muslims are, at the very least, sympathetic to terrorism and incapable of truly belonging in Canada'. This is why they are targeted 'not as individual criminals but as a *group*' (Winter and Previsic, *this volume*, 55). Here again, exclusion is carried out along an ethical-cum-ethnical line in so far as Muslims are perceived as pledging their allegiance to a value system which is not only different but also opposed to 'ours'. In short, they are framed as ethical dissidents, at odds with national values.

Conclusion

Moving from theory to practice, from the philosophical literature on liberal democracy's current challenges to the public debate on citizenship revocation, the diagnosis of dilemmas, and not mere tensions, is growing more tangible. What would now be worth investigating is the ambivalent role of law on such a slippery slope. According to Boeskestein and de Groot (*this volume*, 35), 'the legal analysis cannot provide a definite answer to the policy question of whether states should denationalise (certain) foreign fighters. Instead, it can only establish the human rights limitations to such policies'. Furthermore, as we have seen, the weakening of the liberal dimension of citizenship, associated as it is with cosmopolitanism and pluralism, has made international law and constitutional norms less effective in framing liberal-democratic citizenship. In a context of terrorist threats and growing patriotism, the convergence of the republican and communitarian dimensions and their conjoined impact on morally and culturally thickening citizenship have given increased power to government policies and democratic legislation in setting out the conditions for access to, and exit from, citizenship.

In such a context, law has an essential yet uncertain role to play. It is crucial since its function is to institutionalise the basic principles of justice which, in a liberal-democratic framework, include equal rights, individual liberties and the 'right to have rights'. In that sense, law offers a bulwark against political decisions that may be contradictory to human rights, even if they are in accordance with public opinion and the political preferences of democratic majorities. However, analysis of current discourses and policies on citizenship revocation reveals that the logic of liberal constitutionalism, with its related hierarchy of legal norms, has become highly precarious. As shown by case studies of Australia, Canada and the UK, the exclusionary use of revocation measures has been validated by a number of court decisions, including constitutional courts. Hence, this legal safeguard has proven to be vulnerable to democratic majorities, and even to their illiberal branches. Henceforth, what acts as umpire is no longer universal principles of justice, but the laws, i.e. legislation and governmental decisions, resulting from electoral votes that express majoritarian opinions. The prospect that democracy – as the medium of both popular sovereignty and national identity – will be the final arbiter in debate on the nature, standards and boundaries of liberal citizenship may represent a possible path to re-politicise this debate. Yet, such re-politicisation can go two ways depending on the governments elected. As was the case in Canada (Winter and Previsic, *this volume*), this may lead to the repeal of revocation bills and measures in a spirit of reaffirmed liberalism. Conversely, as in Australia (Irving, *this volume*), it may lead to an escalation of exclusionary use of the language of shared national values. But in any case, the 'return of banishment' (Macklin 2018) as an effective and legitimate means to draw the line between 'us' and 'them', the desirables and the undesirables, good and bad citizens, will certainly continue to put liberal democracy to the test.

Notes

1 On the distinction between 'thick' and 'thin' morality, see Walzer (1994, xi, note 1) where he qualified as 'thick' a 'kind of argument' which is 'richly referential, culturally resonant, locked into a locally established symbolic system or network of meanings', in contrast with a 'thin' argument which refers to 'universalist morality', including procedural principles of justice.

2 These are the words used by then Prime Minister David Cameron in his well-publicised speech at the Munich Security Conference, delivered on 5 February 2011 (www.gov.uk/government/speeches/pms-speech-at-munich-security-conference).

References

Ackerman, B. 1994. "Political Liberalisms." *The Journal of Philosophy* 91 (7): 364–386.
Alesina, A., E. Glaeser, and B. Sacerdote. 2001. "Why Doesn't the US Have a European-Style Welfare State?" *Brookings Papers on Economic Activity* (2): 187–278.

Appiah, K. A. 1997. "Cosmopolitan Patriots." *Critical Inquiry* 23 (3): 617–639.

Ascherson, N. ed. 2006. Special issue "Responses to David Goodhart's Demos Pamphlet from Five Commentators." *Prospect Magazine* (123).

Banting, K., and W. Kymlicka. 2006. *Multiculturalism and the Welfare State: Recognition and Redistribution in Contemporary Democracies*. Oxford: Oxford University Press.

Barry, B. 2001. *Culture & Equality: An Egalitarian Critique of Multiculturalism*. Cambridge: Polity Press.

Bauböck, R. 1994 *Transnational Citizenship. Membership and Rights in International Migration*. Aldershot: Edward Elgar.

Bellamy, R, and D. Castiglione. 2008. "Beyond Community and Rights: European Citizenship and the Virtues of Participation." In *Constituting Communities: Political Solutions to Cultural Conflict*, edited by P. Mouritsen and K. E. Jørgensen, 162–186. Basingstoke: Palgrave Macmillan.

Bobbio, N. [1988] 1990. *Liberalism and Democracy*. Translated by M. Ryle and K. Soper. London: Verso.

Boekestein, T., and G.-R de Groot. 2020. "Discussing the Human Rights Limits on Loss of Citizenship: A Normative-Legal Perspective on Egalitarian Arguments Regarding Dutch Nationality Laws Targeting Dutch-Moroccans" *When States Take Rights Back: Citizenship Revocation and Its Discontents*, edited by É. Fargues, E. Winter, and M. J. Gibney, 26–43. Abingdon: Routledge.

Borevi K., K. K. Jensen, and P. Mouritsen. 2017. "The Civic Turn of Immigrant Integration Policies in the Scandinavian Welfare States." *Comparative Migration Studies* 5 (1).

Bouvet, B. 2015. *L'insécurité culturelle. Sortir du malaise identitaire français*. Paris: Fayard.

Brubaker, R. 1992. *Citizenship and Nationhood in France and Germany*. Cambridge: Harvard University Press.

Brubaker, R. 2001. "The Return of Assimilation? Changing Perspectives on Immigration and Its Sequels in France, Germany and the United States." *Ethnic and Racial Studies* 24 (4): 531–548.

Cohen, E. 2016. "When Democracies Denationalize: The Epistemological Case against Revoking Citizenship." *Ethics & International Affairs* 30 (2): 253–259.

Cohen, J., M. Howard, and M. Nussbaum. ed. 1999. *Is Multiculturalism Bad for Women? Susan Moller Okin with Respondents*. Princeton, NJ: Princeton University Press.

Dworkin, R. 1978. "Liberalism." In *Public and Private Morality*, edited by S. Hampshire, 113–143. Cambridge: Cambridge University Press.

Etzioni, A. 2007. "Citizenship Tests: A Comparative, Communitarian Perspective." *The Political Quarterly* 78 (3): 353–363.

Fargues, E. 2017. "The Revival of Citizenship Deprivation in France and the UK as an Instance of Citizenship Renationalisation." *Citizenship Studies* 21 (8): 984–998.

Fargues, E. 2020. "Simply a Matter of Compliance with the Rules? The Moralising and Responsibilising Function of Fraud-Based Citizenship Deprivation in France and the UK" *When States Take Rights Back: Citizenship Revocation and Its Discontents*, edited by É. Fargues, E. Winter, and M. J. Gibney, 77–92. Abingdon: Routledge.

Fargues, E., and E. Winter. 2020. "Conditional Membership: What Revocation Does to Citizenship" *When States Take Rights Back: Citizenship Revocation and Its Discontents*, edited by É. Fargues, E. Winter and M. J. Gibney, 1–9. Abingdon: Routledge.

Freeden, M. 2017. "After the Brexit Referendum: Revisiting Populism as an Ideology." *Journal of Political Ideologies* 22 (1): 1–11.

Gibney, M. 2013. "Should Citizenship Be Conditional? The Ethics of Denationalisation." *The Journal of Politics* 75 (3): 646–658.

Goodhart, D. 2004. "Too Diverse? Is Britain Becoming Too Diverse to Sustain the Mutual Obligations Behind a Good Society and the Welfare State?" *Prospect Magazine* (95): 30–37.

Graham, G. 1992. "Liberalism and Democracy." *Journal of Applied Philosophy* 9 (2): 149–160.

Habermas, J. [1992] 1996. *Between Facts and Norms: Contributions to a Discourse Theory of Law and Democracy*. Translated by W. Rehg. Cambridge, MA: MIT Press.

Habermas, J. 1998. *The Inclusion of the Other: Studies in Political Theory*. Cambridge, MA: MIT Press.

Herzog, B. 2016. "The Democratic Roots of Expatriations." *Ethics & International Affairs* 30 (2): 261–264.

Irving, H. 2020. "The Concept of Allegiance in Citizenship Law and Revocation: An Australian Study" *When States Take Rights Back: Citizenship Revocation and Its Discontents*, edited by É. Fargues, E. Winter and M. J. Gibney, 93–108. Abingdon: Routledge.
Joppke, C. 2004. "The Retreat of Multiculturalism in the Liberal State: Theory and Policy." *The British Journal of Sociology* 55 (2): 237–257.
Joppke, C. 2007. "Transformation of Citizenship: Status, Rights, Identity." *Citizenship Studies* 11 (1): 37–48.
Joppke, C. 2010. *Citizenship and Immigration*. Cambridge: Polity Press.
Joppke, C. 2016. "Terror and the Loss of Citizenship." *Citizenship Studies* 20 (6–7): 728–748.
Kymlicka, W. 2000. *Multicultural Citizenship: A Liberal Theory of Minority Rights*. Oxford: Oxford University Press.
Kymlicka, W., and W. Norman. 1994. "Return of the Citizen: A Survey of Recent Work on Citizenship Theory." *Ethics* 104 (2): 352–381.
Larmore, C. 1990. "Political Liberalism." *Political Theory* 18 (3): 339–360.
Lenard, P. 2016. "Democracies and the Power to Revoke Citizenship." *Ethics & International Affairs* 30 (1) 73–91.
Macedo, S. 1990. "The Politics of Justification." *Political Theory* 18 (2): 280–304.
Macedo, S. 1992. "Charting Liberal Virtues." In *Virtue*, Nomos XXXIV, edited by J. W. Chapman and W. A. Galston, 204–232. New York: New York University Press.
Macedo, S. 2000. *Diversity and Distrust: Civic Education in a Multicultural Democracy*. Cambridge, MA: Harvard University Press.
MacIntyre, A. 1981. *After Virtue*. Notre Dame: University of Notre Dame Press.
MacIntyre, A. [1984] 2002. "Is Patriotism a Virtue?" The Lindley Lecture, University of Kansas. Reprinted in *Patriotism*, edited by I. Primoratz, 43–58. Amherst, MA: Humanity Books.
Macklin, A. 2018. "The Return of Banishment: Do the New Citizenship Revocation Policies Weaken Citizenship?". In *Debating Transformations of National Citizenship*, edited by R. Bauböck, 163–172. IMISCOE Research Series. Cham: Springer.
Miller, D. 1995. *On Nationality*. Oxford: Clarendon Press.
Miller, D. 2005. "Partiality towards Compatriots." *Ethical Theory and Moral Practice* 8 (1–2): 63–81.
Miller, D. 2016. "Democracy, Exile, and Revocation." *Ethics and International Affairs* 30 (2): 265–270.
Miller, R. 1998. "Cosmopolitan Respect and Patriotic Concern." *Philosophy and Public Affairs* 27 (3): 202–224.
Mouritsen, P., and K. E. Jørgensen. ed. 2008. *Constituting Communities: Political Solutions to Cultural Conflict*. Basingstoke: Palgrave Macmillan.
Mouritsen, P., J. K. Kriegbaum, and S. J. Larin, 2019. "Introduction: Theorizing the Civic Turn in European Integration Policies." *Ethnicities* 19 (4): 595–613.
Müller, J.-W. 2016. *What is Populism?* Philadelphia: University of Pennsylvania Press.
Nathanson, S. 1989. "In Defense of 'Moderate' Patriotism." *Ethics* 99 (3): 535–552.
Nyers, P. ed. 2009. *Securitizations of Citizenship*. London and New York: Routledge.
Orgad, L. 2015. *The Cultural Defense of Nations: A Liberal Theory of Majority Rights*. Oxford: Oxford University Press.
Pathak, P. 2007. "The Trouble with David Goodhart's Britain." *The Political Quarterly* 78 (2): 261–271.
Pathak, P. 2008. *The Future of Multicultural Britain: Confronting the Progressive Dilemma*. Edinburgh: Edinburgh University Press.
Pocock, J. G. A. 1992. "The Ideal of Citizenship since Classical Times." *Queen's Quarterly* 99 (1): 35–55.
Primoratz, I. 2001. *Patriotism*. Amherst, MA: Humanity Books.
Putnam, R. D. 2007. "E Pluribus Unum: Diversity and Community in the Twenty-First-Century." *Scandinavian Political Studies* 30 (2): 37–174.
Rawls, J. 1971. *A Theory of Justice*. Harvard, MA: Harvard University Press.
Rawls, J. 1993. *Political Liberalism*. New York: Columbia University Press.
Raz, J. 1986. *The Morality of Freedom*. Oxford: Oxford University Press.
Sandel, M. 1982. *Liberalism and the Limits of Justice*. Cambridge: Cambridge University Press.

Schnapper, D. [1994] 1998, *Community of Citizens: On the Modern Idea of Nationality*. Translated by S. Rosée. Abingdon: Routledge.

Sher, G. 1997. *Beyond Neutrality: Perfectionism and Politics*. Cambridge: Cambridge University Press.

Skinner, Q. 1992. "On Justice, the Common Good and the Priority of Liberty." In *Dimensions of Radical Democracy*, edited by C. Mouffe, 211–224. London and New York: Verso.

Sykes, P. 2020. "Denaturalisation and Conceptions of Citizenship in the 'War on Terror'". *When States Take Rights Back: Citizenship Revocation and Its Discontents*, edited by É. Fargues, E. Winter and M. J. Gibney, 62-76. Abingdon: Routledge.

Tan, K.-C. 2004. *Justice without Borders. Cosmopolitanism, Nationalism, and Patriotism*. Cambridge: Cambridge University Press.

Taylor, C. 1989a. *Sources of the Self: The Making of the Modern Identity.* Cambridge: Cambridge University Press.

Taylor, C. 1989b. "Cross-Purposes: The Liberal-Communitarian Debate." In *Liberalism and the Moral Life*, edited by N. Rosenblum, 159–182. Cambridge, MA: Harvard University Press.

Tolstoy, L. [1896] 1987. "Patriotism, or Peace?" In *Writings on Civil Disobedience and Nonviolence*, 137–147. Philadelphia: New Society Publishers.

Troy, D. 2020. "Governing Imperial Citizenship: A Historical Account of Citizenship Revocation" *When States Take Rights Back: Citizenship Revocation and Its Discontents*, edited by É. Fargues, E. Winter and M. J. Gibney, 10–25. Abingdon: Routledge.

Viroli, M. 1995. *For Love of Country: An Essay on Patriotism and Nationalism*. Oxford: Oxford University Press.

Waldron, J. 2000. "What is Cosmopolitan?" *The Journal of Political Philosophy* 8 (2): 227–243.

Wall, S. 1998. *Liberalism, Perfectionism and Restraint*. Cambridge: Cambridge University Press.

Walzer, M. 1983. *Spheres of Justice: A Defense of Pluralism and Equality*. New York: Basic Books.

Walzer, M. 1984. "Liberalism and the Art of Separation." *Political Theory* 12 (3): 315–333.

Walzer, M. 1994. *Thick and Thin: Moral Argument at Home and Abroad*. Notre Dame: University of Notre Dame.

Winter, E., and I. Previsic. 2020. "The Politics of Un-Belonging: Lessons from Canada's Experiment with Citizenship Revocation." *When States Take Rights Back: Citizenship Revocation and Its Discontents*, edited by É. Fargues, E. Winter and M. J. Gibney, 44–61. Abingdon: Routledge.

Index

Note: Page numbers in **bold** refer to tables. Footnotes are denoted by n, e.g. 105n8.